INSIDERS, OUTSIDERS

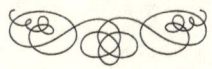

INSIDERS, OUTSIDERS

TOWARD A NEW HISTORY OF SOUTHERN THOUGHT

Edited by Sarah E. Gardner and Steven M. Stowe

THE UNIVERSITY OF NORTH CAROLINA PRESS
Chapel Hill

This book was published with the assistance of the Fred W. Morrison Fund of the University of North Carolina Press.

© 2021 The University of North Carolina Press
All rights reserved
Manufactured in the United States of America
Designed and composition by Kristina Kachele Design, llc
Set in Miller Text with Miller Display Roman
The University of North Carolina Press has been
a member of the Green Press Initiative since 2003.

Library of Congress Cataloging-in-Publication Data
Names: Gardner, Sarah E., editor. | Stowe, Steven M., 1946– editor.
Title: Insiders, outsiders : toward a new history of Southern thought /
edited by Sarah E. Gardner and Steven M. Stowe.
Description: Chapel Hill : The University of North Carolina Press, [2021] |
Includes bibliographical references and index.
Identifiers: LCCN 2021003505 | ISBN 9781469663555 (cloth ; alk. paper) |
ISBN 9781469663562 (pbk. ; alk. paper) | ISBN 9781469663579 (ebook)
Subjects: LCSH: Marginality, Social—Southern States—History. | American
literature—Southern States—History and criticism. | Southern States—
Historiography. | Southern States—Intellectual life. | Southern
States—History. | LCGFT: Essays.
Classification: LCC F209.5 .I67 2021 | DDC 975—dc23
LC record available at https://lccn.loc.gov/2021003505

FOR MICHAEL O'BRIEN

CONTENTS

Acknowledgments ix

Introduction
Sarah E. Gardner and Steven M. Stowe 1

PART ONE: IDEAS IN THE SOUTH

The Insider's Outsider: Edgar Allan Poe
and the Art of Self-Destruction
Stephen Berry 15

The Excitement at Boggy Swamp
Michael T. Bernath 36

Toward a History of Books in the American South
Beth Barton Schweiger 56

The Intellectual Life of a Fantasy: Edwin Wiley Fuller's
Sea-Gift and Postwar Imagination
Timothy J. Williams 76

The Discourse of Conflict in the Reconstruction South:
Land, Labor, and Immigration
Mitchell Snay 94

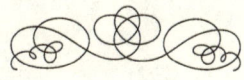

PART TWO: IDEAS ABOUT THE SOUTH

Southern Literature and the Anthropocene
Melanie Benson Taylor 119

The Wrecking Crew: Willie Morris, Larry L. King, Marshall Frady, and the Southern Turn in American Literary Journalism
John Grammer 141

Identity as Debate: The Subintellectual History of Edward A. Pollard's *True Southerners*
Scott Romine 161

Fashioning Insiders and Outsiders: Race and Gender in the Making of *The Library of Southern Literature*, 1900–1920
Jonathan Daniel Wells 182

Tony Judt and Michael O'Brien: Writing History
Michael Kreyling 202

Contributors 225

Index 229

ACKNOWLEDGMENTS

WE JOINTLY thank our contributing authors for their unflagging engagement with this project and for many moments of fresh insight about southern thought and southern thinkers along the way. Several of them have participated over the last three decades in the annual gatherings of the Southern Intellectual History Colloquium. We have benefited greatly from the intellectual excitement of this peripatetic, field-defining group.

As executive editor at the University of North Carolina Press until his retirement in 2020, Charles Grench was present at the inception of this volume, sustaining and improving it in countless ways. We are grateful for his enduring interest and expertise. Mark Simpson-Vos, taking on the project as the press's editorial director, added crucial support both intellectual and practical. Important, too, were the unusually detailed critical comments from two anonymous readers for the press. Both helpfully pressed us to think about the reach and content of each essay, as well as the orientation of the volume as a whole. When all was said but not done, Mary Caviness wisely guided the volume through the final stages before publication.

Dedicating this volume to Michael O'Brien acknowledges his uniquely pathbreaking historical work in intellectual history in and beyond the American South. Michael's commitment to searching scholarship, his sense of the intellectual past as alive with both conflict and harmony, and his friendship continue to inspire us and those who knew him.

Finally, Sarah wishes to thank Todd Leopold for his forbearance. She can get a bit cranky when writing and editing. Steve wishes to thank Naoko Wake for her intellectual companionship and for sharing her own work from another part of history's forest.

INSIDERS, OUTSIDERS

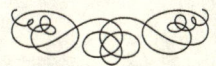

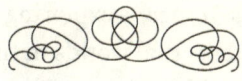

INTRODUCTION

SARAH E. GARDNER AND STEVEN M. STOWE

IN 1963, Richard Beale Davis was very cautious when he framed his now-classic intellectual history of post-Revolutionary Virginia. He tied his book to a great man—it was a history of "Jefferson's Virginia"—and not to all of the writers and institutions that his innovative study in fact considered. His first words of introduction went past modesty to the very rim of doubt. Intellectual life? Readers should not expect his book to put forward an essential southern mind. His study, he said, is "in large part an assemblage of evidence" filled with "minutiae and details" about thinkers who admittedly "have left no great impression in the history of American literature."[1]

Misgivings like this about the local texture of intellectual life, and about the number and variety of texts where the life of the mind may be found, have long since passed away in the field of intellectual history. In fact, the volume before you, *Insiders, Outsiders: Toward a New History of Southern Thought*, takes these features of thought as both starting point and destination, and it aims to show the intellectual history of the South as alive with curiosity and poised for a new maturity. The authors here, historians and literary critics, take it as a given that knowing about ideas in the southern past means knowing about people of all sorts who wrote or used texts to express themselves with conviction and experiment; the authors themselves do much the same thing. Knowing the intellectual past means finding out how thinkers became writers and readers and how this shaped their ideas. It means exploring how ideas were replanted in material as well as in intellectual worlds in the South—and how this in turn generated new words with which to solve the past or imagine what is to come.[2]

The present moment of vibrant interest in the South's intellectual history is marked by a resurgence of intellectual history more broadly. There is new work on European intellectual life in the modern era, as well as work taking the measure of global intellectual history. Scholarship on the intellectual past is easy to find in the programs of major historical societies and associations. On the American scene, professional groups specific to the American intellectual past are now well established and multivoiced, including the Society for U.S. Intellectual History and the African American Intellectual History Society. A leading journal of modern thought acknowledged not long ago that a watershed has been reached in terms of how American intellectual history is conceived and written. As if to seal the moment, two new collections of essays have since arrived on the scene, each serving to bring forward questions that inspire—and perplex—the history of thought and thinking.[3]

For all of the newness, though, much of the work in U.S. intellectual history circles back to a certain turning point in the field some forty years ago. This juncture has become a touchstone in the narrative of U.S. intellectual history as a field, the ancestor in the room where today's intellectual history takes shape, including *Insiders, Outsiders*. Toward the end of the 1970s, a rising interest in social history promised exciting new visions of ordinary Americans and the fullness of their lives. Intellectual history—then inscribed as the history of elite men—began to seem a little pale. It stood apart from the wider world and from the historical struggles to define social reality. Alarmed for their discipline, a group of intellectual historians gathered in Racine, Wisconsin, in 1977 at a Frank Lloyd Wright house commonly known as Wingspread to size up the moment and decide what to do.

In the volume that resulted from the conference, *New Directions in American Intellectual History*, contributors agreed that intellectual history's fading vitality might be countered by shifting the focus from the history of certain covering concepts (the idea of "freedom," for instance) to ideas *in* history. This meant looking at the past as a cultural whole where "intellect" is drawn from a context of values and practices that saturate people's lives. Cultural anthropology is prominent in *New Directions*; Clifford Geertz receives a large number of citations. Intellectual historians such as Quentin Skinner and Thomas Kuhn also are invoked, and future path breakers of a broadly defined field receive notice, Natalie Zemon Davis, Raymond Williams, and Robert Darnton among them. The contributors were much occupied with making the practice of intellectual history a collective scholarly concern, self-consciously shared, although the collective represented by the volume (with one exception) consisted entirely of professional historians. Surprisingly, there were no literary critics among the contributors, despite the fact that American studies had been bringing historians and critics together for two decades. John Higham, in his introduction to the volume, seemed almost puzzled by his essayists' "relative indifference to literature."[4]

Looming large in all this was the figure of Arthur O. Lovejoy and his forty-year-old study of a cross-cultural idea (the Great Chain of Being) that had persisted across vast expanses of space and time. Lovejoy's vision of this idea's journey across the centuries now seemed airless in the Wingspread group's view. Lovejoy's work deserved respect, but its hypnotic timelessness was exactly intellectual history's problem. Contributors to *New Directions* wanted to be free of the impoverishing quest for the consistency of established ideas. They wanted studies that showed how changes in intellectual life have changed the *questions* that matter. The idea of a great chain of being has indeed traveled over time, David Hollinger wrote, but a new intellectual history would recognize that "disregard of the distinctive contexts" of an idea fatally diluted its historical meaning. The Wingspread volume's essays are organized in a way that exactly mirrors the challenge and the proposed solution: an initial "definitions" section followed by "History of Ideas" and "History of Culture." Be critically self-aware; bring culture in.[5]

There is no Arthur O. Lovejoy figure or unified approach to be surmounted by contributors to the two recent collections of essays in American intellectual history, though both volumes take note of what now seems to be the tentative, even mechanical, way of relating ideas to culture in the Wingspread volume. Both argue that it is once again time to take the measure of the present moment in the field's profile and accomplishments. Gone is the fear that intellectual history has become mummified. Instead, there is excitement about how to map its liveliness. In both *The Worlds of American Intellectual History* and *American Labyrinth: Intellectual History for Complicated Times*, the essays are rooted in clear social contexts and explore modes of thinking as well as established thought. Essays grow directly from authors' research, testimony to a self-confident, expanded field. *Worlds* sees the structure of the field in terms of intellectual vantage points that map domains of thought, varying from the functional ("frames," "method") to the topical ("justice," "secularization"). The *Labyrinth* volume aims to capture why ideas matter in terms of how they do their cultural work. Both volumes cover a wide range of intellectual life, from formal thought to what one essayist in *Worlds* terms the "free-range" ideas of popular thought.[6] It is clear from both volumes that scholars in the field have spent much time since 1979 thinking about class, gender, and race and about the critical value of seeing American thought in shared rather than exceptionalist terms. Particular intellectual roots or forebears are harder to find than they were in 1979, but the intellectual arena is much larger, more struggled over, and more heavily peopled. (Strangely, though, as in *New Directions*, literary critics are missing.) Scholars in both volumes agree that the best work in intellectual history puts questions about values up front and refreshes past ideas by letting us see them alive in the present.

The essays in *Insiders, Outsiders* flow from these intellectual waters, though with a southern rhythm that arises from how the history of the South has diverged in telling ways from the American mainstream. For one, the much longer persistence of human bondage in the South, along with the racial violence and segregation that fueled the Civil War and outlived it, created an amorphous but powerful atmosphere encompassing who was (or is) "inside" the South and who was not. For another, the self-awareness of being "southern," in its myriad forms and complications, raises historical questions of who *belongs* inside and who does not and where the threshold is (or could be, or should be). Indeed, the context—and the convergence—of "insiders" and "outsiders" in the South is a key theme of southern difference across the board but not in a simplistic way marked by either the South's departure from national norms or its congruence with them. Instead, southern difference is seen playing out over time in the region's particular experience of regional identity, national belonging, and global relevance.

The slave South was first beheld—and written about—as a distinctive region in the nineteenth century when social and cultural forces bent on stability were stirred up and overwhelmed by the huge national debate over human bondage. It took the Civil War and the downfall of the Confederacy to make the South an object of academic study, although "southern intellectual history" did not have its own niche until the 1960s, some would say the 1970s. Prior to that, the history of southern thought mostly circulated through two main channels: the history of politics and political ideas, and the development over time of a distinctive southern literary tradition. Politics was the fuel of the history wars that broke out over why the Civil War came, whether it was inevitable or induced by extremists, and whether "the South" was culpable. Beginning immediately after the conflict, debate over political organization and ideology dominated scholarly exchanges that zigzagged between the empirical and the polemical. The political South was the white South, and the thinkers who mattered were those intellectuals (largely "insiders" to the South, and male) who formulated the political and constitutional arguments for or against slavery, secession, and Reconstruction. Well into the 1960s, it was political ideas and thinkers who continued to define much of what counted as substantial intellectual debate.[7]

The other stream of interest in southern intellectual life, the South's literary tradition, developed alongside but apart from political history. Sometimes writing as historians of literature, literary critics became important interpreters of southern life and mind, a tradition that continues in *Insiders, Outsiders*. While the history of the South's political ideas moved into the twentieth century still weighed down by the Civil War, its literary history attempted to ease past the war, or to look for intellectual dimensions in or beyond it. From the 1890s into the mid-twentieth century, literary scholars established distinctive southern canons of literature—the plantation romance, the Southern Renaissance, antimodernism, southern local color—that grew from the study of individual authors who had made their marks on the national scene: William Faulkner, most notably, but many others, from Kate Chopin to Thomas Wolfe and Zora Neale Hurston. Critics linked an interest in southern imagination and style to a fascination with the noirish reaches of southern experience and how southern novelists and poets seemed to speak easily to audiences far beyond the South, even beyond the United States.[8]

Since the 1980s, developments in the intellectual history of the South mirror changes in many fields of historical scholarship. While *Insiders, Outsiders* is not a survey of this scholarship, widespread interest in gender, class, and race in southern society and culture has yielded a huge crop of fresh work in which intellectual historians have participated. The same is true for how study of the South has been aired out in the last three decades with insights from social theory and cultural anthropology.[9] Multicultural perspectives and a vision of a global South have cracked open older ideas about what, even *where*, "the South" was and is.[10] In short, views of the South's intellectual past have become more exploratory and nuanced and at the same time more rooted in a wider range of specific events and people.

Literary scholars, too, have continued to challenge assumptions about southern exceptionalism within the nation as well as essentialist modes of thinking that have propped up the idea of a unified southern literary canon. This is particularly true of the New Southern Studies, a body of literary and cultural scholars who see the South as not a discrete, objectified place but a cultural habitat, an imaginary, made from ideas and sensibilities that come from both inside and outside the South's geographic bounds. Indeed, whether the South exists at all is up for debate. That certain groups—academics, editors, journalists, politicians, enslavers—had a vested interest in maintaining the "reality" of the South, however, remains unquestioned, as essays in *Insiders, Outsiders* show.[11]

Creative ties between New Southern Studies scholars and intellectual historians are a distinguishing feature of where we are now in the study of southern thought. Yet *Insiders, Outsiders* is not an overview or synthesis of current conversations between critics and historians. Instead it taps into exchanges that are creatively unstable in the best sense, open-ended and unguarded. Authors speak from their respective disciplines but with the awareness that disciplines overlap. Intellectual approaches change, but they are not erased. The essays fall into two groups. The first, in part 1, highlights an array of past occasions and places for thought *in* the South. Here historians step forward but with the awareness of how distinct settings for intellectual life in the past always raise questions about how historical texts are not simple repositories of historical meaning. Rather, in both their form and content, they make meaning. Part 2 takes up modes of thinking *about* the South. Here literary scholars predominate but in ways that keep the focus on how structures of meaning recombine, but never shed, the historical particulars that gave them birth.

The essays in part 1 thus explore aspects of intellectual life understood as growing from southern ground and negotiating its time-bound material as well as its intellectual features. Shared visions among southerners of the life of the mind appear here, as well as individual struggles to believe and to know. Stephen Berry takes in hand the shape-shifting Edgar Allan Poe—a southerner or not?—to suggest that literary passions mix uneasily on the provincial stage where Poe put himself. The writer's destiny is fame or death (or fame *and* death) and how he echoes less literary folk who are clearly southern. Michael T. Bernath relates a kind of story known in many southern neighborhoods in the late antebellum years—a tale of Yankees let inside the community who become a danger to slavery and everything in white society that rested upon it. But a tale of outing the outsiders turns into a story of a community fracturing from the inside out. Beth Barton Schweiger explores how readers made books in the nineteenth-century South. Renowned for being book starved, readers in the South were in fact much more than accessories to the productions of authors and publishers. A readers' culture tossed books around, put new words into people's mouths, and embraced books as malleable things that transcended themselves in the making of intellectual life. Worldly energies like these seem foreign to the postwar, introspective writing of novelist Edwin Fuller. But as Timothy J. Williams shows, Fuller's novel *Sea-Gift* reads as a subjective counterpoint to the grandiose plans afoot among ex-Confederates reeling from defeat. In the pages of his novel, Fuller cast the white South's fantasy of a powerful nation into intimate emotional terms of yearning and imagined completeness. Mitchell Snay takes up a very different sampling of writers in the South after the war: politicians and journalists who contested what the Civil War had done to change race, labor, and the chances for southern economic recovery. Their debates over immigration as a solution to the South's needs were piecemeal and partisan but all the more powerful for it, framing questions of who belonged in the South, and who did not, in the coming decades.

Insiders, Outsiders' second interpretive path, in part 2, traces modes of thinking *about* the South. The perspective here partakes of a bit more cultural distance on the South, often with a close eye for how it is or has been (or might be) conceptualized and inscribed. Melanie Benson Taylor explores the idea of the Anthropocene and its proposition that we live in a geologic time essentially shaped by human beings—humans and their stories. The concept of the Anthropocene is immense, but it is, after all, a narrative—of the crisis we are in now, of history, and of how we place ourselves in time. Southern writers, in a sense, have for a long while taken up such themes, and their creative unease tells its own story. A crisis of a different sort—of race, civil rights, and journalism—is explored by John Grammer in his look at a trio of southern writers who defined a "southern turn" in the New Journalism of the 1960s and 1970s. Willie Morris, Marshall Frady, and Larry L. King each found themselves drawn to the unfolding civil rights movement in the South, with its unavoidable moral urgency and its ripening political demands. As southerners, these writers were drawn to the movement as insiders. As white men, they stood outside some of the danger stirred up by race and power. Grammer shows how the person-centered New Journalism, with its emphasis on "scenes" and its challenge to the ideal of journalistic objectivity, supplied this trio with the means to write about the South as a homeplace made startlingly new. In his essay on the Civil War–era writer Edward A. Pollard, Scott Romine suggests how we might rediscover Pollard by taking seriously his own rediscoveries of what it meant to be a white southerner living inside the Lost Cause. The inconsistencies and revisions in Pollard's writing are most richly seen not as flaws but as Pollard reinventing for himself the meaning of the new postwar South. If complex, sophisticated writers and texts are the subjects of traditional intellectual history, Pollard is rewarding as a "subintellectual" intellectual, whose thought we approach through the provisional realities of his thinking. Jonathan Daniel Wells's essay shows how ideas about southern insiders and outsiders influenced the critical judgment shaping *The Library of Southern Literature* in the opening decades of the twentieth century. Despite their desire to have southern writing included within the charmed circle of "American" literary excellence, *LSL* editors promoted *regional* assumptions, especially about gender and race, that privileged white men and, increasingly, white women. Whiteness, not gender, was the marker of inclusivity. In this way, the *LSL* emerged as a "new" literary creation—but one with the aspect of a memorial to the South's Confederate past. Writing intellectual history is an elusive pursuit in any case, Michael Kreyling suggests, a hunt without a clear trophy. The metaphor of the fox and the hedgehog—one knowing many things, the other one, big thing—is a playful-serious shorthand for the practice of writing history. Through the work of two pace-setting modern historians, Tony Judt and Michael O'Brien, Kreyling suggests that writing intellectual history means seeking an all-enveloping story but only from within the subtleties that belong to individuals in the past. "History" thus grows from the friction arising from different ways to combine these approaches. In the end, we are all hedgehogs and we are all foxes.

Taken together, this volume's two parts show how pursuing the South's intellectual history makes all of us insiders and outsiders, at one time or another if not all at once. It is hardly place of birth that inclines one toward knowing the South, as many immigrants comfortable in the South have found out—and as many born southerners have discovered in the relief of leaving their native land. Identity and belonging pose questions never quite answered. New thought means circling back in one way or another to what has come before.

NOTES

1. Richard Beale Davis, foreword to *Intellectual Life in Jefferson's Virginia, 1790–1830* (Chapel Hill: University of North Carolina Press, 1964).

2. The once-obscure intellectual history of the South now easily generates panels at the annual meetings of the Southern Historical Association and in professional associations whose scope goes beyond the South. In 2004, Michael O'Brien's study of intellectual life and the antebellum South won the Bancroft Prize and much other recognition. The *Journal of Southern History*, as well as the larger southern state journals such as the *Georgia Historical Quarterly*, regularly publishes new research in the history of thought in and about the South. The Southern Intellectual History Colloquium's annual meetings have taken place nationally and internationally and mark their thirty-third robust year in 2021. Civil War history and the history of African American thought have recently seen new volumes of intellectual history relevant to the southern past. See Michael O'Brien, *Conjectures of Order: Intellectual Life and the American South, 1810–1860* (Chapel Hill: University of North Carolina Press, 2004); Gregory P. Downs and Kate Masur, eds., *The World the Civil War Made* (Chapel Hill: University of North Carolina Press, 2015); and Mia Bay, Farah J. Griffin, Martha S. Jones, and Barbara D. Savage, eds., *Toward an Intellectual History of Black Women* (Chapel Hill: University of North Carolina Press, 2015).

3. See Thomas Bender, "Forum: The Present and Future of American Intellectual History; Introduction," *Modern Intellectual History* 9, no. 1 (April 2012): 149–56. The two recent volumes are Joel Isaac, James T. Kloppenberg, Michael O'Brien, and Jennifer Ratner-Rosenhagen, eds., *The Worlds of American Intellectual History* (New York: Oxford University Press, 2017); and Raymond Haberski Jr. and Andrew Hartman, eds., *American Labyrinth: Intellectual History for Complicated Times* (Ithaca, N.Y.: Cornell University Press, 2018). As part of this recent, generous moment in intellectual history, see Samuel Moyn and Andrew Sartori, eds., *Global Intellectual History* (New York: Columbia University Press, 2013); and Darrin M. McMahon and Samuel Moyn, eds., *Rethinking Modern European Intellectual History* (New York: Oxford University Press, 2014).

4. John Higham and Paul K. Conkin, eds., *New Directions in American Intellectual History* (Baltimore: Johns Hopkins University Press, 1979), quote on xvii.

5. David Hollinger, "Historians and the Discourse of Intellectuals," in Higham and Conkin, *New Directions*, 48. See Arthur O. Lovejoy, *The Great Chain of Being: A Study of the History of an Idea* (Cambridge, Mass.: Harvard University Press, 1936).

Thomas Bender, a participant in the Wingspread conference, much later recalled participants' urgent desire to avoid a march-of-ideas approach, agreeing, wrote Bender, that they "had to either find a way out of the 'American-mind' model or prepare the field for death." Bender, "Forum," 150.

6. Sarah E. Igo, "Toward a Free-Range Intellectual History," in Isaac et al., *Worlds*, 324–42.

7. Two early works of political history that gave attention to political ideas are Frank Owsley, *State Rights in the Confederacy* (Chicago: University of Chicago Press, 1925); and Jesse Carpenter, *The South as a Conscious Minority* (New York: New York University Press, 1930). John Hope Franklin's *The Militant South, 1800–1861* (Cambridge, Mass.: Harvard University Press, 1956) was a path breaker in linking intellectual history directly to the institution of slavery. The first survey of intellectual life in the South that went beyond politics and the war in substantial ways is Clement Eaton, *The Mind of the Old South* (Baton Rouge: Louisiana State University Press, 1964). Politics still matter, of course, but the ways in which historians of ideas have written about southern political thought have changed. See, e.g., Joseph Crespino, *In Search of Another Country: Mississippi and the Conservative Counterrevolution* (Princeton, N.J.: Princeton University Press, 2007); and Joseph Crespino, *Atticus Finch: The Biography; Harper Lee, Her Father, and the Making of an American Icon* (New York: Basic Books, 2018).

8. The one major work of journalist, philosopher, and tale spinner Wilbur J. Cash, published in 1941, was for many years a kind of bridge between literary scholars and the historians who ventured into the history of southern intellectual life in the 1950s and '60s. Cash's volume was secondary source and primary source rolled into one. He was compelling not only for how he captured a dreamy-violent, self-obsessed South but also because his tortured identity as a southern white man recapitulated his sense of a Romantic southern "mind." Race is nearly invisible in Cash and slavery even more so. See W. J. Cash, *The Mind of the South* (New York: Knopf, 1941).

Authors of studies published before the 1980s who set the modern tone for southern literature in a historical setting include Jay B. Hubbell, *The South in American Literature, 1607–1900* (Durham, N.C.: Duke University Press, 1954); Lewis P. Simpson, *The Dispossessed Garden: Pastoral and History in Southern Literature* (Athens: University of Georgia Press, 1975); and Louis D. Rubin Jr., *William Elliott Shoots a Bear: Essays in the Southern Literary Imagination* (Baton Rouge: Louisiana State University Press, 1975). The work of Michael O'Brien has been unparalleled among more recent scholars of the intellectual South for critically bringing together historical and literary studies. For samplers, see his two volumes of collected essays: Michael O'Brien, *Rethinking the South: Essays in Intellectual History* (Baltimore: Johns Hopkins University Press, 1988); and Michael O'Brien, *Placing the South* (Jackson: University Press of Mississippi, 2007). For an overview of this trajectory, see Sarah E. Gardner and David Moltke-Hansen, "The Transformation of Southern Intellectual History," in *Reinterpreting Southern Histories: Essays in Historiography*, ed. Craig Thompson Friend and Lorri Glover (Baton Rouge: Louisiana State University Press, 2020): 534–62.

9. See, e.g., James L. Peacock, *Grounded Globalism: How the South Embraces the World* (Athens: University of Georgia Press, 2007).

10. James L. Peacock, Harry L. Watson, and Carrie W. Matthews, eds., *The American South in a Global World* (Chapel Hill: University of North Carolina Press, 2005); Jon Smith and Deborah Cohn, eds., *Look Away! The U.S. South in New World Studies* (Durham, N.C.: Duke University Press, 2004); Matthew Pratt Guterl, *American Mediterranean: American Slaveholders in the Age of Emancipation* (Cambridge, Mass.: Harvard University Press, 2008).

11. See esp. Jon Smith, *Finding Purple America: The South and the Future of American Cultural Studies* (Athens: University of Georgia Press, 2013); and Scott Romine, *The Real South: Southern Narrative in the Age of Cultural Reproduction* (Baton Rouge: Louisiana State University Press, 2008). Additional recent scholarly works in southern intellectual history may be found throughout the essays in *Insiders, Outsiders*.

PART ONE

IDEAS IN THE SOUTH

THE INSIDER'S OUTSIDER
Edgar Allan Poe and the Art of Self-Destruction

STEPHEN BERRY

> He was altogether a strange and a fearful being, and a true history of his life would be more startling than any of the grotesque romances which he was so fond of inventing.
> —CHARLES FREDERICK BRIGGS (1849)

THE MOST famous poem in American history has its origins in an actual, individual bird. Following the runaway popularity of *The Pickwick Papers*, Charles Dickens settled into work on *Barnaby Rudge*, a book that would prove a troubled labor and a mixed success. With part of the manuscript written, Dickens began publishing *Rudge* in serial installments in his own short-lived magazine, *Master Humphrey's Clock*. He quickly became bogged down, however, not least because his wife was in the midst of a difficult pregnancy. Sitting at his desk for hours and "staring with an appearance of extraordinary interest" at the same page of a book, Dickens occasionally got restless and rambled down to his stable where he kept a pet raven named Grip. The bird had a propensity for biting children on the ankles and burying Dickens's pocket change in the yard, but Dickens wrote off such behaviors as mere play; mostly he found the bird's movements and mimicry hypnotizing. Grip's "accomplishments [have] been daily ripening and enlarging for the last twelve months to the increasing mirth and delight of all of us," Dickens said to a friend.[1]

For whatever reason, Grip's "bouncing about" seems to have leavened Dickens's spirit and inspired him with the idea to immortalize Grip in prose. Writing his illustrator, George Cattermole, in late January 1841, Dickens asked: "I want to know whether you *feel* ravens in general, and would fancy Barnaby's raven in particular. Barnaby being an idiot, my notion is to have him always in company with a pet raven who is immeasurably more knowing than himself. To this end, I have been studying my bird, and think I could make a very queer character of him." With that Dickens was off and running. By February he could proudly proclaim: "I have . . . done a very fair morning's work, at which I have sat very close, and been blessed besides with a clear view of the end of the volume. As the contents of one number usually require a day's thought at the very least, and often more, this puts me in great spirits. I think—that is, I hope—the story takes a great stride at this point, and takes it *well*. Nous verrons. [We shall see.] Grip will be strong."[2]

Sadly just as Grip was being immortalized as a fictional character, he determined to consume the shiny bits of a chaise and four parked at the Dickens stable. Returning from a writing retreat in early March, Dickens found that his pet had "ripped the lining off the carriage and eat[en] the paint off the wheels." If he'd had all summer, "I think he would have eat it all bodily," Dickens laughed. Then Grip began swooning about like Hamlet, having "lost all his mirth and foregone his customary exercises." Dosed with castor oil and fed his favorite gruel, Grip rallied enough to bite Toppings, the coachman, which Dickens took as a promising sign. The next day, however, Toppings appeared at Dickens's writing desk to say that the bird had died. "He did it with great caution and delicacy," Dickens noted, "preparing me by the remark that 'a jolly queer start had taken place'; but the shock was very great notwithstanding."[3]

Dickens sent a note of condolence to circulate among Grip's local admirers. He wittily narrated the bird's final moments in the accepted style, signed the letter "in profound sorrow," and sealed it with black wax, with a depiction, added by his illustrator, of Grip's ascension to heaven. Beneath all the playful insouciance, however, he had loved the bird. In the strange confluence of his own writer's block, his wife's pregnancy, and Grip's oddities of character, there was something that Dickens wanted preserved. And so he had Grip stuffed, encased in glass, and installed in his study to be his permanent writing companion.[4]

Two months later, Grip had a profound effect on another immortal writer, who reviewed the first few installments of *Barnaby Rudge* for the *Saturday Evening Post*. For Edgar Allan Poe, Dickens's decision to make the raven and Barnaby essential to each other—to complete each other in some mystical way—was both "beautiful" and "strikingly original," and he predicted that Grip's "frequently, appropriately, and prophetically heard" croakings were to be responsible "for some of the most exciting incidents of the story." Ten months later, in a second review in *Graham's Magazine*, this time of the whole of *Barnaby*, Poe admitted that he had been *slightly* disappointed in the uses to which Dickens put the raven. Not having Dickens's fondness for the original bird, Poe thought the fictional Grip occasionally too comical when he ought more consistently to have been the prophetic voice of doom.[5]

This criticism Poe offered as one writer to another, and indeed, the whole of his review reads as if he intended Dickens to see in its author a transatlantic peer when it came to narrative strategy. And almost surely this was precisely his intention, because, by the time Poe wrote it, Dickens was at the start of his American tour.

"I can give you no conception of my welcome," Dickens wrote of his arrival in America. "There never was a King or Emperor upon the earth so cheered and followed by crowds, and entertained at splendid balls and dinners and waited upon by public bodies of all kinds. . . . If I go out in a carriage, the crowd surrounds it and escorts me home; if I go to the theatre, the whole house (crowded to the roof) rises as one man, and timbers ring again. You cannot imagine what it is. I have five public dinners on hand at this moment, and invitations from every town and village and city in the United States." Dickens was not exaggerating, but he soon wished he had been, for what began as a gratifying reception swelled into an annoying and alarming lovefest. In Philadelphia a throng of 400 surrounded Dickens's hotel, and he had to suffer "his arm to be . . . shaken off" rather than risk a city riot. So many women wanted snippets of his signature curls that newspapers began joking that there was no way he would make it back to England anything short of bald. "Eying his profuse flow of 'soap locks' with a most envious glance," noted the *Public Ledger*, women seemed to be plotting how the author could be "thrown into a mesmeric sleep, that they could plunder his cranium of its drapery undiscovered." (No worries, noted a savvy advertiser. If the Boz was snatched bald there was a "Balm in Gilead"—the "Balm of Columbia"—which rubbed on any "bald pate [restores] hair to its pristine luxuriance and beauty.") In fairness, no one actually tore locks of Dickens's hair, but during one gala women did bribe a waiter to retrieve his hat from the hat checker and "the lovely dears plucked off all the nap, and put it in their bosoms as a memento." (When Dickens retrieved his hat at the end of the evening, he said "he imagined it had the small-pox.")[6]

Poe was an avid fan of few writers. To the extent that he worshipped anybody, he worshipped Dickens. The question was: How to get the Boz's attention? Surely Dickens didn't need yet another sycophantic American lapping at his heels. (Or as a Philadelphia newspaper critic put it, "Let us dine Boz—let us feed Boz, but not let us lick his dish after he has eaten out of it.") So, like any desperate admirer, Poe decided to take a chance. Instead of purely puffing *Barnaby Rudge*, he decided to read it more closely than any other critic and dare to point out all the little ways in which it might have been *improved*. To make sure that Dickens would take his critique in the right spirit, Poe first noted that with *Barnaby Rudge* the Boz had at last destroyed the publishing "dogma that no work of fiction can fully suit, at the same time, the critical and the popular taste." He also began with a parable. Once upon a time, the god Apollo had written an excellent poem and submitted it to a critic, who had offered up a severe censure of what all knew was a beautiful work of art. Apollo then asked the critic to list some of the beauties of the work, but the critic had "only troubled himself about the errors." In the parable, Apollo then gives the critic a sack of unwinnowed wheat and tells him "to pick out all the chaff for his pains." But "we have not fully made up our minds that the God was in the right," Poe concluded, whereupon he proceeded to compose his clever list of close readings and critical improvements. Rhetorically his review is a work of genius. He flattered Dickens's vanity by calling him a god, but he implied that even gods get lonely—they long to trade secrets and talk shop with true peers who can evaluate and appreciate their work. It was as if Poe said to Dickens: you are a god, but I am a god too, if a smaller one; come play with me.[7]

Dickens might have rewarded Poe with the social equivalent of a sack of unwinnowed wheat. Instead he gave him an interview. With the invitation to meet and a copy of the review, Poe had sent along his own *Tales of the Grotesque and Arabesque*. Dickens had barely noticed it—he "glanced" over it, he said—but he did look "more particularly at the papers to which you called my attention" and concluded, "I have the greater pleasure in expressing my desire to see you on this account." Clearly, Apollo had to cuff the critic a little. But Dickens appended some chatty insider stuff about one of the writers Poe had mentioned in his review: "Apropos of the 'construction' of *Caleb Williams*, do you know that Godwin wrote it backwards,— the last volume first,—and that when he had produced the hunting down of Caleb, and the catastrophe, he waited for months, casting about for a means of accounting for what he had done?" This was a hopeful sign: two gods conversing about a third.[8]

Thus it was with rare happiness and anticipation that Poe attended upon Dickens on March 7, 1842, at his room at the United States Hotel in Philadelphia. In preparation for their talk, Poe had procured an advance copy of Rufus Griswold's forthcoming anthology, *Poets and Poetry of America*. He had wanted the book not only to give him an excuse to read some of his own poetry but to show it displayed alongside the work of such American luminaries as Halleck, Bryant, and Longfellow. Unfortunately, Dickens didn't think much of Americans as a rule. His friend Thomas Carlyle was always making an exception of Emerson; the rest, Carlyle had said, "belong alas, alas, to the species Bore." (Mrs. Carlyle had been even more savage, claiming that Emerson was the only person worth knowing in America.) Thus it seems that Dickens listened politely through one or two of Poe's own poems before asking if the volume contained any Emerson. Poe, with mixed emotions, must have admitted that it did, and thus he began reciting Emerson's ode to "The Humble Bee":

> BURLY, dozing humble-bee,
> Where thou art is clime for me.
> Let them sail for Porto Rique,
> Far-off heats through seas to seek;
> I will follow thee alone,
> Thou animated torrid-zone!
> Zigzag steerer, desert cheerer,
> Let me chase thy waving lines;
> Keep me nearer, me thy hearer,
> Singing over shrubs and vines.

Suffice to say, Poe and Emerson would not have seen eye to eye on the idea of the humble bee as a "yellow-breeched philosopher" (line 53), and probably Poe did not even understand what he was reading when he pronounced, "Wait, I prithee, till I come / Within earshot of thy hum,— / All without is martyrdom" (lines 17–19). Poe himself had said in print, just two months before, that "Emerson belongs to a class of gentlemen with whom we have no patience whatever"—self-enraptured obscurantists whose impenetrable notions become popular precisely because no one understands them. Emerson preached a gospel of self-reliance, Poe the gospel of the self-unreliable. He was unlikely ever to win the Boz over, and yet here he was, in an American hotel room, reading poetry to Charles Dickens. Undoubtedly, he was satisfied at that.[9]

If I could go back in time to one historical moment, I certainly wouldn't spend my single time-travel token on this once-only meeting of two immortal literary minds who could never, would never, see each other whole. Even so, it must have been something to see. Dickens was the insider's insider: beautiful and well-mannered and perfectly at ease. Three years older, Poe would have been twitchy and affected; he had come into the room with disadvantages that had nothing to do with his talent. London was the literary metropole of the Western world, and Dickens stood at its absolute center. Poe was a literary provincial, removed from the metropole by layers he both could see and couldn't, all of which he resented.[10]

Historians and literary critics typically make a hash of Poe's "southernness." This is forgivable; he was a peripatetic character—as unstable geographically as he was psychologically, and his relationship to his native region was particularly complex. Over the course of his (shortened) life, Poe lived, in order, in Richmond, Scotland, London, Richmond, Charlottesville, Richmond, Baltimore, Boston, Charleston, Baltimore, New York, Baltimore, New York, Philadelphia, and New York. He spent the bare majority of his forty years in the South, but he spent the majority of his productive life in the North. Poe, it should be said, would never have defined himself a "southern" writer. His canvas was the cosmos; his settings were supernal, preternatural, and he abhorred "localism" of every stripe; preciousness of place was anathema to him. While he was by aspiration a poet, however, he was by nature a critic—a dismisser, denier, decrier, and deflater—and this particularly extended to the North. In the 1840s, just as New York City was becoming recognizably itself, Walt Whitman walked its wharfs listening to the "varied carols" of the fishermen and poetizing about his "mast-hemm'd Manhattan." At the same time, living only blocks from the Poes, Lydia Maria Child seemed hypnotized anew by each blazing storefront, where "beautiful candelabras gracefully held out their lily-cups of frosted silver, and prismatic showers of cut glass were upborne by Grecian sylphs, or knights of the middle ages, in golden armor." "I look at them, as I do at the stars and the forests," she said rhapsodically, "without slightest wish to appropriate them, and with the feeling that every human being ought to enjoy the fairest creations of Art, as freely as the sunlight and the star-glory, which our Father gives to all."[11]

At the same time, Poe walked the streets of Manhattan with nothing but scorn. It wasn't that Poe couldn't see the ribbons and rainbows of Child's New York. It was that he believed he saw through them. Child, it should be said, was no naïve optimist; as an antislaveryite, she knew as well as anyone the depths of human depravity. But like virtually all Americans, she had a perfect faith in progress. Commerce, she said, "is gradually helping the world onward to a higher and better state. It is bringing the nations into companionship, and it has already taught kings and diplomatists that war is a losing game, even to the conqueror." Poe found such notions laughable. "I have no faith in human perfectibility," he told a friend. "I think that human exertion will have no appreciable effect upon humanity. Man is now only more active—not more happy—nor more wise, than he was 6000 years ago. [And] the result will never vary."[12]

Poe's natural cynicism (or realism) is, I believe, the key to unlocking his character (and his "southernness.") The world, the supernal cosmos, may have been his province and playground as a writer, but his "southernness" was rooted in his opposition to the idea that humans had any sort of existential Manifest Destiny. Standing outside the American mainstream—with all its faith in perfectionism, capitalism, and millennialism—Poe could not help but map his defiance onto the South (just as the South came to map its defiance onto Poe). Locked out of the London and New England cliques, Poe's natural resentfulness mandated that he poke holes in transcendental verities and hypocrisies. What choice did he have? And this is the point: while Poe might not have defined himself as southern, his many critics did; certainly if he wasn't "southern" by reputation, he was "southern" by imputation, a dynamic perfectly calculated to bring out the worst in him. No wonder, then, that Poe's stories typically feature ancient families, bearing dark secrets, embracing a proud sort of decay, even as they collapse into the madness of psychic swamps, shitty land, and inwardly directed vengeance. We're (deservedly) dying, Poe implied of his "existential South," but it isn't because we don't have a mind—or a point.[13]

All of these regional and national realities were both omnipresent and politely denied at this titanic meeting of literary minds in a Philadelphia hotel room in 1842. More than anything, Poe hoped that his new connection with the great Boz could be put to selfish ends. The reality of an American writer's situation was only too well known to him. As he himself had written in 1836, Americans would only read "the productions of our native writers . . . after repeated assurances from England that such productions were not altogether contemptible." (Alexis de Tocqueville had said the same: in making "up their minds upon the merit of their authors, [Americans] generally wait till his fame has been ratified in England.") It was imperative to Poe, then, that he secure an English publisher for an edition of his tales, and given his exorbitant fame, Dickens could have done a great deal for him if he had been inclined.[14]

He was not inclined. Returned to England, Dickens lost Poe's letter, then blamed his secretary, then waited nine months before claiming he had mentioned Poe's book to all the publishers with whom he had any influence and "one and all [had] declined the venture." (In fact, Dickens had written to *one* publisher, Edward Moxon, and then only to secure a rejection he could forward to Poe. "Pray write me such a reply as I can send to the author," he said, that I may "get absolution for my conscience in this matter.") Dickens then assured Poe: "Believe me that it never, for a moment, escaped my recollection [to do] all in my power to bring [this] to a successful issue [and] do not for a moment suppose that I have ever thought of you but with a pleasant recollection." By successively drawing Poe's attention to the very idea he was denying, Dickens seems to have been, as he later proved, disingenuous. The coup de grace came, appropriately, at the end: "The only consolation I can give you," he told Poe, "is that I do not believe any collection of detached pieces by an *unknown* writer, even though he were an Englishman, would be at all likely to find a publisher in this metropolis just now." It is never inspiring to be called an unknown, particularly by an idol. But Dickens was the best-known writer in the English-speaking world, and Poe consoled himself that anyone would be an "unknown" by that standard. And so Poe determined not to read between Dickens's lines and tried not to see in the Boz's protestations of regard the labor of a man who doth protest too much.[15]

And then Dickens published his anonymous review of "American poetry" in the January 1844 issue of *Foreign Quarterly Review*. "Before we close this article," the author promised, "we hope to satisfy the reader that, with two or three exceptions, there is not a poet of mark in the whole [American] Union." Reading the review for the first time, Poe's heart must have quickened. Would he be one of the few singled out for praise? Was it possible there had been a *mutual* recognition of genius in his interview with Dickens? The first prize for originality went to Longfellow, but he had the unfair advantage of a European education, so "we have some doubts whether he can be fairly considered an indigenous [American] specimen." This left a single slot for a truly original American poet, and that went to . . . Emerson and his humble bee. "Without being in the slightest degree an imitation [the poem] constantly reminds us of the gorgeous beauty of L'Allegro," the anonymous critic intoned. And "there is pleasant wisdom hived in the bag of [this] 'yellow-breeched philosopher.'" Emerson had not written much poetry, the critic admitted, but this was to his credit also. "Mr. Emerson evidently cares little about any reputation to be gained by writing verses; his intellect seeks other vents, where it is untrammeled by forms and conditions. But he cannot help his inspiration." His was a native, natural, American genius.[16]

Poe must have been mildly crushed at this. Dickens wouldn't even have known about Emerson's "yellow-breeched philosopher" if Poe hadn't read it to him. Then the review worsened. Where Emerson was an American original who had won a reputation without trying, Poe, the review concluded, was an American "mocking-bird," a semiskilled "imitator" of Tennyson who could sing but "a solitary note" of his own. Though the article went on to handle other poets even more roughly, Poe was devastated. Friends sought to assure him that Dickens hadn't really written it, and there was a great deal of speculation in the press as to the identity of the anonymous critic who could so cavalierly dismiss virtually the whole of American poetry. "THE ARTICLE in the *Foreign Quarterly* . . . is attributed by many to the pen of Dickens," noted the *Spirit of the Times*. "We know not why. It certainly bears not one of his characteristics. We don't believe the rumor." Poe did believe it. "It has been denied that Dickens wrote it," he said to a friend, "but, to me, the article affords so strong internal evidence of his hand that I would as soon think of doubting my existence." "Nearly every thing in the critique," he continued, "I heard from him, or suggested to him, personally. The poem of Emerson I read to him." There could be no doubt. Poe had gone to Dickens's hotel room hoping to find a kindred spirit, but Dickens had chosen Emerson before Poe even stepped in the room.[17]

Poe took the blow relatively well. He continued to believe and to say that Dickens had a "vigorous, glorious *imagination*" and wielded his pen like "the wand of an enchanter." He was also inclined to defend himself and his countrymen. "*We are* a poetical people," he assured his fellow Americans. Yes, the work of taming a continent had taken precedence and given

Americans a reputation for practicality. "But the arena of exertion, and of consequent distinction, into which our first and most obvious wants impelled us, has been regarded as the field of our deliberate choice," Poe noted. "Our necessities have been mistaken for our propensities. Having been forced to make rail-roads, it has been deemed impossible that we should make verse. Because it suited us to construct an engine in the first instance, it has been denied that we could compose an epic in the second."[18]

And so in a mix of homage, showing off, and pain at his rejection, Poe set out to distinguish himself by taking Dickens's own materials and showing him what he had missed. In his review of *Barnaby Rudge*, Poe had said that more might have been made of Grip. Dickens had littered his novel with possibilities. Grip was constantly "conducting himself . . . in a more than usually thoughtful, deep, and mysterious manner"; he was engaged in "his own grave pursuits," burying and unburying things, digging holes to whisper secrets to the earth, though the reader knows they won't stay buried. At one point Barnaby responds to another's curiosity about the bird: "You had good reason to ask me what he is for sometimes it puzzles me . . . to think he's only a bird." And when the bird helps reveal the truth, Barnaby has "a dark cloud [that] overhung his whole previous existence, and never cleared away." Finally "the bird himself advanced with fantastic steps to the very door of the bar, and then cried, 'I'm a devil, I'm a devil, I'm a devil!' with extraordinary rapture." When Grip is first making noise, someone remarks, "What was that—him tapping at the door?" The answer is "'Tis some one knocking softly at the shutter." Yes, in the novel, the bird seems a creepily displaced aspect of Barnaby, but Barnaby is a half-wit: something is obviously missing, damage has too obviously been done by others, by history. But what if the central character was a genius and still not whole? What if the damage is self-inflicted? What if the bird kept burying unburiable secrets in his master's bosom—like the truth about death itself? Dickens had said that Poe was the sort of bird who could croak only a single note. Poe would give him a note to remember, and he would do it from Dickens's dead pet's own throat.[19]

The *American Review* gave Poe nine dollars for "The Raven." Because the journal made it a policy to only "publish poems either unsigned or with pseudonyms," Poe chose "Quarles"—a mash-up of "quarrel" and "Charles" (Dickens). Hoping to get his authorship of the poem on the record, however, Poe asked his employer at the New York *Evening Mirror*, Nathaniel Parker Willis, to run an "advance copy" on the back page of the issue for January 29, 1845. Poe had been so steady that Willis was happy to do it; he even inserted an endorsement: "In our opinion, it is the most effective single example of 'fugitive poetry' ever published in this country; and unsurpassed in English poetry for subtle conception, masterly ingenuity of versification, and consistent, sustaining of imaginative lift and pokerishness [ability to excite fear]. It is one of these 'dainties bred in a book' which we feed on. It will stick to the memory of everybody who reads it."[20]

Willis was right. No poem has ever created, or will ever create, so instantaneous a sensation. Within days it was reprinted in all of the New York papers. Within weeks it had spread to Boston, Philadelphia, Baltimore, and Richmond. ("Everybody reads the poem and praises it," summarized the *New World*. "It is written in a Stanza unknown before to gods, men, and booksellers, but it fills and delights the ear strangely with its wild and clashing music." This was not entirely true—Poe had borrowed the rhyme and rhythm from an Elizabeth Barrett Browning poem—but it certainly *seemed* new.) And within months, the poem had skipped the pond, and Elizabeth Barrett Browning herself was writing to Poe: "Your 'Raven' has produced a sensation, a 'fit of horror,' here in England. Some of my friends are taken by the fear of it and some by the music. I hear of persons haunted by the 'Nevermore,' and one acquaintance of mine who has the misfortune of possessing a 'bust of Pallas' never can bear to look at it in the twilight." (So far as is known, Dickens never commented on the irony of his own Grip returning from the dead to incite a "fit of horror" in his native country. One can hope he had the decency to read the poem to its inspiration, his writing partner, the raven-under-glass.)[21]

Poe had scored other successes in his career, particularly with "The Gold Bug," but, as he put it, the "bird beat the bug . . . all hollow." "The Raven" is "the talk of the town," admitted Julia Ward Howe. "'The Raven' has taken rank over the whole world of literature," echoed the *Southern Literary Messenger*. "Soon the Raven became known everywhere, and everyone was saying 'Nevermore,'" remembered Elizabeth Oakes Smith. Apparently the whole nation had gone stark "Raven" mad. Arriving at a theater, Poe was not long in his seat before one of the actors contrived his lines to place a heavy emphasis on the word "nevermore," and the effect was chilling. The assembly "took up the allusion" en masse, Poe later said. "A thrill seemed to pass through the whole audience, and the sensation, together with its cause, were not to be mistaken." Poe could hardly believe it, perhaps especially because it was what he had always wanted. Toiling for years in various genres, ginning up column inches on whatever nonsense would keep the wolf from the door, grubbing about as a "sub-editor" or assistant editor or assistant to the editor: it all seemed to be coming to an end. With one poetic breakthrough, Poe had forced his contemporaries to notice him anew. "He has squared out blocks enough to build an enduring pyramid," marveled an author for *Graham's*, "but has left them lying carelessly and unclaimed in many different quarries." Seizing the opportunity, Wiley and Putnam issued a volume of Poe's *Tales* in June and a collection of his poetry, *The Raven and Other Poems*, in November.[22]

There were some among his fellow poets who, out of artistic scruple or professional jealousy, found "The Raven" too popular. Fanny Longfellow allowed that "The Raven" was "most artistically rhythmical but 'nothing more.'" Emerson himself could "see nothing in it" and had to have Poe's name repeated twice before exclaiming, "Ah, you mean the Jingle-Man!" Even Poe's own biographer gives his signature effort a rather scathing review:

> To a cold critical eye the dance-craze rhythms and Technicolor alliteration can seem pointlessly deft, verbal equivalents of rolling a half-dollar across one's knuckles. William Butler Yeats, for one, thought the poem "insincere and vulgar." "Analyze the Raven," he said, "and you find that its subject is a commonplace and its execution a rhythmical trick. Its rhythm never lives for a moment, never once moves with an emotional life." For many [of] the most discriminating critics, Poe succeeded all too well in suiting the popular taste, producing a work fatally destined to be Beloved, a poem for people who don't like poetry.[23]

And perhaps that is what the poem has become. But to dismiss it so easily is to dismiss the feelings of the thousands of people who lived through it. "I wish I could convey to you the impression which the 'Raven' has made upon me," confessed John Reuben Thompson, editor of the *Southern Literary Messenger*. "Like Sinbad in the Valley of Diamonds, I find a new jewel at every step. The beautiful rhythm, the mournful cadence, still ring in the ear for hours after a perusal—whilst the heart is bowed down by the outpourings of a soul made desolate not alone by disappointed love, but by the crushing of every hope, and every aspiration." Poe's genius was in implicitly understanding that the human heart might want to practice dying by littles, might want, for a moment, to feel crushed of every hope and aspiration. Read the poem again: again and again the poem's narrator crafts a question whose most devastating answer is "Nevermore." In one of the stranger alchemies of literature, Poe compounded his resentment of Dickens, his emulation of Dickens, his unswerving affection for Dickens, and his overweening desire for Dickens's own popularity to create publishing gold. Wrapped in Grip's skin, his nightly performances of and as "The Raven" were the toast of New York, and he had only to sit back and wait to be admitted into the pantheon of American poetry.

Instead he decided to use his new fame to wage relentless war on the man Dickens had called "unquestionably the first of [America's] poets"—Henry Wadsworth Longfellow.[24]

"What has 'broke loose' in Poe?" George Rex Graham asked Longfellow in a letter. "I see he is down on you in the New York papers." "Down" didn't begin to cover it. For a month, Poe had been hacking at Longfellow with maniacal fury. The "Little Longfellow War," as Poe called it, had begun mildly enough with an article he wrote for the *Broadway Journal* reiterating some of the points he had made in a lecture about Longfellow's imitativeness. But as Poe warmed to his subject, he found that the first article necessitated a second, the second a third, a fourth, and a fifth. His editor, the relatively inexperienced Charles Briggs, stood by somewhat flabbergasted. "[Poe] is bent on riding [his hobby] to death," he complained, but "I think the better way is to let him run down as soon as possible by giving him no check." (Ultimately Briggs would turn the whole of the *Broadway Journal* over to Poe.)[25]

Unchecked, Poe's criticism of Longfellow's imitativeness gradually morphed into accusations of literary larceny on an unprecedented scale, and he capped off his self-destructive run with the single-most damaging public appearance of his career. In the middle of Poe's escalating tirade against Longfellow, the editor of the *Boston Daily Atlas* offered him a challenge: "If [Poe] were to come before a Boston audience with such stuff," she said, "they would *poh* him at once." Perversely, Poe then not only accepted an invitation to appear in Boston but agreed to deliver an original poem. He had been savaging Longfellow and the Boston clique for months—he had told the world that one of Boston's favorite sons was the "Great Mogul" of imitative art—and now he would voluntarily stand before a Boston audience and invite them to critique an original poem *he did not have*.[26]

Poe's performance was a perfect disaster. Far more than the ridiculous stunt of deciding to read his impenetrable, sophomoric poem "Al Aaraaf," he capped this disaster with a homicidal rant about getting drunk and cutting the throat of his grandmother. He seemed from the outside to be gleefully blowing up his own celebrity. Byron had done this kind of thing too, but Byron had had a fortune and a title and a European public that half admired a good Romantic scandal. America was more puritanical, and Poe's self-destructiveness seemed more embarrassing than grand.[27]

Martin Farquhar Tupper knew none of this at the end of November when he wrote the editor of the London *Literary Gazette*. He had received a volume of Poe's short stories—the stories Dickens had "glanced" over—and he wanted to offer up his judgment: "I volunteer a critique for your *Gazette*: the book is worth all I say of it: if you find the extracts too long, you can shorten them; but perhaps you will find room for all. I have no other cause to serve in this . . . except to give a foreign genius some encouragement amongst us Britishers. . . . How say you? Shall we, or shall we not, make Edgar A. Poe, famous?"[28]

Poe became infamous instead. "Edgar Allan Poe is dead," noted the *New-York Tribune* on October 9, 1849. "This announcement will startle many, but few will be grieved by it." Immediately after publishing "The Raven," the Raven burned himself out on a national stage. Given the chance to achieve everything he had dreamed of, he chose instead to get drunk and to finish the work of killing himself that began in earnest the night his wife, Virginia, sang to him and started bleeding.[29]

It is for just such utter lack of self-control that Poe has earned the enmity of critics. His poems could be so singsongy that Emerson derisively dubbed him "The Jingle Man." His tales could be so overwritten that James Russell Lowell pronounced him "two fifths sheer fudge." As a literature critic, Poe was probably more guilty of every crime he ever accused better writers of committing. And though it is a low blow, aimed at emasculating him, W. H. Auden is probably correct in guessing that Poe's love life was "largely confined to crying in laps and playing house." But to everything Poe was ever accused of, he bleakly responded, "I did it"—and not merely because he did do it but because, having pointed the finger at himself so long and so ably, he was ever ready to confess to anything.[30]

Poe was not perfect. He did things and was things that perhaps shouldn't have been forgiven. "One of the strange points of his strange nature," said a friend after his death, "was to entertain a spirit of revenge toward all who did him a service. His pecuniary difficulties often compelled him to solicit aid, and he rarely, or never, failed to malign those who befriended him." Poe bit every hand that ever tried to feed him. Grim, prim, and clad invariably in black, Poe, it was said, could suck the light out of a room. His body was "slightly... formed," his head was "massive" with a forehead "exquisitely white." He seemed, said one witness, like a pale balloon tethered to earth by a narrow black string. And when Virginia died, that string was cut, and Poe drifted, not up, toward heaven, but out, into an eternal and meaningless cold.[31]

Importantly, Poe took his countrymen with him. Even as they sat comfortably reading their beloved "fireside poets," Poe's contemporaries instinctively responded to his spectacular self-destruction. The poet Hart Crane later noted that if America was like a shining train, ever on the go, Poe was the reeking hobo haunting the cars and stations whose mad ravings unnerved the passengers enough to invite their scorn but not their sympathy. This is brilliant but not quite true, and not quite fair, particularly to Poe's contemporaries. "Money (to tell a useless truth)," noted one leading magazinist of the day, "could not be better laid out for the honor of this period of American literature—neither by the government, by a society, nor by an individual—than in giving Edgar Poe a competent annuity, on condition that he should never write except upon impulse, never dilute his thoughts for the magazines, and never publish anything till it had been written a year." Poe's countrymen recognized his genius, and the desperate penury that drove his hackwork, and from the beginning, they were drawn to the way he drew the abyss.[32]

By 1850, Americans had watched their country double in size twice (once with the Louisiana Purchase and again with the Mexican Cession); they had won two wars against the most powerful country in the world (Britain); their population was doubling every twenty-two years (at twice the rate of Britain); and their economy was modernizing quicker than any in history. And everyone from Wall Street stockjobbers to backwoods hog drovers was feeling the effects. "Histrey cold not relate aneything to excell the progress," goggled one Tennessee pig herder, and "we are still going ahead."[33]

And the pig herder was right. The country had made a startling debut, and by 1850 most Americans believed that their nation either was or would soon become the greatest civilization ever to grace the earth. Traveling to New York in September 1858, South Carolina planter William Elliott was present for a two-day celebration of the laying of the first

Atlantic cable (between Ireland and Newfoundland). Looking down from the upper window of his hotel on "the thronging multitudes that—filling the streets—were distributed on the very house tops," he began to sob. "[I] remembered this City as I had known it in 1806," he wrote his wife, and "whether it was patriotism or what other feeling—I know not—but the tears streamed down from my eyes. Possibly it was a commendable pride at witnessing the extraordinary progress of the Country." Americans had for years told brazen tales about their special destiny as a people; by 1850 it was beginning to seem as if the tales might be true. No longer a passive exemplar—a City upon a Hill—America began to dream itself an empire for the ages.[34]

To the observers living the dream, however, the country's rapid growth seemed often more frenetic and disorienting than directed and progressive. The attainments were lofty, the rhetoric loftier, but still there was something in the speed of the advancement that seemed reckless in itself. Americans were a simple, republican people at heart. Their progress, while fortuitous, had also gotten beyond their ability to assimilate and make sense of it. The economy, while booming, was also volatile and easily overheated. The first sharp contraction came in 1819. While Europe had been at war and grain prices were high, Americans had sunk their fortunes into western land. Then Napoleon went to Elba, the grain market collapsed, investors dumped what they could, the banks foreclosed on the rest and battened down the credit, and suddenly America's first economic bubble had burst. In Philadelphia, unemployment reached 75 percent, and 1,800 workers were imprisoned for debt. Tent cities ringed Baltimore. No one yet knew it, but it was the beginning of the business cycle, and every twenty years the dragon would return for its tribute—in Panics of 1837, 1857, 1873, and 1893 that rounded out the century. "Oh for a snug little farm," a planter lamented in 1846, "where I could indulge my fondness for the country . . . without the anxiety created by the idea that the 'main chance' depends on having every screw tight & and the whole machinery moving on clock-work principles."[35]

Faced with a clockwork life, the number of communal experiments and utopian societies ballooned. The Millerites went up their mountain . . . and came back down to their "Great Disappointment." Despite their country's success, indeed because of it, Americans hungered for a more authentic experience. "The present state of the world is most momentous," noted one editorial, "and to one that can look back for the last thirty years, the changes they have brought with them are beyond the wildest imaginings.

[N]ew and extended powers . . . together with the wonderful inventions of man, have added to his nature, have made him almost another being." The writer needn't have said "almost." What was being born in America *was* a new being: the Romantic self—the deserving, questing, unsatisfied, aspiring, ever-dreaming, ever-dying Romantic self.[36]

Looking at this state of affairs, some Romantics turned into transparent eyeballs. Some found a pond and made love to it. Some sang the body electric. Some retreated to their rooms to write little poems about birds and wrap them in red ribbons. Only Poe decided to destroy himself—and that's why he's immortal—because sometimes, at three in the morning, his countrymen (and we) grow perversely certain that his is the proper response.

Poe's biographers have turned him into a dreamer and a dark Romantic compelled by mommy issues into a "mournful and never ending remembrance." In truth, Poe was a shameless, shameful, sometimes vile creature who burned every bridge, bit every hand that fed him, and cried out in a great existential rage: fuck you, fuck God, fuck this country and fuck Longfellow, fuck this emerging capitalist age, and most of all, fuck me, fuck me forever.

It is for his vast condemnation of being that Poe has earned the affection of his fans. "I came into this world without my knowledge or consent," wrote one of Poe's contemporaries. "If . . . a Superior and Designing Being created me and placed me here; if this is *all* or the best, *I do not thank him*. I wish I had been let alone. I should not object—hating the pain and lurking fear of death, to be remanded at once to my original nothingness, for this is a world of ineffable misery and from my experience I abominate it and most that it contains. If there is a Hereafter, then the God who placed me here owes me large compensation for the sufferings I have *involuntarily* undergone on Earth."[37]

As well as any writer ever, Poe captures the rage we feel at our very smallness before death, at the performing-monkey way we go about our mortal work. Poe is the patron saint of *every* jingle man, *every* hypocrite, *every* man not quite good enough for the glitterati, *every* dying soul who ever threw an infantile tantrum at the desolating kick in the pit of the soul and unleashed a plaintive groan at the stupidity of a life both too miserable and too short. "The mass of men lead lives of quiet desperation," said Thoreau—but Poe refused to be quiet. And, to his credit and his shame, he raged not against the dying of the light but against the light itself and against the God who would give such light, only to take it away.

"My whole nature," he supposedly said, "utterly *revolts* at the idea that there is any Being in the Universe superior to myself." He did not mean that he thought so greatly much of himself. He meant that he thought so greatly little of a God who could heap upon his children such needless pain.[38]

NOTES

1. Charles Dickens and John Forster, *The Works of Charles Dickens* (London: Chapman and Hall, 1899), 215.

2. *The Letters of Charles Dickens* (London: Chapman and Hall, 1880), 1:39; Dickens and Forster, *Works of Charles Dickens*, 143–44.

3. *The Letters of Charles Dickens* (London: Oxford University Press, 1969), 304.

4. Pet preservation had come into its own in England in 1829 when George IV lost his beloved giraffe, a gift from the pasha of Egypt.

5. Edgar Allan Poe, review of *Barnaby Rudge*, by Charles Dickens, *Saturday Evening Post*, May 1, 1841.

6. *Letters of Charles Dickens* (1880), 1:59; William Clyde Wilkins, *Charles Dickens in America* (London: Chapman and Hall, 1911), 161.

7. George Lippard, "The 'Boz' Fever in Philadelphia," *Spirit of the Times* (New York), February 7, 1842; Edgar Allan Poe, review of *Barnaby Rudge*, by Charles Dickens, *Graham's Magazine*, February 1842. For more on Poe and Dickens, see Undine, "Poe and Charles Dickens," *The World of Edgar Allan Poe* (blog), March 1, 2013, http://worldofpoe.blogspot.com/2013/03/poe-and-charles-dickens.html.

8. Dickens to Poe, March 6, 1842, Edgar Allan Poe Society of Baltimore, https://www.eapoe.org/misc/letters/t4203060.htm, accessed October 19, 2018.

9. Joseph Slater, ed., *The Correspondence of Emerson and Carlyle* (New York and London: Columbia University Press, 1964), 345n2; Edgar Allan Poe, "An Appendix of Autographs," *Graham's Magazine*, January 1842, 49. It continues to be Poe's peculiar fate to be unfavorably compared to Emerson. As Harold Bloom noted: "Poe, a true Southerner, abominated Emerson, plainly perceiving that Emerson (like Whitman, like Lincoln) was not a Christian, not a royalist, not a classicist. . . . If you dislike Emerson, you probably will like Poe. . . . Emerson, for better and for worse, was and is the mind of America, but Poe was and is our hysteria, our uncanny unanimity in our repressions." Harold Bloom, *Edgar Allan Poe* (New York: Chelsea House, 2006), 1.

10. On "Anglophilia" and the antebellum American writer, see Christopher Hanlon, *America's England: Antebellum Literature and Atlantic Sectionalism* (London: Oxford University Press, 2016); and Elisa Tamarkin, *Anglophilia: Deference, Devotion, and Antebellum America* (Chicago: University of Chicago Press, 2008).

11. While not usually identifying as "southern," Poe was quite defensive of southern literature and occasionally positioned himself rhetorically as "southern." During a literary dustup with James Russell Lowell, for instance, Poe called Lowell "one of the most rabid of the Abolition fanatics" and advised that "no Southerner who does not

wish to be insulted, and at the same time revolted by a bigotry the most obstinately blind and deaf, should ever touch" one of his volumes. "It is a fashion among Mr. Lowell's set to affect a belief that there is no such thing as Southern Literature," Poe continued. "Northerners—people who have really nothing to speak of as men of letters—are cited by the dozen, and lauded by this candid critic without stint, while Legare, Simms, Longstreet, and others of equal note are passed by in contemptuous silence." Edgar Allan Poe, "A Fable for the Critics," *Southern Literary Messenger*, March 1849, https://www.eapoe.org/works/harrison/jah13c16.htm. While I have suggested that historians have made a hash of Poe's southernness, I do not mean to imply that academics have done a poor job generally of historicizing Poe. In 2001, J. Gerald Kennedy published *A Historical Guide to Edgar Allan Poe* (New York: Oxford University Press, 2001) and has generally helped to lead a renaissance in historically inflected Poe studies. See, e.g., J. Gerald Kennedy, *Strange Nation: Literary Nationalism and Cultural Conflict in the Age of Poe* (New York: Oxford University Press, 2016).

Walt Whitman, "Crossing Brooklyn Ferry," in *The Portable Walt Whitman* (New York: Penguin, 2003), 154; Lydia Maria Child, *Letters from New York* (New York: C. S. Francis, 1846), 97.

12. Child, *Letters from New York*, 255; Poe to James Russell Lowell, July 2, 1844, Edgar Allan Poe Society of Baltimore, https://www.eapoe.org/works/letters/p4407020.htm, accessed August 24, 2019.

13. This obviously raises the issue of Poe's position on slavery, which has also been debated deeply. In three tales—"A Predicament," "The Man That Was Used Up," and "The Gold Bug"—Poe presents ludicrous and deeply offensive enslaved characters that also seem perfectly at home in the sadly *American* tradition of blackface and minstrelsy. In *The Narrative of Arthur Gordon Pym*, Poe loads black and white with symbolic meanings—whiteness symbolizing the mystical, sacred, and by novel's end, godly, while blackness is portrayed as the color of the murderous natives. More interesting, from a regional perspective, are those stories in which Poe identifies with, and borrows energy from, the racialized other, portraying black figures as a shrewd and resourceful force of vengeance. This is nowhere more apparent than in Poe's final published tale, "Hop-Frog," in which an enslaved black jester avenges himself on a white king and his court, hauling them to the top of a ballroom and setting them on fire. The jester then bounds out of the throne room with the exclamation "This is my last jest"—Poe's last published words as an author.

14. Edgar Allan Poe, review of *The Culprit Fay, and Other Poems*, by Joseph Rodman Drake, and of *Alnwick Castle, with Other Poems*, by Fitz-Greene Halleck, *Southern Literary Messenger*, April 1836; Sidney P. Moss, "Poe's 'Two Long Interviews' with Dickens," *Poe Studies* 11, no. 1 (June 1978), 10–12; Alexis de Tocqueville, *Democracy in America* (New York, 1843), 2:58. For a sense of the broader literary landscape in which Poe wrote, see David S. Reynolds, *Beneath the American Renaissance: The Subversive Imagination in the Age of Emerson and Melville* (New York: Knopf, 1988); Robert Weisbuch, *Atlantic Double-Cross: American Literature and British Influence in the Age of Emerson* (Chicago: University of Chicago Press, 1989); and Kennedy, *Strange Nation*.

15. Dickens to Poe, November 27, 1842, Edgar Allan Poe Society of Baltimore, https://www.eapoe.org/misc/letters/t4211270.htm, accessed October 16, 2018.

16. "American Poetry," *Foreign Quarterly Review* 32 (January 1844), 291–324. Controversy surrounds the precise authorship of this takedown, but the point here is that Poe believed Dickens wrote it. See Gerald G. Grubb, "From 'Sketches by Boz' through 'Barnaby Rudge,'" pt. 1 of "The Personal and Literary Relationships of Dickens and Poe," *Nineteenth-Century Fiction* 5, no. 1 (June 1950): 1–22; and Gerald G. Grubb, "'English Notes' and 'The Poets of America,'" pt. 2 of "The Personal and Literary Relationships of Dickens and Poe," *Nineteenth-Century Fiction* 5, no. 2 (September 1950): 101–20.

17. "American Poetry," 175; *Spirit of the Times*, January 31, 1844, 2, col. 3; Poe to James Russell Lowell, March 30, 1844, in *The Collected Letters of Edgar Allan Poe*, ed. John Ward Ostrom, Burton R. Polin, and Jeffrey A. Savoye (Staten Island, N.Y.: Gordian, 2008), 1:256–59. Poe persisted in believing Dickens was behind the review; responding to the Brook Farm *Phalanx*, he explained his reasons for publishing juvenilities in a volume of collected poetry: "Our foot-note . . . has reference to an article written by Charles Dickens in the London 'Foreign Quarterly Review' in which Mr. Dickens had paid us some injudicious compliments, among them that 'we had all Tennyson's spirituality, and might be considered as the best of his imitators'—words to that effect." See also Sidney P. Moss, *Poe's Literary Battles: The Critic in the Context of His Literary Milieu* (Durham, N.C.: Duke University Press, 1963), 205.

18. Edgar Allan Poe, review of *The Poets and Poetry of America*, by R. W. Griswold, *Boston Miscellany of Literature and Fashion*, November 1842, 218–21. Again, Poe was responding directly to the *Foreign Quarterly Review* article, which had concluded, "We repeat, however, that it is a matter of regret, and not of censure, that America should be destitute of a national literature." "American Poetry," 176.

19. Charles Dickens, *Barnaby Rudge: A Tale of the Riots of 'Eighty* (London: Chapman and Hall, 1841), 266, 263.

20. Edgar Allan Poe, "The Raven," *Evening Mirror* (New York), January 29, 1845, 4. See also Joseph Jackson, "Poe's Signature to the 'The Raven,'" *Sewanee Review* 26, no. 3 (July 1918): 272–75.

21. Edgar Allan Poe, "The Raven," *Southern Literary Messenger*, March 1845; Edgar Allan Poe, "The Raven," *Howard District Press* (Ellicotts, Md.), February 15, 1845; Edgar Allan Poe, "The Raven," *Pennsylvania Inquirer and National Gazette* (Philadelphia), February 15, 1845. For other contemporary reprints and excerpts of "The Raven" in the popular press, see "Edgar Allan Poe—'The Raven,'" Edgar Allan Poe Society of Baltimore, http://www.eapoe.org/works/info/pp073.htm, accessed July 31, 2020.

22. Elizabeth Oakes Smith, "Autobiographic Notes: Edgar Allan Poe," *Beadle's Monthly*, February 1867, 147–56; James Russell Lowell, "Our Contributors, No. XVII: Edgar Allan Poe," *Graham's Magazine*, February 1845. "There is indeed but one other—the 'Humble Bee' of Ralph Waldo Emerson, which can be ranked near it." John Moncure Daniel, "Edgar Allan Poe," *Southern Literary Messenger*, March 1850, 184.

23. Fanny Longfellow to Samuel Longfellow, February 13, 1845, in *Mrs. Longfellow: Selected Letters and Journals of Fanny Appleton Longfellow*, ed. Edward Wagenknecht (New York: Longmans, Green, 1956), 116; Edwin Watts Chubb, *Stories of Authors, British and American* (New York: Sturgis and Walton, 1910), 285;

Kenneth Silverman, *Edgar A. Poe: Mournful and Never-Ending Remembrance* (New York: HarperCollins, 1991), 239.

24. John R. Thompson, "The Late Edgar A. Poe," *Southern Literary Messenger*, November 1849; "American Poetry," 316.

25. Graham to Longfellow, March 11, 1845, in Mary Elizabeth Phillips, *Edgar Allan Poe: The Man* (Chicago: J. C. Winceton, 1926), 978; Briggs to Lowell, March 8, 1845, in George Edward Woodberry, *Edgar Allan Poe* (1885), 227. On the "Little Longfellow War," see also Perry Miller, *The Raven and the Whale: The War of Words and Wits in the Era of Poe and Melville* (New York: Harcourt Brace, 1956).

26. *Boston Daily Atlas*, March 3, 1845.

27. See Ghislaine McDayter, *Byromania and the Birth of Celebrity Culture* (New York: SUNY Press, 2009).

28. George Haven Putnam, *George Palmer Putnam: A Memoir, Together with a Record of the Earlier Years of the Publishing House Founded by Him* (New York: G. P. Putnam's Sons, 1912), 395. Tupper did end up reviewing Poe's book. See Martin Farquhar Tupper, review of *Tales of the Grotesque and Arabesque*, by Edgar Allan Poe, *Literary Gazette and Journal of the Belles Lettres*, January 31, 1846, 101–3, https://www.eapoe.org/papers/misc1827/lg460131.htm.

29. Rufus W. Griswold, "The Death of Edgar A. Poe," *New-York Daily Tribune*, October 9, 1849, 2.

30. James Russell Lowell, *A Fable for Critics; or, Better, a Glance at a Few of Our Literary Progenies from the Tub of Diogenes; a Vocal and Musical Medley, That Is, a Series of Jokes* (New York: G. P. Putnam, 1848), 78; W. H. Auden, *Edgar Allan Poe: Selected Prose, Poetry, and Eureka* (New York: Rinehart, 1950), xv.

31. "Topics of the Month," *Holden's Dollar Magazine* 4 (1849), 766.

32. Nathaniel Parker Willis, "Odd Poem," *Home Journal*, April 28, 1849.

33. John Shofner to Michael Shofner, August 28, 1834, Michael Shofner Papers, Southern Historical Collection, University of North Carolina at Chapel Hill.

34. William Elliott to Ann Elliott, September 3, 1858, in Beverly Scafidel, "The Letters of William Elliott" (PhD diss., University of South Carolina, 1978), 914–15.

35. James Henry Hammond to William B. Hodgson, January 1, 1846, quoted in Drew Gilpin Faust, *James Henry Hammond and the Old South: A Design for Mastery* (Baton Rouge: Louisiana State University Press, 1985), 231.

36. "The Days We Live In," *Southern Literary Messenger*, December 1854, 758.

37. Carol K. Bleser, *Secret and Sacred: the Diaries of James Henry Hammond, a Southern Slaveholder* (New York: Oxford University Press, 1988), 263.

38. Poe's comment was described by John Henry Hopkins Jr. in a letter to a Mrs. Shew, February 9, 1875. See John Carl Miller, *Building Poe: Biography* (Baton Rouge: Louisiana State University Press, 1977), 100–101.

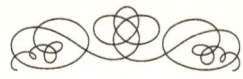

THE EXCITEMENT AT BOGGY SWAMP

MICHAEL T. BERNATH

THIS STORY may be familiar. In the wake of John Brown's raid on Harpers Ferry in 1859, concerned residents of Williamsburg District, South Carolina, met at Boggy Swamp to expel two northerners, W. J. Dodd and R. A. P. Hamilton, who had been working as teachers in their neighborhood. "Nothing definite is known of their abolition or insurrectionary sentiments," the local paper, the *Kingstree Star*, admitted, "but being from the North, and therefore necessarily imbued with doctrines hostile to our institutions, their presence in this section has been obnoxious, and, at any rate, very suspicious." A committee of twelve was dispatched to inform the teachers that they had four days to leave and that if they did not, measures of a "coercive character" would be taken. The teachers subsequently left for New Jersey.[1]

This story may be familiar because it appears with some regularity in the standard accounts of the period, used to illustrate the antinorthern hysteria that swept through the South following Brown's raid and the closing of southern ranks in opposition to the perceived abolitionist threat.[2] Certainly the panic was real, and at a glance, the excitement at Boggy Swamp would seem to be simply one incident among many. (But only at a glance.) Vigilance committees sprang up across the South, and southern papers were filled with reports of suspicious northern persons and their sometimes forcible removal. The reaction was particularly intense in South Carolina. "Notwithstanding the warnings from the press growing out of the present state of the country, stragglers from the North continue to visit and tarry in our town ... whose real object may be to act as spies and abolition emissaries," the people of Sumter declared in justifying the formation of a vigilance committee to drive them out.[3] In Pickens County, book subscription agent Israel Haile was deemed "a suspicious character, hailing from Massachusetts—the hot-bed of abolition." While "nothing was found to criminate him in any way" following a search of his possessions, he was forced to leave anyway. "Said Haile is of medium size, light hair and whiskers and moustache of same color," the editor of the *Keowee Courier* informed his readers, urging them, ominously, to "pass him to his 'native land.'"[4] Likewise, already having received "a coat of tar and feathers" near Bamberg, South Carolina, for his alleged "sympathy for the Abolitionists," intrepid northerner T. A. Salvo took a job in a piano store in Augusta, Georgia. Quickly detected, he was told that "if he did not leave the city before night he would be presented with another suit." "This is the way to deal with these abolition miscreants," the editor of the *Augusta Dispatch* applauded. "Let them find no place in the South whereon to lay their perfidious heads."[5] At the end of November 1859, the vigilance committee of Orangeburg, South Carolina, expelled four northerners from its town. "They all, as a matter of course, plead innocence of anything like guilt," the *Orangeburg Southron* reported. The committee members conceded that "their plea might be true, for all they knew . . . yet the present condition of affairs rendered it of the highest importance . . . that hereafter none will be allowed to remain in the community unless satisfactory evidence can be given that they are not inimical to its interest."[6]

While all northerners living in the South, especially those recently arrived, could become objects of suspicion in the wake of Harpers Ferry, northern teachers came under particularly intense scrutiny. There were a number of reasons. For one, northern teachers were the most numerous and most visible Yankees working in the South.[7] For another, while other northern-born southern residents often were concentrated in southern towns and cities, northern teachers were spread throughout the entirety of the southern countryside, especially the slaveholding plantation regions.[8] Unlike other suspicious northerners such as peddlers, book and subscription agents, and itinerant preachers, northern teachers lived within southern households, slave-owning households, and as such had direct, intimate, and often unsupervised contact with susceptible young southern minds and corruptible slaves.[9] Finally, northern teachers fell under additional suspicion after Harpers Ferry because documents uncovered following Brown's capture, and widely republished throughout the country, directly implicated them as subversive abolitionist agents. The infamous "Thatcher's Letter," written to Brown by an ardent supporter, spoke of an extensive network of radical abolitionists quietly embedded throughout the southern states. It included the advice of one such agent, a teacher in Tennessee, to "send out more well-qualified men to the South as school teachers, and work them in everywhere." "*Southern people are easily gulled*," he urged, and "there is no avocation in which a man can do so much good for our cause as that of school-teaching."[10]

"Gulled" no longer, the southern public's reaction was swift. "We are arming, and have need to do so; and the Southern States all had better be rousing," Virginia governor Henry Wise advised in a letter. "*Drive out pedlers [sic] and schoolmasters (not well known) from Yankeedom.*"[11] In Maryland, a teacher from Vermont was disturbed to read a "spirited article" in the local paper urging all citizens to "examine closely into the opinions and *antecedents* of every schoolteacher" in the name of "public safety."[12] In December 1859, a bill was introduced in the Alabama legislature "to protect the State against Abolition teachers" by forbidding licenses to be issued "to any person, male or female, to teach [public] school, unless the applicant has been a resident of the State for ten years."[13] Abolitionists could take many forms, the residents of St. John's Berkeley Parish in South Carolina warned, but few were so insidious as that of "the school master warmly welcomed to the family hearth."[14]

Not surprisingly, such rhetoric made northern teachers targets for vigilance committees and mob action. "A schoolmaster from the land of wooden nutmegs [Connecticut] was tarred and feathered and rode on a rail the other day at Helena [Arkansas], and then set [*sic*] adrift on the turbid waters of the Mississippi on a log, for ventilating his views [*sic*] rather too freely concerning the peculiar institution," a Vicksburg, Mississippi, paper reported, before adding, "Served him right."[15] In Richmond, Virginia, "two intelligent young ladies" from Boston and Hartford had together established a private school in September 1859. Immediately following Brown's raid, however, "they were waited upon by some very respectable gentlemen, who informed them that Northern school-mistresses, however amiable and competent, were not the proper persons to teach the children of Southern parents and guardians." Their school was closed. They applied for new teaching positions in another Virginia city, only to be informed that their applications had been "immediately rejected, as soon as the fact became known that you were both from the North."[16] Invited by prominent local residents, Meigs Case of Otsego County, New York, arrived in Salem, Alabama, in September 1859 to take charge of Alabama Female College. He set to work reorganizing the school and importing teachers and textbooks, and he planned to commence the new term with the beginning of the year. His school never opened. In the wake of Harpers Ferry, he was waited upon by a "Committee on the safety of the Union" who informed him that "public opinion ... had undergone such remarkable changes, that it was now no longer expedient to permit the residence of a Northern man in a Southern community." The committee ordered Case to leave immediately, "intimating that they could not be responsible for his safety if he remained longer than twenty-four hours." A local doctor, who had been one of Case's strongest supporters, told him in parting that "if you had been introduced to our citizens by the Governor of the State, and were as staunch a Democrat as any in Alabama, you still could not be sustained amid the excitement that now pervades all classes of the community."[17] Across the South, northern teachers found themselves closely watched. Many were driven out of their classrooms, often with the implied or explicit threat of violence to speed them on their way. Even if "nothing definite" was known of their alleged abolitionism, as a vigilance committee told D. Heagle, a teacher from New York working in Orangeburg, South Carolina, the "exigencies of the times" demanded that "the innocent had to suffer with the guilty."[18]

When viewed within this context, the incident at Boggy Swamp seems entirely unexceptional and historians' use of it to demonstrate antinorthern hostility quite understandable, especially given the eminent quotability of the *Kingstree Star*'s coverage. But there was something strange about what happened at Boggy Swamp, as those historians who have looked closely at South Carolina during this period have noticed.[19] Indeed, one witness declared "this lamentable occurrence" to have been so unusual as to be "without a precedent in the annals of our Southern history."[20] For the teachers did not leave when they were told. Instead, they were vigorously defended by their wealthy slave-owning employers, who "oppose[d] the action of the meeting, as reflecting upon them," and vowed to resist, by force of arms, "even if it jeopardized them their lives in the attempt."[21] The teachers' accusers were largely nonslaveholders and small slaveholders, and they rallied the district to their cause to the point where, on November 26, the day set for the teachers' expulsion, anywhere between 15 and 250 (the accounts vary wildly) men "armed with muskets, rifles, pistols, bowie knives &c." descended upon Kingstree determined to drive the northerners out.[22] In the end, "to avoid the horrors of civil war," a face-saving compromise was struck.[23] The teachers would leave but not until their respective terms of employment expired (Hamilton's on December 1, Dodd's on December 15). While violence was averted, "greater excitement [had] never prevailed since the days of the Revolution," one witness reported, and the bitter internal divisions opened at Boggy Swamp would not soon be healed.[24]

Those historians who have examined this incident, albeit in passing, have pointed to the ways in which the intense emotions produced by the sectional conflict, and John Brown's raid in particular, challenged traditional class deference and threatened to overwhelm elites. Or, as Stephanie McCurry put it, the "vigilantes had provoked altogether too much excitement among the people."[25]

But there was even more going on in Williamsburg than a case of popular enthusiasm run amok. Beneath the surface lay a complicated story involving long-standing community and class divisions and a nasty private quarrel. What the excitement at Boggy Swamp truly revealed was how sectional hostility could be employed and exploited in the service of class conflict and preexisting personal and political animosities. It also spoke to the unique and usually privileged position that northern teachers had occupied within southern society. Given their attachment to powerful slave-owning families, teachers enjoyed a certain degree of protection, except at moments such as these when sectional hostilities permitted others to target them as proxies for their wealthy, and otherwise untouchable, patrons, all in the name of southern rights and the protection of slavery.

The causes of the "excitement" and the motives behind it immediately became matters of public dispute, fought out not only on the streets of Kingstree but also in the pages of the Charleston newspapers. The teachers' defenders were among the wealthiest and most powerful men in Williamsburg. W. J. Dodd taught in the family of planter Henry D. Shaw, long-standing elder in the Williamsburg Presbyterian Church, the most respectable church in town, and owner of 113 slaves.[26] According to the 1860 census, the value of Shaw's personal and real estate holdings exceeded $111,500.[27] R. A. P. Hamilton lived on S. J. Bradley's plantation. Only thirty-four years old, Bradley owned twenty slaves, but he, too, was an elder in the Presbyterian church, and most vitally, he came from one of the most politically prominent families in the area. His father, Dr. James Bradley, had been the outspoken leader of the Unionists in Williamsburg during the nullification crisis.[28] Along with nine other signers, Shaw and Bradley presented their version of events of the Boggy Swamp incident in a lengthy letter to the *Charleston Mercury* on December 22, 1859. Those fellow supporters included the two other elders from the Presbyterian church, and collectively, these eleven planters owned at least 564 slaves.[29]

Finding themselves "stigmatized as the harborers of abolitionists," the teachers' employers eagerly declared their loyalty to the South, their support for its institutions, and their enmity for those who threatened them. "We are willing and ready, at any time, to co-operate with our fellow-citizens in putting off from amongst us Northern abolitionists," they insisted, but what had happened at Boggy Swamp had nothing to do with northern abolitionists, John Brown, or sectional tensions. While much "capital" had been made from the heightened passions following Harpers Ferry, this was merely pretense, a smoke screen, designed to conceal the true conflict that lay at the heart of the matter: a bitter personal dispute between one of the teachers, R. A. P. Hamilton, and Richard Columbus Logan, the twenty-seven-year-old editor of the *Kingstree Star*. Hamilton, a Pennsylvanian, had arrived in Williamsburg two years earlier to teach the children of five neighboring slaveholding families, in whose homes he boarded. "His demeanor was unobjectionable, and his conduct was not such as to awaken in the minds of his employers any fear that his principles were tinged with abolitionism," his supporters testified. "But he had his peculiarities," they admitted, including a fondness for writing, especially about religion, and this, not his northern birth or his views on slavery, was what led to trouble.

When he tried to get a provocative article criticizing two local ministers, which he signed "Not a Baptist," published in the local paper, Logan, the editor, refused, but he did run his own editorial condemning Hamilton's article and making "severe strictures" upon its author. Hamilton wrote a response and confronted Logan in person, demanding that he publish it. Instead, Logan beat him.[30] Or, as Logan himself later put it, "he assailed me in terms that I would not rest under. I chastised him."[31] The teacher, "not being skilled in pugilism, and being a crippled man, did not come off triumphant in the *melee*," his supporters explained, but he subsequently filed charges against Logan for assault and battery. This all took place at the beginning of August 1859, "a long time before the Harper's Ferry affair," the signers noted, and it was then, not coincidentally, that "the treachery and danger of Northern school teachers" became "frequent themes" in the editorials of the *Kingstree Star*.[32]

In short, Logan was plotting his revenge, and Harpers Ferry provided the perfect opportunity for him to take it. It was Logan who spoke out most vigorously against the teachers at Boggy Swamp; it was Logan who was appointed chairman of the committee charged with driving the teachers out; and it was Logan who used the *Kingstree Star* to fan the flames of antinorthern hostility and then to direct them toward targets of his choosing.

As for W. J. Dodd, the other teacher, he was collateral damage in Logan's campaign against Hamilton, his defenders argued. Dodd had been in Williamsburg for only ten or eleven months and had done nothing to suggest any "Abolition proclivities," according to his employer, Henry Shaw. Admittedly, he did receive a large volume of mail from the North, and one package, in particular, had attracted the notice of the suspicious local postmaster. On the outside, someone, presumably the Richmond, Virginia, postmaster, had drawn pictures of a fish and a hook, along with the cryptic message "take care, old fellow, that you are not caught." While admittedly bizarre, and later pointed to as definitive proof of abolitionist conspiracy, his defenders dismissed these signs as merely playful chiding for insufficient postage paid. In any case, this had occurred in May or June of 1859, long before the excitement commenced.[33]

No, Dodd's true crime was being a northerner and living in the same neighborhood as Hamilton, his defenders insisted. "It would be entirely too barefaced to attack HAMILTON without including him also in the matter," they speculated. "The intention would then be too plain for argument, and DODD being included, the real cause of the animosity might be better concealed." Misled as they were, many of their fellow citizens who demanded the teachers' removal had been "actuated by patriotic [southern] principles," the teachers' defenders conceded, but "we cannot say so of all."[34]

The planters objected to the precipitant haste with which the Boggy Swamp accusers acted, the lack of evidence presented, and the ways in which Logan and his allies intentionally excited the "animosity" of the people to the verge of violence. But mostly, they objected to the impudence of the upstart Logan and their younger, poorer neighbors, who should have deferred to their social betters, granting them the respect that "we conceive to be due to us and to our position as slave owners, and having an interest in Southern institutions, and being of sound Southern principles." The teachers' accusers did not even bother to inform, let alone consult, the planters before taking action. The Boggy Swamp meeting was held only three miles outside Kingstree, "yet the slave-owners, in whose employment these obnoxious persons were engaged, and whose slaves . . . were in danger of being corrupted by the machinations of these suspicious personages, are not invited to attend it."[35]

Their repeated self-identification as "slave-owners" was neither accidental nor incidental. By emphasizing their large slave ownerships, they sought to draw a sharp distinction between themselves and their adversaries. Those who had assembled at Boggy Swamp were of a different sort. They were younger men, many in their twenties. Some did not appear in the 1860 census, but of those who did, few had yet to become heads of households and fewer still owned slaves.[36] The accusers, too, sent a long letter to the *Charleston Mercury*, published on January 6, 1860, as rebuttal.[37] They, too, assembled a list of signatories, but whereas the teachers' eleven defenders owned at least 564 slaves, the twelve men who stood behind R. C. Logan could muster only twenty-five. As for Logan himself, he had been born in Sumter, South Carolina, and had come to Kingstree only in 1856. Earlier in 1859, he had married into a local slave-owning family, but he remained an editor and printer by trade. Strangely, Logan does not seem to have been listed in the 1860 census, although the communicant records from the Williamsburg Presbyterian Church suggest that he owned at least one slave at some point.[38]

In responding to the accusations against him, Logan both minimized his own role in the affair and lashed out at the teachers and especially their employers. As "they have singled me out . . . as a particular target," Logan was ready to return fire. It was true, he admitted, that there had been a "private difficulty" between Hamilton and himself, but "what has that to do with the matter?" The assault and battery charges had been dismissed by the grand jury in the fall court session. Logan had been vindicated and Hamilton had succeeded only in giving evidence "of not being a gentleman." "My cup of satisfaction was full, and why should I inaugurate a plot . . . for Hamilton's expulsion from the District?" Logan asked innocently. In any case, "can any man in his senses suppose that I could exert so much influence as to call together so large and respectable a body of gentlemen to revenge a private quarrel?" No, he maintained, the banishment of Dodd and Hamilton had been a popular movement by true-hearted southerners, in which he had taken only a small and not very significant part.[39]

The planters' attacks on Logan and his supporters were nothing but "miserable subterfuges" designed to distract from "the true issue": that is, "whether the citizens of Williamsburg District acted properly in driving from their midst two Northern men, whom they had reason to believe were Abolitionists." Clearly, the answer was yes. By January 1860, Dodd's and Hamilton's abolitionism was no longer a matter of suspicion, Logan argued; it was established fact. Perhaps not "positive proof sufficient to satisfy a sworn jury," he admitted, but certainly enough to justify extralegal action. The mysterious markings on Dodd's packages more than merited his removal, and Logan dismissed out of hand the accusation that those at Boggy Swamp had "no purer motives at heart . . . than of ordering Dodd to leave the community, because I had a fight with Hamilton." As for his nemesis, Hamilton, Logan reported that he had subsequently convicted himself, by comments he made, privately, to a local "gentleman" in Sumter by which he "showed enough of 'the cloven foot'" to convince the hearer that "he was *not sound* on the slavery question." What these comments were or who this witness was Logan did not say, but this vague secondhand account confirmed, for Logan at least, that Hamilton was indeed an abolitionist, rightly expelled.[40]

Dodd and Hamilton, however, were no longer Logan's primary targets, if indeed they ever were, and he directed the bulk of his "investigation" to the "*opinions*" of the planters who had defended them and to the "vast deal of *spurious corruption*" with which they had polluted the community. Motivated by "unfriendly feelings towards me," these men had backed Hamilton's legal suit against Logan and then stood by the teachers in defiance of Williamsburg's, South Carolina's, and the South's vital interests.

The men who had met at Boggy Swamp were right not to invite the planters. "Suppose the people had gone to Messrs. Shaw and Bradley, what would have been the result?" Logan demanded. "They would have been assured that Dodd and Hamilton were innocent." However, subsequent "evidence," such as the questionable account of Hamilton's confession, had shown that, knowingly or not, Bradley had been harboring an abolitionist. As for Shaw, Logan gleefully revealed that not only had he shielded the suspicious Dodd, but he also had entertained as a guest in his home for many years the northern teacher and surveyor Harold Wyllis, who had just recently been arrested in Greenville for exciting "a servile insurrection" (specifically for distributing copies of Hinton Helper's *Impending Crisis*).[41] As such, Bradley, Shaw, and their supporters were dupes or they were disloyal. Logan did not say which, but either way, their opinions were not to be trusted and certainly not when "set up in opposition to nearly the whole District."[42]

And here was Logan's main point. Regardless of what motivated the attack on these teachers or whether they really had been abolitionists, and notwithstanding the respectability of their employers, the accusers had numbers on their side, and in the end, that was all that mattered. "I hazard nothing in saying that not fifty men in Williamsburg District will endorse their [the planters'] course," Logan boasted. While the *Kingstree Star* had lost "about a dozen subscribers" as a result of the controversy (nine of whom had signed the letter to the *Mercury*), "I have one hundred new ones, all residents of this District." The men of the Cedar Swamp Troop (a local militia unit) now refused to muster under Capt. D. E. Gordon because he was one of the signatories supporting the teachers. The planters had erred in assuming their wealth, status, and authority would carry the day. "I hold this," Logan declared, "that Dodd and Hamilton were both suspicious characters, from free States . . . that they are abolitionists in *principle*, and they ought not to be trusted *in practice*. We are taught that those 'who are not for us are against us,' and acting on this maxim, I think the people were right in removing them."[43]

There is more that could be said about what happened in Williamsburg, but the question is, so what? Apart from those interested in the local history of Kingstree, why does the excitement at Boggy Swamp matter? I argue that it matters for a few reasons. For one, both the incident's origins and its subsequent fame/notoriety reveal much about the role and power of the partisan press during the sectional crisis. Not only had a newspaper editor played a central part in publicizing and, according to some, orchestrating the incident in the first place, but also the expulsion of Dodd and Hamilton became big news at the time, both locally and nationally. Newspapers across South Carolina closely followed the excitement and the public dispute that arose after it, and the reactions of the editors, like those of the residents of Williamsburg, were divided. Some applauded the expulsion of these "two worthless abolition characters" and voiced their support for the *Kingstree Star* and its maligned editor.[44] Vigilance committees across the state took inspiration from Boggy Swamp and urged their fellow citizens to act in like fashion.[45] Other editors, however, expressed their reservations. The *Lancaster Ledger*, for instance, regretted "to hear of a serious disturbance in Williamsburg District, which came near resulting in bloodshed," noting that "the ground upon which they [the teachers] were suspected does not appear" in the accounts.[46] The most interesting reaction came from the *Charleston Mercury*, in whose columns the public dispute between Logan and the planters unfolded. Editor Robert Rhett found the incident to be highly unsettling, and though hardly known for his moderation or restraint, he now urged both. Clearly siding with the planters, Rhett lamented the "sad state of things" in Williamsburg and worried what it portended. "In our indignation at the aggressions of the North, we are in danger of dealing with men as if they were guilty, without proof," he cautioned. But even worse, indeed "the very worst effect of Northern Abolitionism must be that it divides us amongst ourselves," and this is what Logan and his supporters had wrought by "frittering away the strength of Southern sentiment in insignificant and mischievous efforts, productive of no extensive or permanent good results."[47] The southern press should use its power to fan the flames of sectionalism and southern nationalism in a single direction, Rhett believed, and Logan's misuse of that power threatened to set a dangerous fire in the rear.

It was in the northern press, however, that the excitement at Boggy Swamp would have its second life. In making their case to the southern public, the teachers' defenders had worried that "Northern newsmongers and abolitionists may, for a time, rejoice over our differences."[48] They were partially right. Northern newsmongers certainly took notice, but southern internal division was not the headline.[49] As had been the case since its inception, what had happened in Williamsburg was open to multiple interpretations, and those interpretations could be made to serve divergent sectional and partisan ends. Under banners such as "Another Exhibition of Southern Chivalry," "The Irrepressible Folly," "Public Meetings of the Chivalry," and "Barbarism Rampant," Republican newspapers and especially the abolitionist press trumpeted the Kingstree affair as a prime example of recent antinorthern atrocities and used it to mock the gentlemanly pretensions of the southern slave-owning "chivalry."[50] For them, this was a story of unoffending northerners victimized by southern thuggishness and proslavery hysteria. In its annual report, the American Anti-Slavery Society cited the Williamsburg incident specifically as proof positive of "the chronic malady of lawless barbarism, so long notoriously prevailing" throughout the South, which had sunk so low as to target innocent "school-teachers, thinking only of their spelling-books and grammars."[51] W. J. Dodd, now safely back in Jersey City, New Jersey, told his harrowing tale to William Cullen Bryant's *Evening Post*. He reported that in the wake of Brown's raid, despite "attending to his own business, without a thought of harming or being harmed by any of his neighbors," he had received a letter signed "Many Citizens," warning that "we have reason to believe, and do believe, that you are one of the treacherous scoundrels who have been sent here for the purpose of exciting our slaves to rebellion and insurrection," and "if you are detected you will receive what you richly merit, viz.: a coat of tar and feathers and a riding on a rail, and perhaps a cowhiding." While the northern coverage occasionally noted that the teachers' employers had resented the accusations "as reflecting upon them" and the *Evening Post* added that "the most respectable men in Kingstree" later had issued a statement "totally exculpating Mr. Dodd from all charges made against him," little mention was made of the spirited defense mounted by the planters, and the implication was that it had been the slaveholders, "the chivalry," who led the charge to drive the teachers out.[52]

The Democratic *New York Herald* was outraged. It accused the "Northern incendiary prints" of concocting "a lying story" out of the Kingstree affair. When properly understood, what this incident truly revealed was "that the slaveholders in this district are more liberal to the North than are the other whites" and that southern nonslaveholders were "in fact more pro-slavery than the planters themselves." "Continually" publishing and compiling "every act of violence" against northerners, the abolitionist press intentionally "dress[ed] up and exaggerate[d] those outrages with the view of exasperating the North against the South," the *Herald* charged. By distorting such incidents as the Kingstree excitement and exploiting them for propagandistic purposes, the abolitionists recklessly jeopardized northerners living in the South, threatened northern trade, and worst of all, encouraged southern secession. In the aftermath of the Union's destruction, there would be a fearsome reckoning, the *Herald* warned, as northerners rose up to violently punish not southerners but the abolitionist journals for their irresponsible lies.[53]

The *Herald*'s was a lonely voice, however, as most northern readers (and future historians) encountered a far less nuanced account of what had happened in Williamsburg. Reading the northern papers on the Maryland plantation where she taught, worried Sarah Hagar wrote home to Vermont, "Some quiet Northern teachers in Williamsburg S.C. have been threatened & ordered to leave. . . . Is it not a fine specimen of Southern *chivalry*. Just like them though."[54]

But the significance of the excitement at Boggy Swamp lies not solely in its use as fodder in a sectional propaganda campaign. This incident also reveals much about the special place that northern teachers, in particular, had long occupied within southern society. While there were thousands of northerners teaching throughout the slave states, they almost invariably taught and lived in the homes of slave owners. Planters provided many important services for their poorer nonslaveholding neighbors. They shared their trade connections and their cotton gins. They loaned money; dispensed agricultural, legal, and medical advice; and exerted political influence on behalf of the local community. They hired out, and even sometimes lent out, their slaves. But one thing that planters did not share was their teachers. To be able to hire a northern teacher was a clear marker of class. These teachers, tutors, and governesses taught the planter's children, and perhaps those of his friends and relatives, but they were not there to benefit the community at large.[55] As such, northern teachers could serve as objects of both class and sectional resentment for southern white nonslaveholders struggling with limited educational opportunities for their own children.

Yet throughout most of the antebellum period, northern teachers generally had remained shielded from hostilities arising from the growing sectional divide by virtue of their intimate associations with slave-owning families. While northern laborers, sailors, and peddlers could be run out of town with relative impunity, teachers had powerful allies. But as sectional tensions escalated to the breaking point, that protective sphere began to crack, and employers found that the presence of northern teachers in their homes could become a liability and even an indirect means of challenging their own authority. As secession and war approached, incidents such as Boggy Swamp became more common as antinorthern hostility invited non-elite southerners to target these teachers in spite of, and perhaps because of, their very visible connections to wealthy slave-owning families. In Virginia in 1861, planter Jesse Maury received a visit from a local Baptist preacher demanding that he send away the "horrid Yankee girl" who taught his children. Hearing that a "committee of gentlemen" was coming "to warn off that dangerous Yankee woman," Maury vowed to "set the dogs" on any who dared approach.[56] In Mississippi, a similar group of concerned vigilantes successfully made it to the door of Thomas Smith Dabney's "Burleigh" plantation with accusations that his northern tutor was a spy and demands for his immediate dismissal.[57] Invited by a prominent local planter and carrying a letter of introduction attesting to his friendship and support, Massachusetts native William Brewster arrived in Somerville, Alabama, to take charge of an academy in September 1860. He did not last a day. Tipped off that a "Wendell Phillips rascal" was en route to their town, the residents surrounded Brewster and, amid cries of "Hang him!" and "Shoot him!" charged the teacher with being "a G-d d——n black-hearted Abolitionist. You came from Boston, and that is proof enough against you!" Brewster fled town on foot trying to make it to the plantation of his patron, when he was overtaken by three men on horseback, who threatened to hang him but instead "pitched" him into a nearby pond and then held him there with a long stick. When he finally reached the safety of the plantation, he found the planters of the neighborhood assembled and armed, as "my assailants had threatened to burn down Mr. Giers's house, if he sheltered me." Brewster slept that night "with a loaded revolver under my pillow, which weapon was given me by a noble-hearted youth, himself the son of an extensive slave-owner." Despite their temporary protection, the planters "could not advise me, under the circumstances, to remain," and Brewster left immediately for Boston.[58] While no mob threatened to burn down novelist William Gilmore Simms's Woodlands plantation, his neighbors found another way to punish him for his northern governess. Simms had hoped to represent his district in South Carolina's Secession Convention and to cast his vote for disunion personally, only to be defeated at the polls. Simms knew why. As he wrote to a northern friend in March 1861, "Did I mention that her presence in my house, as Teacher, is reported to be the cause of my defeat for the convention. It is the feeling of the common people towards Northern teachers."[59] Like at Boggy Swamp, the special relationship between wealthy slave owners and northern teachers had become a vulnerability, and declarations of southern patriotism and accusations of disloyalty concealed a multitude of hidden motives and resentments. What seemed on the surface a clear-cut conflict between southerners and northerners, insiders and outsiders, was in fact, very often, an internal dispute between southerners with far deeper roots than Harpers Ferry.

Finally, the excitement at Boggy Swamp helps to illuminate the complicated relationship between southern intellectual life and the larger social and political environment in which it operated. What began as an editorial dispute arising from a religious controversy between two men who could be considered public intellectuals (at least within their local context) escalated, with the catalyst of Harpers Ferry, into a widespread social and class conflict. A squabble of words and ideas became a "civil war" of guns and bowie knives, or at least the brandishing of them. The incident showcases the power and perceived importance of the printed word in the Old South.[60] R. C. Logan adeptly had utilized his position and his printing press to marshal support, sway public opinion, and ultimately rally armed forces. In the aftermath of the affair, both the teachers' defenders and accusers rushed to get their version of events published in the newspapers of record: the *Charleston Mercury* and the *Charleston Courier*. After reaching for their guns, they picked up their pens. That they felt compelled to do so shows the central role that print played in antebellum southern life as both sides recognized that the conflict at Boggy Swamp would be ultimately won or lost on the printed page.

Back in Kingstree, editor R. C. Logan emerged triumphant from the controversy. In his response to Hamilton's and Dodd's supporters, he had scoffed at the notion that he alone had incited the people against them. "I, who have been a citizen of this District but three years, must indeed have risen rapidly into power, and now exercise more than it is safe that one citizen of this free country of ours should, if this be true."[61] Still in his twenties, Logan indeed had risen rapidly, and that ascension would accelerate in the wake of Boggy Swamp. As the 1860 presidential election approached, Logan continued to rail against all things Yankee and beat the secessionist drum. "Depend upon it," he wrote in October 1860, "we of the South have a most heartless, fiendish foe to fight."[62] Following Lincoln's victory, he was chosen as one of Williamsburg's three delegates to South Carolina's Secession Convention and often is credited, mistakenly, as the state's youngest signer of its Ordinance of Secession (he was the second youngest).[63] When Williamsburg's first military unit, the Wee Nee Volunteers, marched off to defend South Carolina on January 4, 1861, R. C. Logan was at its head as its second-ranking officer. In command was Samuel W. Maurice, the chairman of the Boggy Swamp meeting, and many of the other officers had played prominent roles in the teachers' expulsion.[64] Logan would survive the war and, thereafter known as "Colonel Logan," would live out the rest of his days as one of Kingstree's most prominent and respected citizens.[65]

Secession and the coming of the war seemingly painted over Williamsburg's divisions in Confederate gray as nearly all the men, the teachers' defenders and accusers, marched off to battle. However, there were indications that bitterness lingered and that the men did not march off arm in arm. According to the 1860 census, planter John A. Salters, a Presbyterian elder, owner of 119 slaves, and one of the teachers' most public defenders, kept in his house as teacher one Eunice Dodd of New Jersey, W. J. Dodd's younger sister. How or when she came to the Salters' plantation is unknown, but her presence there in 1860 certainly could be seen as an act of continuing defiance.[66] What was more, the teachers' defenders and their sons did not go off to fight under the command of R. C. Logan or the other Boggy Swamp participants. Instead, many of them joined the Williamsburg cavalry troop, which would eventually become part of the Fourth South Carolina Cavalry. This unit, one local historian noted, "was composed largely of the wealthier young men of the State. When they arrived in Richmond for participation along the battle line, nearly every individual soldier in the regiment had a negro servant attending him."[67]

Perhaps the most suggestive indication that the excitement at Boggy Swamp was not forgotten or forgiven was to be found not in the actions of the men involved but in those of their wives. In August 1861, women in Williamsburg formed the Cedar Swamp Soldiers' Aid Society to provide boxes of food, clothing, and other necessities for their soldiers. Many of the officers and members were the wives and relatives of the teachers' accusers. Almost immediately, a rival organization, the Lower Bridge Soldiers' Aid Society, sprang up, its officers composed almost exclusively of the wives of Hamilton's and Dodd's most prominent supporters.[68] With the men off to war, the rift, it seems, would continue in the parlors of the women they left behind.

NOTES

1. Reprinted from *Kingstree (S.C.) Star* in "Public Meeting," *Charleston (S.C.) Mercury*, November 26, 1859.

2. See, e.g., James M. McPherson, *Battle Cry of Freedom: The Civil War Era* (New York: Oxford University Press, 1988), 213; and Allen Nevins, *The Emergence of Lincoln* (New York: Charles Scribner's Sons, 1950), 2:107–8.

3. Reprinted in "Public Meeting," *Camden (S.C.) Weekly Journal*, November 29, 1859; and "Public Meeting," *Sumter (S.C.) Watchman*, November 29, 1859.

4. "Taken Up," *Keowee (S.C.) Courier*, December 17, 1859.

5. Reprinted in "Another Abolition Emissary," *Edgefield (S.C.) Advertiser*, November 30, 1859.

6. Reprinted in "Warned to Leave," *Laurensville (S.C.) Herald*, December 2, 1859. For other examples, see "Meeting of the Citizens of Abbeville," *Abbeville (S.C.) Banner*, December 1, 1859; "Rode on a Rail" and "A Suggestion," *Camden Weekly Journal*,

November 29, 1859; "Public Meeting," *Edgefield Advertiser*, November 30, 1859; and "A Southern Vigilance Association," *Laurensville Herald*, December 2, 1859.

7. On the presence of northern teachers in the late antebellum and Civil War South, see Michael T. Bernath, "Our Yankee: The Uncertain Fate of Northern Teachers in the Seceded South," *Civil War History* 64, no. 3 (September 2018): 272–303. See also Elizabeth Brown Pryor, "An Anomalous Person: The Northern Tutor in Plantation Society, 1773–1860," *Journal of Southern History* 47, no. 3 (August 1981): 363–92; Elizabeth Brown Pryor, "An Anomalous Person: The New England Tutor in Southern Plantation Society, 1785–1860" (MA thesis, University of Pennsylvania, 1978); David Ross Zimring, *To Live and Die in Dixie: Native Northerners Who Fought for the Confederacy* (Knoxville: University of Tennessee Press, 2014); and Christie Anne Farnham, *The Education of the Southern Belle: Higher Education and Student Socialization in the Antebellum South* (New York: New York University Press, 1994).

8. Randall M. Miller, "The Enemy Within: Some Effects of Foreign Immigrants on Antebellum Southern Cities," *Southern Studies* 24, no. 1 (1985): 30–53; William W. Chenault and Robert C. Reinders, "The Northern-Born Community of New Orleans in the 1850s," *Journal of American History* 51, no. 2 (September 1964): 232–47; Fletcher Melvin Green, *The Role of the Yankee in the Old South* (Athens: University of Georgia Press, 1972); Frank J. Byrne, *Becoming Bourgeois: Merchant Culture in the South, 1820–1865* (Lexington: University Press of Kentucky, 2006).

9. On northern peddlers, see Joseph T. Rainer, "The 'Sharper' Image: Yankee Peddlers, Southern Consumers, and the Market Revolution," *Business and Economic History* 26, no. 1 (October 1997): 27–44; and Joseph T. Rainer, "The Honorable Fraternity of Moving Merchants: Yankee Peddlers in the Old South, 1800–1860" (PhD diss., College of William and Mary, 2000).

10. Joseph A. Turner, "What Are We to Do?," *De Bow's Review*, July 1860, 70; "Thatcher's Letter," *Unionville (S.C.) Times*, November 25, 1859. See also C. Vann Woodward, "John Brown's Private War," in *The Burden of Southern History*, 3rd ed. (Baton Rouge: Louisiana State University Press, 1993), 64.

11. Wise to William Scott, November 25, 1859, in *Southern Notes for National Circulation* (Boston: Thayer and Eldridge, 1860), 81.

12. Sarah Hagar to unidentified, [December 16, 1859], Hagar Family Papers, University of Vermont Libraries Special Collections, Burlington.

13. "Abolition School Teachers," *Columbia (S.C.) Banner*, December 21, 1859. See also *Southern Notes*, 83–84.

14. As quoted in Manisha Sinha, *The Counter-revolution of Slavery: Politics and Ideology in Antebellum South Carolina* (Chapel Hill: University of North Carolina Press, 2000), 212.

15. "Tarred and Feathered," *Tri-weekly South Carolinian* (Columbia), December 17, 1859; *Southern Notes*, 131.

16. *Southern Notes*, 71–72.

17. Reprinted from *New York Independent* in "An Exile from Alabama," *Liberator* (Boston), January 27, 1860; *Southern Notes*, 83–84.

18. "Public Meeting," *Charleston Mercury*; *Southern Notes*, 88–90; "Warned to Leave."

19. Stephanie McCurry, *Masters of Small Worlds: Yeoman Households, Gender Relations, and the Political Culture of the Antebellum South Carolina Low Country* (New York: Oxford University Press, 1995), 295-96; Sinha, *Counter-revolution of Slavery*, 211-12; Steven A. Channing, *Crisis of Fear: Secession in South Carolina* (New York: W. W. Norton, 1974), 32-33; Howell Meadoes Henry, "The Police Control of the Slave in South Carolina" (PhD diss., Vanderbilt University, 1914), 162-64.

20. T. B. Logan, "Great Excitement in Williamsburg," *Charleston (S.C.) Tri-weekly Courier*, December 1, 1859.

21. "Excitement in Williamsburg," *Daily South Carolinian* (Columbia), November 30, 1859; Logan, "Great Excitement in Williamsburg."

22. "Excitement at Williamsburg," *Lancaster (S.C.) Ledger*, December 7, 1859. On the varying estimates of the heavily armed men, see Logan, "Great Excitement in Williamsburg"; "For the Mercury," *Charleston Mercury*, December 22, 1859; Sinha, *Counter-revolution of Slavery*, 211; and Henry, "Police Control," 163.

23. "For the Mercury."

24. Logan, "Great Excitement in Williamsburg."

25. McCurry, *Masters of Small Worlds*, 295.

26. Of the Williamsburg Presbyterian Church, Samuel McGill recalled that its members were "wealthy Christian people, refined and cultured in their general appearance, equipages and splendid horses." Samuel D. McGill, *Narrative of Reminiscences in Williamsburg County* (Kingstree, S.C.: Kingstree Lithographic Company 1952), 253.

27. U.S. Bureau of the Census, *1860 Census: Population of the United States* (Washington, D.C.: Government Printing Office, 1864).

28. U.S. Bureau of the Census. There is evidence to suggest that at least some of the divisions exposed during the Boggy Swamp incident dated back to the nullification crisis and perhaps earlier. The correspondence is not exact, but as a general matter most of the families that supported the teachers had sided with the Unionists, while many of the accusers' families had been nullifiers. See William Willis Boddie, *History of Williamsburg* (Columbia, S.C.: State Company, 1923), 268-69; and McGill, *Narrative of Reminiscences*, 49, 67-76.

29. The other signers were E. P. Bradley, J. A. Gordon, D. E. Gordon, W. B. Gordon, J. W. Gordon, J. Watson, J. A. Salters, W. K. Lane, and J. M. Braddey [Bradley?]. "For the Mercury"; U.S. Bureau of the Census, *1860 Census*.

30. "For the Mercury." Apparently, Hamilton subsequently published his article as a "circular" and distributed it "over the District." Unfortunately, I have been unable to locate a copy. "To the Public," *Charleston Mercury*, January 6, 1860.

31. "To the Public."

32. "For the Mercury."

33. "For the Mercury."

34. "For the Mercury."

35. "For the Mercury."

36. By contrast, all of the teachers' supporters appear in the 1860 census.

37. As one would expect, the expulsion of Dodd and Hamilton and the controversy surrounding it received extensive coverage in the *Kingstree Star*. Unfortunately, none

of the issues from this period have survived, but many articles from the *Star* were reprinted in newspapers throughout South Carolina and Georgia.

38. U.S. Bureau of the Census, *1860 Census*; "Minutes, Williamsburg Presbyterian Church, 1834–1931," 24, copied by Elizabeth Rogan Rice, Historical Records Survey Division of Women's and Professional Projects, Works Progress Administration, in possession of church clerk, Williamsburg Presbyterian Church, Kingstree, South Carolina; Boddie, *History of Williamsburg*, 521–22; Eleanor Winn Foxworth, *South Carolina's Williamsburg: A Collection of Articles Appearing in the News of Kingstree, South Carolina* (Spartanburg, S.C.: Reprint Company, 2007), 359–61.

39. "To the Public."

40. "To the Public."

41. "To the Public"; "Imprisoned for Circulating Helper's Book," in Francis Vincent, *Vincent's Semi-annual United States Register: A Work in Which the Principal Events of Every Half-Year Occuring in the United States Are Recorded, Each Arranged under the Day of Its Date. This Volume Contains the Events Transpiring between the 1st of January and 1st of July, 1860* (Philadelphia: Francis Vincent, 1860), 261.

42. "To the Public."

43. "To the Public." See also "Where Ignorance Is Bliss, 'Tis Folly to Be Wise" and "Still They Come," *Charleston (S.C.) Courier*, December 20, 1859.

44. "Exchanges," *Keowee Courier*, December 17, 1859.

45. See, e.g., "Dear Editor," *Sumter (S.C.) Watchman*, November 29, 1859.

46. "Excitement at Williamsburg." See also "The Arrest at Abbeville," *Edgefield Advertiser*, December 7, 1859; and "Vigilant Enough," *Edgefield Advertiser*, December 21, 1859.

47. "The Excitement in Williamsburg," *Charleston Mercury*, November 30, 1859; Channing, *Crisis of Fear*, 33. For additional newspaper coverage, see "Excitement in Williamsburg," *Daily Morning News* (Savannah, Ga.), December 2, 1859; "Excitement in Williamsburg," *Daily South Carolinian*; "Excitement in Williamsburg," *Keowee Courier*, December 3, 1859; and "The Excitement in Williamsburg," *Yorkville (S.C.) Enquirer*, December 8, 1859.

48. "For the Mercury."

49. For northern coverage, see "Expulsion of Northern Teachers from South Carolina," *Philadelphia Inquirer*, December 2, 1859; "Excitement in Williamsburg, S.C.," *New York Herald*, December 5, 1859; "Excitement in Williamsburg," *Commercial Advertiser* (New York), December 7, 1859; "Mr. Fisk Tarred and Feathered," *Evening Post (New York, N.Y.)*, December 7, 1859; "More Martyrs of Northern Incendiarism—the Beginning of the End," *New York Herald*, January 14, 1860; "Another Exhibition of Southern Chivalry," *Evening Post*, January 24, 1860; "The Irrepressible Folly: More Banishments from Virginia," *New-York Tribune*, January 27, 1860; and *Southern Notes*, 32–34.

50. "Another Exhibition"; "Irrepressible Folly"; *Southern Notes*, 32–33; *Annual Report of the American Anti-Slavery Society by the Executive Committee for the Year Ending May 1, 1860* (New York: American Anti-Slavery Society, 1861), 166–91.

51. *Annual Report*, 166, 168.

52. "Another Exhibition."

53. "More Martyrs."

54. Sarah Hagar to sister Kate, [December 1859], Hagar Family Papers, University of Vermont Libraries Special Collections, Burlington.

55. As historian Vernon Burton has noted, "The southern aristocrat's sense of noblesse oblige did not extend to the education of the common people." Orville Vernon Burton, *In My Father's House Are Many Mansions: Family and Community in Edgefield, South Carolina* (Chapel Hill: University of North Carolina Press, 1985), 80–81. See also Harry L. Watson, "The Man with the Dirty Black Beard: Race, Class, and Schools in the Antebellum South," *Journal of the Early Republic* 32, no. 1 (Spring 2012): 1–26.

56. That "Yankee girl" was Caroline Morrill of Maine. Caroline Morrill Brown, "War-Time Memories by an Old Lady Who Was Then Young," *Magazine of Albemarle County History* 30 (1972): 36–37.

57. Dabney had little choice but to send the unoffending man away. Susan Dabney Smedes, *Memorials of a Southern Planter*, ed. Fletcher M. Green (New York: Knopf, 1965), 184–85.

58. "Ruffianly Treatment of a Massachusetts Man in Alabama," *Liberator*, October 19, 1860; "The Reign of Terror," *Liberator*, November 16, 1860.

59. Simms to James Lawson, March 17, July 4, August 20, 1861, in *The Letters of William Gilmore Simms*, ed. Mary C. Simms Oliphant and T. C. Duncan Eaves (Columbia: University of South Carolina Press, 1955), 4:352–53, 370, 373.

60. On southern reading, see Beth Barton Schweiger, *A Literate South: Reading before Emancipation* (New Haven, Conn.; Yale University Press, 2019); Beth Barton Schweiger, "The Literate South: Reading before Emancipation," *Journal of the Civil War Era* 3, no. 3 (September 2013): 331–59; Timothy J. Williams, *Intellectual Manhood: University, Self, and Society in the Antebellum South* (Chapel Hill: University of North Carolina Press, 2015), chap. 4; and Timothy J. Williams, "The Readers' South: Literature, Region, and Identity in the Civil War Era," *Journal of the Civil War Era* 8, no. 4 (December 2018): 564–90.

61. "To the Public."

62. "What the South Must Contend With," *Kingstree Star*, October 31, 1859.

63. Boddie, *History of Williamsburg*, 341, 521; Foxworth, *South Carolina's Williamsburg*, 360.

64. Boddie, *History of Williamsburg*, 343.

65. Boddie, 521; McGill, *Narrative of Reminiscences*, 270–71.

66. U.S. Bureau of the Census, *1860 Census*.

67. Boddie, *History of Williamsburg*, 355.

68. Boddie, 370.

TOWARD A HISTORY OF BOOKS IN THE AMERICAN SOUTH

BETH BARTON SCHWEIGER

ASK ABOUT the history of books in the South, and sooner or later you will hear about Governor William Berkeley of Virginia. Remarkably, a man who purchased the governorship in 1641, navigated the treacherous politics of civil war, and survived Nathaniel Bacon's bloody rebellion is at least as famous for what he said about books as for being the longest-serving governor in Virginia's history. His boast—"I thank God, there are no free schools nor printing . . . for learning has brought disobedience, and heresy, and sects into the world. . . . God keep us from both!"—has been cited repeatedly to contrast a southern sensibility about books with that of New England.[1] A century after his death in 1677, it appeared in the earliest histories of the American Revolution, it was called to service in numerous antebellum histories, and it was enlisted to show that two "antagonistic civilizations"—a bookish North and an illiterate South—coexisted in the era of the Civil War. The quote continues to appear in school textbooks, lectures, and histories.[2]

In fact, Berkeley was not hostile to print nor was his colony bereft of books, as David D. Hall has shown. The governor's views were a commonplace among seventeenth-century royalists, who presumed that printing should be regulated by church and state. The Chesapeake did not have a printing office until the 1680s, no merchants in Virginia or Maryland specialized in bookselling, and only a few stores carried more than a tiny selection of titles. Nevertheless, the region was awash in scribal publications. Handwritten "books" and legal documents were abundant at a time when "to publish" meant to read aloud.[3]

The enduring impulse to quote a royalist governor underscores how hard it is for us to remember a time when reading did not seem to promote liberty. The American Revolution was one of the events in the early modern Atlantic world that recast printing from the bastion of imperial and ecclesiastical authority it had been for centuries into the lifeblood of human liberty. The printed book has been an ideologically charged ally of freedom in both the popular and scholarly imagination ever since. In the colonial era, it was never illegal to teach Virginia slaves to read. After the Revolution, the Virginia General Assembly made it illegal in 1819 to gather slaves to teach them to read, and the law was strengthened in 1831 in the wake of Nat Turner's bloody rebellion. Ralph Waldo Emerson showed how this new ideology of literacy was defined in opposition to slavery. "Slavery is no scholar, no improver," he said in 1844. "It does not love the whistle of the railroad, it does not love the newspaper, a mail bag, a college, a book . . . everything goes to decay." Similarly, the North Carolina polemicist Hinton Rowan Helper wrote in 1857 that "slavery is the parent of ignorance" and is "inevitably hostile to literary culture."[4] Since Emerson and Helper's generation, this ideology's powerful hold on our imagination has been hard to measure. Americans have rarely considered that books can be instruments of social control in the hands of tyrants—something obvious to people in other societies. We send our children to public libraries not to be indoctrinated but to learn how to be free.

To write a history of books in the South, some space needs to be cleared to allow critical perspective on this ideology. The claims of black and white abolitionists to the contrary, the southern states counted more readers than almost any other western society in 1850. While rates of illiteracy were somewhat higher there than in New England, a large majority of free people, and probably 10 percent of enslaved people, learned to read. Very few of these readers were trained in what scholars call "schooled literacy" until after the Civil War. It is well known that law and custom suppressed literacy among enslaved people and free blacks—often cruelly so—but a straightforward correlation between literacy rates and slavery cannot be made for white Americans. Population density, rather than the presence of enslaved people, determined literacy rates across a young nation. Meanwhile, making the picture more complex, proslavery theorists melded biblical rhetoric with racist and political ideologies to develop a printed canon by 1850. Literacy was as much an ally as a foe of chattel slavery.[5]

Recent work has affirmed the complicated story of books and readers in the South. Intellectual and social historians have found generous access to books and various uses of literacy across the region.[6] Yet many areas of inquiry remain. What kinds of print circulated across the South? Where was it produced? Who were southern printers and where did they get their ink, type, and paper? How did editors and publishers in eastern cities or across the Atlantic reach customers in the southern states? Answers to such questions will help us to better understand the place of rural societies in two key developments in nineteenth-century global history: the unprecedented increase in the availability of printed texts and the spread of mass literacy.

A full accounting will move beyond the conventions of American book history. This diverse and diffuse field remains, four decades on, "one in the making" even as it has been embraced around the globe. As Robert Darnton pointed out more than thirty years ago, book history is "interdisciplinarity run riot," and this has proven both a boon and a bane. Like southern studies, it is full of disjointed conversations in which participants tend to "talk past" one another. Leon Jackson has shown that book history rarely engages African American literary and cultural history and vice versa. Book historians and bibliographers continue to eye each other suspiciously, while many historians seem content to defer to literary scholars.[7]

Nevertheless, book history has broadly reinterpreted how culture worked in the American past. To take but two examples, we now know that nineteenth-century readers' tastes never fell strictly along class lines, contradicting those who have seen the development of high and low cultural modes in the nineteenth century. Moreover, a thriving export-import business shipped books back and forth across the Atlantic to sustain Anglo-American culture well into the late nineteenth century. Books ignored national boundaries, preferring to travel wherever the market might take them. In both cases, book historians have shown that cultural production, distribution, and consumption rarely accords with the ordered narratives and crisp categories preferred by scholars. Joan Shelley Rubin has suggested that the very unruliness of these conclusions better reflects the complexity of human lives.[8]

It is still in its early days, but a history of books in the South will likely unsettle things further. Not only does this highly literate slave society disrupt the liberal consensus that reading promotes liberty, but it also defies at least two other conventions of book history.

First is the question of how region affected the workings of American culture. The South's experience with books refutes the orthodoxy that culture respected the border between free and slave states. Close studies of New England and eastern cities have dominated the field, but evidence from the southern states suggests that region mattered less than we have thought.[9] African Methodist Episcopal hymnbooks printed in Philadelphia spread spirituals across the southern states, while sacred songsters full of revival tunes created in Tennessee spread them into New England. Maine humorist Seba Smith found an audience in Appalachia, while Augustus Baldwin Longstreet of Georgia was welcomed into Cincinnati parlors. Slaves and freedmen and women favored Noah Webster's Connecticut speller, while almanacs and Sunday school tracts knew no boundaries.

Second is the question of what readers did with books. Like rural people around the globe in an age of Western imperialism, people in the South got their books from other places. In spite of a beginning that stressed the holistic nature of the book from authors to printers, booksellers to readers, book history has exhibited a "materialist fetish" that has examined production at the expense of distribution and use.[10] Reading was not an end in itself. Rather, it was a means of cultural formation as people absorbed, memorized, criticized, copied, or even decried the novels and blue-back spellers that made their way across the country one box at a time. Verbal texts can be spoken, sung, imprinted in ink on rag paper, or digitally reproduced; they are always subject to the context in which they are made, transmitted, and used. In the nineteenth century, books were most often voiced. Texts were not signs pressed into rag paper and bound in boards as much as sound waves propelled by the human breath. People told new stories, poems, and songs, along with those that were generations old. Some of these were eventually set into type to be read and memorized before moving back into oral tradition. Anthropologists and folklorists have long argued that it is folly to divide speech from print in studies of culture.[11]

This essay briefly suggests how the malleability of both regional and cultural boundaries shaped the history of books in the southern states before the Civil War. I focus on this era because it is what I know best, but I hope what is offered here will inspire students of other periods and places. As a rural region that did not make many books, the American South was not an outlier but the norm in the nineteenth century. The history of Africa and Asia has shown how printing and literacy often produced unexpected results. Allowing for similar contingencies will enhance accounts of books and readers in the United States.

REGION AND AMERICAN CULTURE

It is difficult to square the estimation that "the South was a place into which torrents of print poured," as Michael O'Brien observed, with Robert Gross's view that "the great majority of white southerners . . . lived in a world . . . where presses and newspapers were seldom seen, public schools and libraries nonexistent, and itinerant peddlers carried only an occasional pamphlet or book among their notions."[12] The former suggests that boundaries mattered little in the circulation of books and periodicals, while the latter claims that the South was a "world" cut off from the rest of the nation. By this telling, regional boundaries not only demarcated free and slave states but also designated sharp differences in culture.

Books themselves don't offer much help in resolving this confusion. The Bibles that eventually lent the South one of its most familiar names—the Bible Belt—were printed in Philadelphia, New York, Cincinnati, and London. The shape-note tune books that have become synonymous with the South were first published in Philadelphia. Were Bibles that rendered ancient texts in Elizabethan English "southern" books? Were tune books full of songs originating in western Massachusetts and eastern Tennessee and printed in the mid-Atlantic in any sense "southern" books? Answers will be found not in the books themselves but in understanding how they were used.

O'Brien and others have shown that the southern states were teeming with print, much of it made in other places. Daughters of Tidewater planters and Appalachian yeomen read magazines edited in Philadelphia and Cincinnati that reprinted articles from Edinburgh and London. A Mississippi governess originally from western Pennsylvania took solace during her lonely exile in French periodicals and editions of Dickens. Intellectuals in the southern states conversed literally and by post with those in Britain and on the Continent, drawing on their immersion in books that were by turns American, English, or European. Jonathan Wells found that families across the region were enamored of New York papers and Philadelphia magazines on the eve of secession.[13]

Scarcity *was* an apt description of many enslaved and free African Americans' experience with books. The handful of first-person accounts of slavery that survive, and those written by white allies, focus on how enslaved people were deprived of education and punished for reading. In particular, the eighty-seven slave narratives that survive from the pre–Civil War period have deeply influenced how we view the relationship between enslaved people and books since the mid-twentieth century. They borrowed them, stole them, surreptitiously opened them behind white people's backs, and carefully studied them under cover of darkness. These narratives tell that books were always in short supply, and in the worst cases, when found by white owners in the hands of black readers, they led to physical maimings or beatings.[14]

Yet African Americans' experience with reading and the ability to acquire books was complicated. They did not use literacy to simply imitate or resist white power. Books and readers enabled the strengthening of religious communities in creative ways, and literate preachers were able to serve as mediators for their communities. Free black men and women used literacy skills for political and personal gain, corresponding with family members and scouring the papers for word of any changes in their precarious legal position. They sometimes found access to literacy, and even schooling, easier in places such as Baltimore, where whites did not fear that the institution of slavery was under imminent threat. Likewise, white attitudes toward black reading varied widely. Nineteenth-century literacy had a range of meanings; it could be regarded as a skill like any other, it could be infused with high moral purpose, or it could be both simultaneously. The ability to read, write, or figure numbers both warranted a higher price on the auction block and was considered necessary for colonizing Liberia. Some whites were indifferent to black literacy. A man in Yazoo, Mississippi, admitted to a visitor in the 1850s that enslaved people on his place purchased books from peddlers with their own money. Above all, many black and white Christians deemed reading to be necessary for religious practice. All of these activities required things to read, and there is evidence that African Americans often found them.[15]

In addition to the image promoted by slave narratives, the South has seemed empty of books because of the practice of quantifying culture based on census returns. Because so few case studies of readers, printing shops, or booksellers exist, census counts of illiterate free people, schools, libraries, and printing offices have characterized the region as a whole.[16] These numbers offer a rough picture of the state of things. Southern states counted fewer newspapers per capita than northern states and were never home to major publishing houses. Public schools were rare, albeit growing in number by the 1850s. The region counted significantly more academies than northern states, but it had fewer private library societies, circulating libraries, and college and university libraries, with fewer volumes held, than in the northeast.[17]

None of this indicates a scarcity of things to read. Static numbers gleaned from the census ignore a critical quality of printed texts, that is, their ability to move across the landscape. They focus exclusively on books, ignoring the printed ephemera that circulated freely across the region. Nor did the South's high rates of literacy depend on the institutions that historians have identified as critical to fostering a reading public elsewhere. People in the southern states had ways of learning to read and of using books that continued eighteenth-century patterns. Most learned to read outside of school, with family members or friends or on the job. Books remained expensive—book prices remained steady into the 1840s in spite of technological changes—and bookshops were limited to large cities.[18]

People in counties without printing offices relied on their wits and publishers' marketing strategies to get things to read. We have anecdotal evidence that they acquired these via the post and private couriers from booksellers in regional cities and beyond. They found a limited stock of inexpensive steady sellers such as hymnbooks, schoolbooks, almanacs, and testaments at local stores and pooled funds with neighbors for periodical subscriptions. They found tracts, testaments, and hymnbooks in Sunday school libraries and bought periodicals and books from preacher peddlers.[19] Frank Richardson, who grew up near Knoxville, Tennessee, before the Civil War noted how his Methodist parents added regularly to their small library of standard works by buying from itinerant ministers.[20] Heads of rural academies and seminaries ordered boxes of books from eastern publishers, selling them to students and offering what remained to neighbors. Advertisements from New York publishers appeared in even the smallest of newspapers, offering premiums for postmasters and agents who drummed up subscribers. While every major town or city had at least one printing office that issued cheap ephemera, most of this output did not survive. One distinguished bibliographer has estimated that as much as 80 percent of the work produced in such establishments has been lost.[21]

Readers had access to a wide variety of magazines and newspapers that arrived via the burgeoning network of postal routes, while more than 700 magazines began publishing in southern towns in the century before the Civil War.[22] Readers in Rocky Mount, North Carolina, on the Tar River in the eastern part of the state, subscribed to at least ninety-four different newspapers and magazines in the fifteen months after July 1859. More than 400 different subscriptions to more than 200 readers were received by the postmaster. Several had paid subscriptions to between seven and ten titles. Subscribers included laborers, clerks, artisans, women, planters, and at least two "servants" who subscribed to Primitive Baptist periodicals.[23]

The old orthodoxy that the South was bereft of print ignores how far and how fast books moved across the nation's landscape. The geography of production never aligned precisely with consumption.[24] Readers were customers, and publishers, editors, printers, and booksellers paid less attention to regional borders than historians have. They ignored them for a simple reason—profit—and used creative ways to meet customer demands, seeking them wherever they might be found. Teamsters, agents, wholesalers, booksellers, the railroads, colporteurs, peddlers, the mails, and private express services all took part in "getting the books out" across the vast expanse of the young nation.[25] Distribution of print took a central place in the "communication circuit" that laid an early foundation for book history, but it has not received the attention of other topics. There is good reason for this. As the legendary dealer Madeleine Stern observed, sellers of books are shadowy figures who are far more difficult to find in archives than the publishers and printers whose names are inscribed at the foot of title pages.[26] Nevertheless, until we know more about how a growing national publishing distribution system used jobbing firms to send books wholesale via a growing network of railroad lines, trade sales, post offices, and express firms, any generalizations about books and readers will remain provisional.[27] Unfortunately, some questions will never be answered. There is, for example, the tantalizing suggestion that the majority of the business of J. B. Lippincott of Philadelphia lay south of the Mason-Dixon Line before the Civil War, but the early nineteenth-century records of the publishing house have not survived.[28]

Restoring the presence of books in the South will emphasize the energy of the printing and publishing market as part of a broader story of the region. Histories of the book have not yet reckoned with the recent turn in southern studies away from the view that the plantation South was precapitalist. This work has deemphasized southern distinctiveness, arguing that slavery was a variant of market capitalism. Most historians now agree that slavery and its northern allies were the engine for much of the economic growth of the nation in the nineteenth century. Integrating these findings with the study of books will breathe life into the study of printing offices, paper mills, post offices and private couriers, and transportation routes. Nearly every town of some size had a small printing office, and many had more than one.

In the South as elsewhere, urban people were the engines of the printing and publishing trades and comprised most of the region's readers. Two examples will suffice. Charleston, South Carolina, emerged early as a critical seat of importance for intellectual activity in the region, and the work there was supported by a host of institutions and printers, as well as the port city's easy access to imported volumes and magazines from Britain and Scotland. The city saw more than fifty periodicals founded in the eight decades before secession. Many were religious organs, including the nation's first Catholic periodical and Protestant periodicals of all stripes. The city also produced a number of medical, agricultural, and law journals, along with a large cohort of literary periodicals, some with national reputations.[29] Nashville also became an important center of printing and publishing. In 1850, the city was home to sixty-four printers, editors, and publishers, along with eleven booksellers. In 1854, however, the game changed when the Methodist Episcopal Church, South, established its publishing house in the city, setting up four Adams power presses and a Hoe cylinder press in several large four-story buildings. In five years the number of presses doubled, and the workforce employed more than 130 people. In 1858, the city produced product worth more than $600,000 and had six daily papers. Overall, Nashville saw more than sixty periodicals established by 1861.[30]

Book historians have some familiarity with colonial printers in Annapolis, Williamsburg, and Charleston but far less with the printing and papermaking trades far from the eastern seaboard in the nineteenth century.[31] One exception is the comprehensive study by Catherine A. Baker of the printing trades in Mobile, Alabama, in 1850–65.[32] Baker found a flourishing trade that supplied the city and surrounding area with newspapers, magazines, pamphlets, and even some books. S. H. Goetzel and Company, owned by an Austrian who had probably worked in New York, opened in Mobile in the late 1850s as a bookseller and publisher. Baker not only documents the city's industry in detail, but she also debunks myths about the paper used in Confederate printing, finding that the books produced during the Civil War in Mobile were not printed with "wrapping" but instead were made with a finer-grade newsprint. Until we know more about printers such as Goetzel and his supply chains and customers, we cannot tell an adequate story of print in the South.

BOOKS AND THE HUMAN VOICE

Looking south can also restore the human voice to the story of books. If there ever was an "age of print," as nineteenth-century editors and publishers repeatedly proclaimed, then it flourished alongside an "age of oratory" and an "age of song." Speech is critical to the story of how printed texts were disseminated and even created. Stories, songs, and poems passed into the oral tradition when they were read aloud, remembered, and repeated. Similarly, oral tradition passed into print, becoming inspiration for new work scribbled in journals and commonplace books or spontaneously voiced aloud. This meant that the pens of literate people *and* the voices of those who could not read contributed to the body of printed texts. "We did not stop speaking when we learned to write, nor writing when we learned to print, nor reading, writing or printing when we entered 'the electronic age,'" the bibliographer D. F. McKenzie observed.[33]

The complementarity of speech, manuscript, and print has been a constant in the story of American books. In British North America, seventeenth-century Puritans, elites and commoners alike, knew well stories of monstrous births and freakish bolts of lightning spread by word of mouth, some of which were recorded in student notes at Harvard College and eventually passed into print. Twentieth-century residents of the Blue Ridge Mountains told "Jack tales" that had been passed down for generations, including the ancient "Jack and the Bean Tree," which had long been in print.[34] In the 1940s, the folklorist Richard M. Dorson argued that "stories in the United States travel interchangeably through the spoken and the printed word."[35] He explained that because American culture was birthed among a people with high rates of literacy at a time of technological change, print was more important to American folklorists than to their European peers. Nineteenth-century sacred song, of which I will say more below, offers a good example of a genre that incorporates the human voice into the history of books.

Opening up the relationship between print and speech will challenge book history's reliance on the concept of "print culture." As far as I can determine, Elizabeth Eisenstein coined the phrase in her two-volume study of early modern printing, *The Printing Press as an Agent of Change*, published in 1979. The study was a sensation and was credited with opening the field of book history. Over the next decade, "print culture" began to feature in studies ranging from Cuba to England and the United States. Use of the term shows no signs of flagging; in the last two years alone, it appeared in the title of at least fifty books and almost 100 articles.[36]

Historians of books in America have been particularly enthusiastic. The term features prominently, if unevenly, in all five volumes of *A History of the Book in America* (2000–2015), where it acquires a striking range of qualifiers, including African American, socialist, American, Hispanic, Jewish, Catholic, Protestant, Southern, German American, evangelical, and republican. Print culture is accorded ideologies, boundaries, and contours; it is radical, national, local, oppositional, and even sinful. The South is one of only two regions that is credited with having a separate print culture.[37]

The phrase "print culture" can imply that books *created* a culture. This determinist view is rooted in early studies by Marshall McLuhan and Walter J. Ong, but it found its most influential advocate in Eisenstein. The character of printing *itself* changed history, she argued, enabling developments in early modern science and the Protestant Reformation that would have been impossible with handwritten texts. Print changed the direction of cultural movements, she wrote, "as suddenly and completely as a prism bends a beam of light."[38] Her critics, including Americanist Michael Warner and European historian Adrian Johns, argue that print both conditioned history and was conditioned *by* history; people invested meaning and authority in printed texts over time. Some have even called print culture a myth, calling for studies that instead consider "the impact of society on the book."[39]

Even now, print culture lacks definition, and it is not clear precisely what the culture is that print makes. But several key traits have emerged. First, it commonly designates the creation and use of texts based on racial and ethnic identity. Hence, for example, Germans, Latinxs, and African Americans have been deemed to have a print culture. Scholars have tried to shoehorn region into this scheme. A recent volume of *The Oxford History of Popular Print Culture*, for example, treats southern imprints and readers in a section called "Segmentation and Diversity," which also includes chapters on Catholics, children, Native Americans, women, and Spanish speakers, even though people in all of these groups lived in the southern states. This affords a striking example of how book historians create a national norm by defining a subnational region.[40] Print is not a stable technology that creates identity. Not all Germans, Catholics, or southerners used print in the same ways or drew the same conclusions from their reading. Nor is "southern" the equivalent of an ethnic or racial identity.[41]

The dominance of "print culture" has also encouraged book history's alliance with history and literary studies at the expense of other fields. "Interdisciplinary" in the context of American book history has nearly always meant conversations between these two fields, with occasional contributions by bibliographers, scholars of communications or journalism, sociologists, and librarians.[42] To study the ways that readers used texts, however, requires the methods of anthropologists, linguists, musicologists, and folklorists to understand how speech created and disseminated printed texts. Scholars of African Americans and Native Americans have been open to methods that incorporate the oral, visual, and handwritten into the study of printed texts.[43] Book historians should follow their lead, recognizing the importance of oral culture to European Americans even in the age of the steam press.

Boundaries between speech and print were particularly weak in the nineteenth century. Periodicals and pamphlets were full of speechmaking. These were customarily read aloud, offering multiple performances and varied interpretations months and even years after they were first delivered. Every ambitious preacher had sermons typeset, printed, and stitched into pamphlets. Some later collected them into volumes that were nearly always printed outside of the South. The proceedings of religious assemblies—local, regional, and national—were distributed verbatim in thousands of pamphlets and religious periodicals. Debates from oratorical and literary societies, some from academies and colleges, some town based, found their way into print. Political speeches covered several columns or even entire pages of newspapers. In this way, people listened to Daniel Webster, John Calhoun, or William Lamb in parlors, on porches, and at town gatherings. The most memorable (or notorious) lines or phrases in these were remembered and repeated until they entered oral tradition. Primitive Baptists, who loosely organized themselves in a schism of the 1830s, had a long tradition of an oral version of the Bible that coexisted with the printed text. They held that "spoken scripture" was so important "that it is possible to grow up 'knowing' the Bible without being a reader." The printed text, in other words, needed to be spoken to have meaning in this community.[44]

In the nineteenth century, "to read" meant to recite from the page. People ignored the new Romantic image of a silent reader absorbed in a text, if they knew about it at all. Knowledge passed freely from conversation into writing and then into print and back again into speech. Conversation often disseminated information more efficiently than print.[45] Songs, stories, and poems from the diverse oral traditions of the southern states—Native American, African and African American, and European—made their way into print to be disseminated and memorized.[46] Texts were spoken within communities, particularly families, who gathered to hear stories, poems, jokes, toasts, and Bible passages read aloud. In schoolrooms, students were rewarded not for silent reading but for recitation that was sometimes gleefully shouted out in unison. Schoolbooks printed "conversations" that reproduced the catechetical tradition quite literally in their pages.

A good example of the interaction between speech and print can be seen in the tradition of sacred song. Its history has been recorded not by book historians but by a cadre of diligent musicologists and folklorists who have doggedly pursued the sparse record of early southern printing offices. From the earliest days, territorial printers produced songsters, hymnbooks, and pamphlets, highlighting their importance to the printing trades' profits. The first book printed by the noted Lexington, Kentucky, printer John Bradford was a ninety-eight-page duodecimo that recounted a fierce quarrel among Presbyterians about whether they should sing psalms or hymns in worship.[47] Hymnbooks printed in Baltimore, Philadelphia, and Cincinnati appeared in "staggering" numbers of editions and copies to spread across the country.[48] Tens of thousands (by some estimates hundreds of thousands) of copies of pamphlets and songsters were printed to be distributed one saddlebag or box at a time. Eventually, new technologies enabled musical notation (which had been particularly difficult to typeset) to appear in almanacs, dancing manuals, jokebooks, and guides to freemasonry.

Printed song, both tune and text, often circulated in songbooks, pamphlets, and broadsides before it moved into oral tradition.[49] In other cases, slave and master, pietist and Calvinist, weaver and miner learned songs by ear even if they had no books or read poorly or not at all. Enslaved people were particularly fond of hymns by the English Nonconformist Isaac Watts, and they memorized them in worship services, adapting them to their own tunes and uses, while spiritual songs composed in the midst of camp-meeting fervor circulated first by ear and later in print.

African American spirituals were sung into being by those who combined African traditions with imagery, stories, and language from the King James Bible. The musicologist Eileen Southern has found that spirituals originated not in the fields of southern plantations but in the worship of independent black congregations in the Philadelphia area. The critical source is the first collection of African American hymns, Richard Allen's *A Collection of Spiritual Songs and Hymns, Selected from Various Authors* (Philadelphia, 1801), which featured pieces from the English hymn composers John Wesley, Isaac Watts, and John Newton along with songs from the oral tradition. The first printed collection of sacred song highly regarded by African American Christians, it was also the first to include "wandering choruses," simple refrain lines appended to Anglo-American hymns in the oral tradition. A single copy of the first edition has apparently survived. Of the sixty-four songs in the second edition, almost half were from the Anglo-American tradition. The rest were camp-meeting spirituals by American-born authors including Allen himself; he altered some lines in others.[50]

Allen's hymnbook spread through the influence of his Philadelphia congregation—Bethel Church, known as "Mother Bethel"—the most important independent black congregation in the nation. The African Methodist Episcopal Church spread Allen's hymnbooks as far south as Charleston, South Carolina. In the two decades after the book appeared, at least ten other popular compilations used by white and black singers appeared that included a large number of the texts chosen by Allen. There was a particularly close relationship between songs in Allen's book and what became known as the Baltimore Collection, the anonymously compiled *Hymns and Spiritual Songs for the Use of Christians* (Baltimore, 1801), one of the most influential collections of camp-meeting songs in the period. Eileen Southern has traced texts in the first printed compilation of African American spirituals, *Slave Songs of the United States* (1867), collected on the South Carolina coast by northern troops and teachers during the Civil War, back to Allen's hymnbook. This single text offers a marvelous example of how songs from the oral tradition found their way into print only to return to oral tradition.

CONCLUSION

Song has the unnerving tendency to ignore regional boundaries. Confident assertions that a particular song, or collection, is "northern" or "southern" are often impossible in light of the way song was passed along by word of mouth and in print. Many of the sources for what has become known as "southern song" were first printed on northern presses. The most influential shape-note tune book among southern singers before the Civil War, William Walker's *Southern Harmony* (1835), was first printed in New Haven, Connecticut, with later editions produced in Philadelphia. *The Sacred Harp* (1844), compiled by Georgian Elisha J. King and South Carolinian Benjamin Franklin White, was also initially printed in Philadelphia.[51]

The inability to claim a strict regional origin for hymnbooks and songsters is true of a great many printed texts. Books are supremely portable objects. Their history in the South will focus on how they moved into the region from other places at a time in which no one, not even those who could not read, could escape the implications of print.

What is a history of books in the South?[52] It is one that focuses on the uses and distribution of printed texts rather than on how they were produced. It tells of how people created and circulated both printed *and* spoken texts, recognizing that many printed texts originated in oral tradition and that others entered oral tradition off the page. A history of books in the South will hew as closely to linguistics, anthropology, and musicology as it does to literary studies and history. It will unshackle culture from technology, accounting for the range of texts made by both the highly literate and those who could not read and write well, or at all. It will encourage us to write a "cultural history of print" rather than a history of print culture, resulting in a more comprehensive history of human creativity in the American past.[53]

NOTES

1. Berkeley quoted in William Waller Hening, "Extracts from the Legislative and Judicial Proceedings of the Governor and Council of Virginia, as Contained in the Records of the General Court," in *Statutes at Large: Being a Collection of All the Laws of Virginia* (New York: R. & G. & W. Bartow, 1823), 2:517.

2. George Chalmers, *Political Annals of the Present United Colonies from Their Settlement to the Peace of 1763* (London: J. Bowen, 1780), 1:328; John Lendrum, *A Concise and Impartial History of the American Revolution* (Boston: I. Thomas and E. T. Andrews, 1795), 131. Antebellum histories that quote Berkeley include Theodore Parker, *A Letter to the People of the United States Touching on the Matter of Slavery* (Boston, 1848), 65; T[imothy] S[hay] Arthur and W. H. Carpenter, *The History of Virginia* (Philadelphia: Lippincott, 1852), 173; Benson J. Lossing, *A Pictorial History of the United States for Schools and Families* (New York: Mason Brothers, 1860), 89; and Charles Campbell, *Introduction to the History of the Colony and Ancient Dominion of Virginia* (Richmond, Va.: B. B. Minor, 1847), 79. For the Civil War era, see *Cleveland (Ohio) Leader*, May 19, 1864, quoted in Lee Soltow and Edward Stevens, *The Rise of Literacy and the Common School in the United States: A Socioeconomic Analysis to 1870* (Chicago: University of Chicago Press, 1981), 154.

3. David D. Hall, "The Chesapeake in the Seventeenth Century," in *Cultures of Print: Essays in the History of the Book* (Amherst: University of Massachusetts Press, 1996), 99–101.

4. Ralph Waldo Emerson, "Address Delivered in Concord on the Anniversary of the Emancipation of the Negroes in the British West Indies, August 1, 1844," quoted in David Brion Davis, *Slavery and Human Progress* (New York: Oxford University Press, 1984), 110; Hinton Rowan Helper, *The Impending Crisis of the South: How to Meet It* (New York: Burdick Brothers, 1857), 406.

5. Beth Barton Schweiger, "The Literate South: Reading before Emancipation," *Journal of the Civil War Era* 3, no. 3 (September 2013): 340, table 4; Michael O'Brien, *Conjectures of Order: Intellectual Life and the American South* (Chapel Hill: University of North Carolina Press, 2004), 965. In 1850 white adults were twice as likely to be illiterate if they lived in a county with slaves, but those who lived in rural areas in all regions of the country were four times more likely to be illiterate than those in urban areas.

6. Beth Barton Schweiger, *A Literate South: Reading before Emancipation* (New Haven, Conn.: Yale University Press, 2019); Christopher Hager, *I Remain Yours: Common Lives in Civil War Letters* (Cambridge, Mass.: Harvard University Press, 2018); Christopher Hager, *Word by Word: Emancipation and the Act of Writing* (Cambridge, Mass.: Harvard University Press, 2013); Timothy Williams, *Intellectual Manhood: University, Self, and Society in the Antebellum South* (Chapel Hill: University of North Carolina Press, 2015); Michael Bernath, *Confederate Minds: The Struggle for Intellectual Independence in the Civil War South* (Chapel Hill: University of North Carolina Press, 2010); Jonathan Daniel Wells, *Women Writers and Journalists in the Nineteenth-Century South* (New York: Cambridge University Press, 2011); Jonathan Daniel Wells, *The Origins of the Southern Middle Class, 1800–1861* (Chapel

Hill: University of North Carolina Press, 2004); Amy M. Thomas, "Literacies, Readers, and Cultures of Print in the South," in *The Industrial Book, 1840–1880*, ed. Scott E. Casper, Jeffrey D. Groves, Stephen W. Nissenbaum, and Michael Winship, vol. 3 of *A History of the Book in America* (Chapel Hill: University of North Carolina Press, 2007), 373–90; O'Brien, *Conjectures of Order*.

7. David D. Hall, preface to *The Colonial Book in the Atlantic World*, ed. Hugh Amory and David D. Hall, vol. 1 of *A History of the Book in America* (Chapel Hill: University of North Carolina Press, 2007), xiii; Robert Darnton, "What is the History of Books?," *Daedalus* 111, no. 3 (1982): 67; Coleman Hutchison, "Book History," in *Keywords for Southern Studies*, ed. Scott Romine and Jennifer Rae Greeson (Athens: University of Georgia Press, 2016), 248; Leon Jackson, "The Talking Book and the Talking Book Historian: African American Cultures of Print—the State of the Discipline," *Book History* 13 (2010): 251–308. On southern studies, see Michele Grigsby Coffey and Jodi Skipper, eds., *Navigating Souths: Transdisciplinary Explorations of a U.S. Region* (Athens: University of Georgia Press, 2017). On bibliography, see G. Thomas Tanselle, "The History of Books as a Field of Study," in *Literature and Artifacts* (Charlottesville: Bibliographical Society of the University of Virginia, 1998); and David L. Vander Meulen, "How to Read Book History," *Studies in Bibliography* 56 (2003–4): 171–94.

8. Joan Shelley Rubin, "What is the History of the History of Books?" *Journal of American History* 90, no. 2 (September 2003): 566–67, 572.

9. Matthew Pethers, Phillip H. Round, Graham Thompson, John Fagg, and Evan Brier, "Online Roundtable: *A History of the Book in America*," in "Special Issue on Oil Cultures," *Journal of American Studies* 46, no. 2 (2012): 19.

10. Peter D. McDonald, "Semper Aliquid Novi: Reclaiming the Future of Book History from an African Perspective," *Book History* 19 (2016): 384–98, quote on 387.

11. G. Thomas Tanselle, "A Bibliographer's Creed: The 100th George Parker Winship Lecture," *Harvard Library Bulletin* 25, no. 1 (Spring 2014): 7; Donald F. McKenzie, "Speech—Manuscript—Print," in *New Directions in Textual Studies*, ed. Dave Oliphant and Robin Bradford (Austin, Tex.: Harry Ransom Humanities Research Center, 1990), 86–109.

12. O'Brien, *Conjectures of Order*, 488; Robert Gross, "Reading for an Extensive Republic," in *An Extensive Republic: Print, Culture, and Society in the New Nation, 1790–1840*, ed. Robert A. Gross and Mary Kelley, vol. 2 of *A History of the Book in America* (Chapel Hill: University of North Carolina Press, 2010): 525–26. In a survey of rural printers in the early United States, Jack Larkin writes that print was marginal to the conduct of life in the South. Jack Larkin, "'Printing Is Something Every Village Has in It': Rural Printing and Publishing," in Gross and Kelley, *Extensive Republic*, 157.

13. Michael O'Brien, *An Evening When Alone: Four Journals of Single Women in the South, 1827–1867* (Charlottesville: University of Virginia Press, 1993); Schweiger, *Literate South*; O'Brien, *Conjectures of Order*; Wells, *Origins*.

14. William L. Andrews, "Introduction to the Scholarly Bibliography of Slave and Ex-slave Narratives," Documenting the American South, http://docsouth.unc.edu/neh/biblintro.html, accessed December 7, 2020. Elizabeth McHenry has shown

how these narratives tell only part of the story of African American readers in *Forgotten Readers: Recovering the Lost History of African American Literary Societies* (Durham, N.C.: Duke University Press, 2002).

15. Grey Gundaker, "African Americans, Print, and Practice," in Gross and Kelley, *Extensive Republic*, 483–84; Janet Duitsman Cornelius, *When I Can Read My Title Clear: Literacy, Slavery, and Religion in the Antebellum South* (Columbia: University of South Carolina Press, 1991); Hager, *Word by Word*; Michael P. Johnson and James L. Roark, eds., *No Chariot Let Down: Charleston's Free People of Color on the Eve of the Civil War* (New York: W. W. Norton, 1986); Hilary Moss, *Schooling Citizens: The Struggle for African American Education in Antebellum America* (Chicago: University of Chicago Press, 2009); Randall M. Miller, ed., *"Dear Master": Letters of a Slave Family* (Ithaca, N.Y.: Cornell University Press, 1978); Frederick Law Olmsted, *A Journey in the Back Country, 1853–54* (New York: Schocken Books, 1970), 144.

16. An example of how these numbers have been used is Ronald J. Zboray, *A Fictive People: Antebellum Economic Development and the American Reading Public* (New York: Oxford University Press, 1993), which reproduces a table from Helper, *Impending Crisis*, without critical analysis. Helper's numbers were abstracted from J. D. B. De Bow's 1854 compendium of the seventh census. Zboray, *Fictive People*, 197, table 22.

17. On newspapers, see John L. Brooke, "To Be 'Read by the Whole People': Press, Party and Public Sphere in the United States, 1789–1840," *Proceedings of the American Antiquarian Society* 110 (April 2000): 41–118. On schools, see Sarah L. Hyde, *Schooling in the Antebellum South: The Rise of Public and Private Education in Louisiana, Mississippi, and Alabama* (Baton Rouge: Louisiana State University Press, 2016). On libraries, see O'Brien, *Conjectures of Order*, 488–525.

18. James N. Green, "The Rise of Book Publishing," in Gross and Kelley, *Extensive Republic*, 126.

19. Anne Boylan's important history of Sunday schools underestimates their number in the South, where most never affiliated with the American Sunday School Union. Anecdotal evidence suggests a significant number of Sunday school libraries across the South. Anne M. Boylan, *Sunday School: The Formation of an American Institution, 1790–1880* (New Haven, Conn.: Yale University Press, 1988).

20. Frank Richardson, *From Sunrise to Sunset: Reminiscences of Bristol, Tennessee* (Bristol, Tenn.: King, 1910).

21. Wells, *Women Writers and Journalists*, 65; John Cook Wylie, comp., *Preliminary Checklist for Abingdon 1807–1876* (Richmond: Virginia State Library, 1945), 5. The titles preserved in libraries probably represent no more than one-fifth of the actual products of Abingdon, Virginia, presses. So little is known of southern printers that a recent survey relied on a single unfinished manuscript study of North Carolina. Larkin, "'Printing Is Something.'"

22. Schweiger, *Literate South*; Wells, *Women Writers and Journalists*, 67.

23. Helen R. Watson, "A Journalistic Medley: Newspapers and Periodicals in a Small North Carolina Community, 1859–1860," *North Carolina Historical Review* 60, no. 4 (October 1983): 457–85.

24. One study concluded that the South was "less biblically centered and biblically literate" because few Bibles were printed there. Paul C. Gutjahr, *An American Bible:*

A History of the Good Book in the United States, 1777-1880 (Stanford, Calif.: Stanford University Press, 1999), 6.

25. Michael Hackenberg, ed., *Getting the Books Out: Papers of the Chicago Conference on the Book in 19th-Century America* (Washington, D.C.: Center for the Book, 1987).

26. Darnton, "What Is the History"; Madeleine B. Stern, "Dissemination of Popular Books in the Midwest and Far West during the Nineteenth Century," in Hackenberg, *Getting the Books Out*, 76.

27. Michael Winship, "'The Tragedy of the Book Industry?': Bookstores and Book Distribution in the United States to 1950," *Studies in Bibliography* 58 (2007-8): 145-84.

28. J[ames] C[ephas] Derby, *Fifty Years among Authors, Books, and Publishers* (New York, 1884), 387. My thanks to Michael Winship, who catalogued the Lippincott papers at the Historical Society of Pennsylvania, for this reference.

29. David Moltke-Hansen, "The Expansion of Intellectual Life: A Prospectus," in *Intellectual Life in Antebellum Charleston*, ed. Michael O'Brien and David Moltke-Hansen (Knoxville: University of Tennessee Press, 1986), 3-44; Gertrude C. Gilmer, *Checklist of Southern Periodicals to 1861* (Boston: F. W. Faxon, 1934), 16, 92-95.

30. David Kaser, *A Directory of the Book and Printing Industries in Ante-bellum Nashville* (New York: New York Public Library, 1966), 13-16; Gilmer, *Checklist of Southern Periodicals*, 16.

31. Calhoun Winton, "The Southern Book Trade in the Eighteenth Century," in Amory and Hall, *Colonial Book*, 224-46.

32. Catherine Ann Baker, "The Press That Cotton Built: Printing in Mobile, Alabama, 1850-1865" (PhD diss., University of Alabama, 2004).

33. McKenzie, "Speech—Manuscript—Print," 238.

34. David D. Hall, *Worlds of Wonder, Days of Judgment: Popular Religious Belief in Early New England* (Cambridge, Mass.: Harvard University Press, 1989). 85, Richard Chase, *The Jack Tales: Folk Tales from the Southern Appalachians* (1943; repr., Boston: Houghton Mifflin, 1971), vii-viii.

35. Richard M. Dorson, "Print and American Folktales," *California Folklore Quarterly* 4, no. 3 (1945): 207-15, reprinted in Richard M. Dorson, *American Folklore and the Historian* (Chicago: University of Chicago Press, 1971), 174.

36. Elizabeth Eisenstein, *The Printing Press as an Agent of Change* (New York: Cambridge University Press, 1979). Eisenstein mistakenly read the term "print culture" back into earlier works by Walter J. Ong and Jack Goody (9n16). For a critical inquiry of the early modern period, see Harold Love, "Early Modern Print Culture: Assessing the Models," in *The Book History Reader*, ed. David Finkelstein and Alistair McCleery, 2nd ed. (New York: Routledge, 2006), 74-86.

37. The other is New England.

38. Anthony Grafton, "The Importance of Being Printed," *Journal of Interdisciplinary History* 11, no. 2 (Autumn 1980): 265-86, quote on 267.

39. Michael Warner, *The Letters of the Republic: Publication and the Public Sphere in Eighteenth-Century America* (Cambridge, Mass.: Harvard University Press, 1990); Adrian Johns, *Nature of the Book: Print and Knowledge in the Making* (Chicago: Uni-

versity of Chicago Press, 1998), 35; Joseph A. Dane, *The Myth of Print Culture: Essays on Evidence, Textuality, and Bibliographical Method* (Toronto: University of Toronto Press, 2003); Thomas R. Adams and Nicolas Barker, "A New Model for the Study of the Book," in Finkelstein and McCleery, *Book History Reader*, 49.

40. Ronald J. Zboray and Mary Saracino Zboray, eds., *U.S. Popular Print Culture to 1860*, vol. 5 of *The Oxford History of Popular Print Culture*, ed. Gary Kelly (Oxford: Oxford University Press, 2019); Jennifer Rae Greeson, "Nation," in Romine and Greeson, *Keywords for Southern Studies*, 34. See also Thomas, "Literacies, Readers, and Cultures," and Jeannine Marie DeLombard, "African American Cultures of Print," in Casper et al., *Industrial Book*, chap. 10, 360–73, 373–90.

41. Hall, *Worlds of Wonder*; Lawrence Levine, *Highbrow/Lowbrow: The Emergence of Cultural Hierarchy in America* (Cambridge, Mass.: Harvard University Press, 1990); Alice Fahs, *The Imagined Civil War: Popular Literature of the North and South, 1861–1865* (Chapel Hill: University of North Carolina Press, 2003).

42. An overwhelming majority of contributors to the five volumes of *A History of the Book in America*, for example, were trained in history or literature.

43. Lara Langer Cohen and Jordan Alexander Stein, eds., *Early African American Print Culture* (Philadelphia: University of Pennsylvania Press, 2012), 7.

44. Brett Sutton, "Literacy and Dissent," *Libraries and Culture* 26, no. 1 (Winter 1991): 193–94.

45. David Shields, "Eighteenth-Century Literary Culture," in Amory and Hall, *Colonial Book*, 434–76.

46. Philip Round, "Mississippian Contexts for Early American Studies," *Early American Literature* 53, no. 2 (Spring 2018): 445–73.

47. W. H. Venable, *Beginnings of Literary Culture in the Ohio Valley: Historical and Biographical Sketches* (Cincinnati, Ohio: Robert Clarke, 1891), 44–45.

48. Stephen Marini, "Hymnody as History: Early Evangelical Hymns and the Recovery of American Popular Religion," *Church History* 71, no. 2 (June 2002): 273–306, 279n14.

49. Phillips Barry, "The Transmission of Folk-Song," *Journal of American Folklore* 27, no. 103 (January–March 1914): 67. Twentieth-century collectors who searched for a "pure" oral tradition found songs that had been circulated by print or phonograph recording before they reentered the oral tradition. David C. Rubin, *Memory in Oral Traditions: The Cognitive Psychology of Epic, Ballads, and Counting-Out Rhymes* (New York: Oxford University Press, 1995), 264–65.

50. Eileen Southern, *The Music of Black Americans: A History*, 2nd ed. (New York: W. W. Norton, 1983); "An Origin for the Negro Spiritual," *Black Scholar* 3, no. 10 (June 1972): 8–13.

51. David Warren Steel, *The Makers of the Sacred Harp*, with Richard Hulan (Urbana: University of Illinois Press, 2010).

52. This question follows from Darnton, "What Is the History."

53. Adrian Johns, "How to Acknowledge a Revolution," *American Historical Review* 107, no. 1 (February 2002): 106–25, quote on 116.

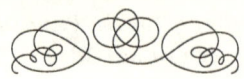

THE INTELLECTUAL LIFE OF A FANTASY

Edwin Wiley Fuller's Sea-Gift *and Postwar Imagination*

TIMOTHY J. WILLIAMS

THIS IS a story about an obscure author, his little-known novel, and the power of historical imagination. Few twenty-first-century readers have probably heard of the North Carolina author Edwin Wiley Fuller or his autobiographical novel *Sea-Gift* (1873).[1] He appears nowhere within the established canon of southern arts and letters, save for one encyclopedia entry. And why should he? *Sea-Gift* received tepid reviews following publication; it was only reprinted once, in 1940. It was, however, resuscitated in the early twenty-first century, when the indefatigable staff of the University of North Carolina at Chapel Hill's Documenting the American South project digitized the text. Published by E. J. Hale and Son, a North Carolina team living in New York, *Sea-Gift* is purportedly the first American novel set in Chapel Hill, North Carolina. According to the book's online summary, "Fuller offers detailed descriptions of the University buildings and grounds" and "humorously describes the rowdy behavior of the Carolina 'scholars.'"[2] Although Fuller attended Chapel Hill for a brief time, he graduated from the University of Virginia. At the end of the book, we learn a little bit about antebellum college life in Chapel Hill but very little about Fuller's life beyond childhood. We do, however, learn a great deal about his postwar imagination and the influence that Confederate defeat and Reconstruction had on it.

The world Fuller created in *Sea-Gift* is, at its core, a Lost Cause romance. Narrated by the protagonist, John Smith, *Sea-Gift* contains every important element of this genre: it emphasizes the South's revolutionary legacy, paints a rosy picture of slavery, and valorizes Confederate soldiers. In the process, it indemnifies abolitionism and legitimates white supremacy. Smith is a classic southern gentleman, an eager secessionist, and a heroic Confederate soldier. He fights Yankees, disavows turncoats, and vindicates his family's honor. As the war progresses, his childhood nemesis joins the Union army and helps burn Smith's house to the ground. Smith's mother is struck by a wooden beam as she escapes the fire; the injury ultimately kills her but not before Smith says farewell while on a two-day furlough. In the meantime, his father dies in prison and his best friend dies in battle. Only his adopted Cuban sister turned wife, Carlotta, remains (more on this provocative twist later). Emancipation and Republican control of the South convince the couple to flee North Carolina for Cuba, where they begin a new life. This story, however, was pure fiction. Edwin Fuller neither had nor married an adopted Cuban sister. What's more, he remained in the South his entire life and never saw battle. Only fourteen years old in 1861, Fuller came of age in wartime but not in war. Yet he can imagine another story through the characterization of John Smith, who enters manhood while fighting for the Confederacy. Both author and protagonist thus experience parallel transitions from the Old South to the postwar period.

A close reading of the novel elucidates important themes in broader Reconstruction-era literature, which has recently seen a modest renaissance, in which literary outsiders of various sorts have received fresh scrutiny.[3] The first theme concerns gender, especially masculinity. By marrying real experience with fiction, Fuller's genre-bending novel adds a literary dimension to the history of southern masculinity, particularly its transformation during the Civil War and Reconstruction. After all, it is a war story of a young man who fought, written by one who did not. War had an impact on men's perceptions of themselves as men and as southern men especially. James J. Broomall has argued that Confederate soldiers inhabited their own "private confederacies" where they "grappled with personal demons while also readjusting to wartime and postbellum life."[4] This paradigm is equally apt for noncombatants, for so much of living on the home front involved *imagining*—imagining camp, battle, hunger, disease, filth, captivity, victory, and defeat. These men must also have had to imagine themselves as part of war stories, though they encountered them only in letters and newspapers and by word of mouth. Through social and intellectual life, in other words, they entered the distorted stories of honor, self-sacrifice, heroism, and patriotism that Confederates told about themselves.

Of course, secession and war did not create these masculine values. A robust scholarship on the purported values of elite white southerners proves that elite white men were motivated by ambition for greatness, and some historians have argued that this was a driving force behind secession.[5] Their masculine fantasies stemmed from the certainty of their own heroic potential.[6] Educated young men such as Fuller, for instance, knew what a hero did in wartime and what heroism meant for a community and a nation. They wrote about, and tried to emulate, the traits they studied.[7] Civil War historians, however, have largely focused on why Confederates fought and not on those young men who remained at home.[8] As Fuller's *Sea-Gift* suggests, these men likewise incorporated values and ambitions into their own "private confederacies."

Second, at the same time Fuller draws on past modes of thought about gender and region, he also underscores the future-oriented perspective of these men caught in transition. The historical record swells with the fantasies of men who confronted (or not) a future they always feared—one defined by an abolitionist world view and a northern political economy. In this context, too, masculinity was on the minds of many veterans. One Confederate kept a diary that began and ended with common masculine fantasies. At the front of the volume, he pasted a poem he'd cut out of a newspaper. "We're *the men*, though our clothes are worn," the poem begins. "We're the men who will triumph again." The diary's final page reveals a vision for the future that placed him as master of his own small world, however humble that world might be: "Utopia—mine—Missouri. A plantation pigs cows, etc. etc."[9] Another fantasy altogether removed men and their families from the South. "I won't be reconstructed! . . . So I'm off for the frontier, soon as I can go," went one popular song. "I'll prepare me a weapon and start for Mexico."[10] Few southerners actually emigrated to places such as Mexico, Brazil, Cuba, Canada, and Europe. Instead, most found escape in literature.[11]

This point leads to the third theme in Reconstruction-era literature that an inquiry into *Sea-Gift* illuminates: the relationship between social and individual imagination and postwar literary genres. Memoirs and novels were popular Lost Cause genres for this work and had become ubiquitous by the time Edwin Fuller published *Sea-Gift* in 1873. Memoirists and novelists drew on a pervasive impulse to memorialize Confederate war dead and to vindicate the cause for which they died (a slave society).[12] The historian Wolfgang Schivelbusch has characterized this postwar "culture of defeat" as a "dreamland state": a social phenomenon "in which all blame is transferred to the deposed tyrant and the losing nation feels cathartically cleansed, freed of any responsibility of guilt."[13] Since the nation's founding, he argues, southerners aligned themselves not so much with English loyalists as with Cavaliers and the fiercely independent Scots, whom they read about in the works of Sir Walter Scott. Relying on classic—albeit flawed—interpretations of southern exceptionalism, Schivelbusch holds to the party line: southerners romanticized chivalry and fought for their honor when challenged.[14] According to Schivelbusch, these prewar obsessions naturally precipitated a nostalgic literature after Lee's surrender at Appomattox. In his rendering, however, individuals and their families disappear from the story. The real pain of loss that motivated southerners to create and consume Lost Cause literature is absent in his explanation. Thus author, text, and context become abstractions and the Lost Cause nearly inevitable.

Tied as it is to both memoir and fiction, Fuller's *Sea-Gift* tests the relationship between concepts so vague as "dreamland" and so idiosyncratic as "private confederacies." The novel reveals that "dreamland" is at once about the individual and about society. This is particularly true for the period of Reconstruction. Utopian visions characterize numerous texts published during Reconstruction.[15] That fact has prompted the literary scholar Cody Marrs to argue that "to read Reconstruction aright . . . demands approaching it as a utopian formation—as an era marked as much by what did *not* happen as by what actually *did*."[16] In other words, Marrs compels historians to read the literary and historical archive for insight into the ways in which the future remained open for imagining the postwar fulfillment of prewar ambitions.

Prewar future-oriented attitudes about manhood, region, and nation especially shaped postwar life. Civil War scholars have demonstrated broad and insidious manifestations of white masculine fantasies in the forms of vigilante violence against freed persons and institutional white supremacy, but we have only begun to dig into the inner, emotional lives of white southerners.[17] Many of these southerners wrote their way through war and Reconstruction and drew on nationalist sentiment within the

Confederacy and postwar South.[18] Building on that work, I argue that Fuller's fictional autobiography is most powerful at the moments when autobiographical suggestions become fiction and vice versa. Here the memoirist's *imagination* becomes the subject of inquiry and can explain that which the social historical record cannot: Fuller's masculine fantasies. In particular, this essay explores how ambitions for greatness—steeped in a long-held colonizing dream of slaveholders—function in his semiautobiographical text.

This approach relies on a broad understanding of intellectual history that is tied as much to a single text as to its social context and its intended audiences. "A convincing intellectual history must, at once, reach into biography, but also into social history," Michael O'Brien writes. "Texts are the necessary core, but where they come from, where they go to, ought to be a matter of interest."[19] We know a bit about where texts such as *Sea-Gift* went: a national reading public interested in wartime stories written by the men who endured them. Civil War fiction and memoir accelerated in the late 1860s and reached their peak in the 1870s, just as *Sea-Gift* hit the market. In particular, it followed Sidney Lanier's popular novel *Tiger-Lilies* (1867), which offers a pastiche of memoir and fiction similar to that found in *Sea-Gift*.[20] Any novel, semiautobiographical or otherwise, draws on the cultural milieu in which the author lives. For Fuller, this milieu was dominated by veteran reminiscences, histories of the Civil War, and wartime poetry, songs, and stories.

Throughout Reconstruction, white veterans particularly encountered an eager market for both memoir and fiction as they sought to find a heroic answer to their wartime defeat. But what of those who hadn't fought but had stories they wanted to tell, a war they wanted to claim as theirs regardless of whether they took up arms? We know less about where the imaginative core of autobiographical novels such as Fuller's *Sea-Gift* originated, however. Despite the novel's obscurity and oddness compared to other Reconstruction texts, this individual novel and its author can reveal a great deal about the broader cultural landscape of Reconstruction. So let us begin with our author, trace where and how his imagination may have developed, and determine how the published manifestation of that imagination—*Sea-Gift*—can offer an intellectual history not only of one man's "private confederacy" but also of the world of arts and letters in the Reconstruction-era South.

Edwin Wiley Fuller was born on November 30, 1847, in Louisburg, North Carolina. His father, Jones Fuller, was a successful cotton merchant, and his mother, Anna Long Thomas, was the daughter of another local slaveholding family. In 1852, Edwin's sister Anna was born.[21] Meanwhile, his mother schooled him at home. In 1857, when he was ten years old, he began attending a local school. In early 1861, amid the crisis of secession and onset of war, he matriculated at the leading preparatory school in the area, the Louisburg Male Academy.[22] In 1864, he matriculated at the University of North Carolina at Chapel Hill. He was seventeen years old. With the South deep in war, the student body was negligible, but classes met, the literary societies held regular business, and Fuller joined the Delta Psi fraternity. Only when Union troops occupied Chapel Hill between April 17 and May 3, 1865, did the university's regular business cease.[23] At the same time, the Union army also occupied Louisburg. Edwin's mother watched the army march along the streets playing music, and Union soldiers made camp at the academy Fuller had attended just three years earlier.[24] As townsfolk witnessed Yankees facilitate the emancipation of local enslaved persons, his mother wrote, "The Negroes are availing themselves of their freedom, by leaving their former owners and setting up for themselves, greatly to the discomfort of both parties. Lucy left us this morning."[25] Not surprisingly, when Anna Fuller accommodated two Union officers in her home that same month, she "felt cramped and ill at ease."[26]

This was Edwin Fuller's Civil War. Shortly after Union occupation of Louisburg, he returned home for the summer and thereafter began a second year at Chapel Hill but only for a short time. His father required assistance running his store in Louisburg. By 1867, business affairs had apparently stabilized enough for Fuller to return to college but this time at the University of Virginia. He studied natural philosophy, history and literature, and moral philosophy. He participated in student life and published original poetry and short fiction in the *Virginia University Magazine*.[27] After he graduated in 1868, Fuller again returned home to assist his father but did not abandon his writing. He revised one of his college compositions, a blank-verse poem entitled "The Angel in the Cloud," and prepared it for publication. At the same time, he tried to figure out his life after college. He did not want to follow in his father's footsteps and become a merchant, so he considered both the law and, as a devout Methodist, ordained ministry. In 1870, however, his father died, and Edwin Fuller carried on the family business. Still, he kept writing. In 1871, he married Mary E. Malone, daughter of a Mississippi farmer, and also published *The Angel in the Cloud*.[28] A lengthy meditation about a young man's moral education, the book was well received and introduced Fuller to a national reading public that praised his erudition.[29] No doubt pleased with his publishing success, he wrote and shared drafts of his manuscript of *Sea-Gift* but admitted to being "dissatisfied with it."[30] With encouragement of friends and family he eventually published the novel in 1873 and dedicated it to his wife.

If Fuller's first book revealed the fruits of a classical liberal arts education, the second underscored his regional education. Nationally, reviewers emphasized the book's southernness. The *Historical Magazine* characterized *Sea-Gift* as "[a] novel founded on Southern life and Southern incidents, and, as far as it is political, with Southern tendencies."[31] *Publishers Weekly* described it as "a novel of southern life, previous to the late rebellion," which was "evidently the production of a sympathizer, from the rather strong eulogies the 'stars and bars' come in for."[32] In a private letter to the author, one reader praised the regional perspective, writing, "Dickens may have known English character, but you certainly have been round in North Carolina, and understand well the ways and doings of her people. . . . Your book is as true as life."[33] Clearly, the reviewer bought into the blend of memoir and fiction and took *Sea-Gift* as a legitimate vision of North Carolina in the era of the Civil War. This was, indeed, the purpose of Lost Cause literature: to make a mythologized time and place real. Fuller accomplished this by appealing to prevailing nostalgia for the Old South, especially a nostalgia that appealed to popular antebellum attitudes about gender, slavery, and nation. Here, Fuller's protagonist, John Smith, and his wartime adventures are most illuminating.

When the Civil War ends, John Smith's slaves become free persons and appeal to him for work, but he denies them and hires other freed persons instead. But his tenure as employer, rather than master, is short-lived. He and Carlotta pack their bags and head to the latter's ancestral land. Perhaps they establish something that looks like a plantation in Cuba—Smith admits to living in wealth—but the novel ends before we know whether exile really brought all it promised them. Instead, we find Fuller in quiet discernment of the past and future, homes new and old. "I am still gazing far over the gray waters towards the land that I fought for," the novel's protagonist explains before characterizing what the South had become and what it once was: "A land where orphans' tears meet widows' wails, and maidens wear the mournful pledge of battle-broken troth—a land where want and woe are rife, and the burdened people bow beneath the yoke of conquest." War, defeat, and Reconstruction made North Carolina hardly recognizable, a mere shade of its prewar self. Yet Smith cannot let go. He says, "And yet, from all the wealth and luxury that surround me, my Southern heart turns with all the yearning of a child back to my Southern Home."[34]

Fuller's protagonist/literary alter ego articulates common themes related to the deep meaning of the "southern home." Many historians will grimace at allowing a fictional character to lead us down his author's "memory lane," but not to do so discredits the work of art he produced, which, as art tends to be, is a part of its creator's own story. Reading backward from John and Carlotta's willing exile to Cuba to the young boy's childhood thus reveals that *Sea-Gift* is, indeed, a single yearning whose component parts reveal a wartime fantasy rooted in the Old South ideal of a "southern home." Rather than set sail on unknown waters to a place he may have only read about in books, Fuller escaped the ponderous moment by writing a nostalgic vision of home and probes what southern manhood meant to him as he grew up in the midst of war. Fuller's choice to connect his story—and that of the South—to Cuba reveals the persistence of antebellum ways of understanding masculinity on both a personal and a social level. Home was at the center—men longed to be masters of worlds small and large—masters of themselves, dependents, enslaved persons, government, and empires. Those ambitions were in the air they breathed, visible to them as palpably as the "castles in the air" about which they daydreamed as youth.[35]

Southerners, the dream went, were destined for greatness by virtue of the nation's southern origins. A reading of any of the Confederacy's founding documents proves that these were men who viewed themselves as guardians of the spirit of 1776, as "real" Americans.[36] So, too, in *Sea-Gift*. John Smith—a rather apt literary nod to ancestral clout—is weaned on stories of his own legacy. He studies the family tree in his father's library and discovers the lines between generations that connect him to the famed Capt. John Smith of the Virginia Company and Jamestown. "Father used to take me on his knee, when I grew old enough to listen," he explains, "and tell me long stories about my brave relative, who had fought with the Turks, slept on straw ... dared the Indians, looked calmly at Powhatan's lifted club, and then flirted with his gentle protectress, Pocahontas."[37] Fuller understood this narrative in a sectionalized way that was common among young white Americans at the time. One Mississippi youth reflected on American history in his diary, for instance, and praised American patriots of the Revolutionary War for their "manliness, the disinterested devotion to their country." He pondered, "Can any man conscientiously detract the first iota from the glory of our Washingtons, Greens, Sullivants, Putnams, Marions, and Schulers by saying that they deserve less renown than the ancient generals?"[38] He only listed *southern* heroes of the Revolutionary era. Similarly, another young man went further back to Jamestown, praising the "illustrious Capt. John Smith" and named him "the Father of Virginia, and the first who planted the Saxon race within the bounds of the United States."[39]

Fuller's protagonist likewise views whiteness as paramount to southernness. When he learns that Pocahontas's Virginia descendants "always claimed kin with our family," his first reaction is disbelief. John Smith believed that brown or black skin was uncivilized and that there were countless words adults used to set these people apart. "I remember well that I did not wish to recognize, as relatives, the children of the mulatto her picture represented her to be," he recalls. But then he learns that "many of them had become distinguished." He confesses to his readers, "And while it was quite a disgrace in society to have had a dark ancestor with kinky hair, it was quite an honor to have had a dark ancestor with straight hair."[40] Perhaps Fuller adds humor to diffuse the loudest whisper of early and antebellum America: interracial sex occurred and often forcibly. Yet John Smith learns about race at a very young age—and not without some dreamy cultural hairsplitting.

Enslaved persons occupy the pages of *Sea-Gift* and Fuller's "southern home" just as they do the ubiquitous minstrel plays and songs of the era. Fuller had been thinking about race and southern civilization for some time prior to publishing his novel and certainly in college during Reconstruction. In "An Elegy," published in one of his college publications, Fuller paints a playful picture of student life on the Virginia campus, where enslaved persons occupy the background. In one noteworthy passage he describes a scene in which students publicly perform a poem or a play as "the darkies laugh at their quaint disguise."[41] Similarly, *Sea-Gift*'s black characters—referred to as "servants" (not slaves)—speak in racialized dialect. Some had names such as Tildy, Winny, or Horace; others appear simply as "two or three excited negroes" or "some of my negroes." In Fuller's imagination, slavery was a benevolent institution. Because his mother "put her [Christian] faith in constant practice," the household was a model for enslaved persons. Smith explains, "Our servants refrained from any insolence and disobedience out of the purest respect for her—a perfect anomaly in slavery." Similarly, Smith treats enslaved persons compassionately, if not empathetically. When he leaves for college, he gives his slaves parting gifts of "half a dollar each."[42] He was becoming the benevolent master commonly depicted in both antebellum proslavery texts and Lost Cause histories.

When John Smith returns to his war-torn hometown, Fuller's mythologizing becomes at once grander and more defensive. Fuller writes, "Eighteen hundred and sixty five! Annuis irae! Year of blood and tears, famine and oppression!" Smith laments, "Could one behold, as in panorama, the South of '60 and the South of '65, even a devil would weep over the ruin wrought in five years." He juxtaposed these sights with his old southern home: "Wide-spreading fields with waving, luxuriant crops, worked by throngs of joyous light-hearted negroes, who sing, in a resounding chorus, as they guide their sleek teams up and down the fertile furrow." In that world, writes Fuller, Smith "would see long villages of negro quarters, each house with its garden and patch, its pig and chickens, and its happy children playing at the door."[43]

Fuller's literary depiction of the southern civilization contains familiar assumptions about white southern masculinity. According to Stephen W. Berry, young men of the late antebellum years felt "pressure to live up to the version of civilized patriarchy that had become so integral to the South's sense of self and to the defense against the North." They were motivated by "romantic ideals of civilizing manhood."[44] For John Smith, the hero's journey began in youth with ambitious dreams. Like the youthful voyager in Thomas Cole's popular series of paintings *The Voyage of Life* (1842), Smith is motivated by the future eminence of his ancestral namesake but in the world he knows: the plantation South where men asserted their independence, protected dependents, and became "masters of small worlds."[45] As a boy, Smith "would fall asleep only to rebuild and embellish in my dreams the magnificent air castles of my waking hours."[46]

Fuller probes the possibilities of this worldview in what is perhaps the novel's dreamiest scenario—the arrival of the "sea gift" on the shores of North Carolina's Outer Banks. Walking along the Wilmington coast after a thunderstorm, Smith and his friends discover a shipwreck. The bodies of a man and a girl are strewn upon the shore. They presume both people to be dead, but before fetching "the negroes and the big boat" to carry the bodies home, they inspect each body and ascertain that the man is dead, but the girl is not. "We cut the cords that held her to the door [of the boat], and lifted her up," explains Smith as he describes their discovery in almost erotic detail. Fuller's description reads like a Victorian memento mori: "Never had I dreamed of such beauty! Her face was as colorless as marble, but showed more perfectly for that its exquisite outline. . . . Her eyes were closed, but the lids atoned by their rose-leaf texture and long black fringe. Her mouth was partially open, as if gasping, but made up for this slight disfigurement by disclosing the clearest smoothest teeth." When the girl awakened and "drew her breath," Smith reflects, "What a moment for our heroism!" After "four stout negroes" brought the bodies into the house, the boys ponder what will become of the girl left fatherless by the shipwreck. The question puzzles Smith and his friend Ned, who "considered her ours by right of discovery," evoking the fifteenth- and sixteenth-century papal and European charters granting adventurers from Columbus to Walter Raleigh and John Smith the right to Indian lands. After dinner that night, the boys "retired only to dream of shipwrecks, and corpses, and half drowned girls."[47]

The shipwrecked girl—Carlotta—moves the novel's plot in just that direction. Ultimately, the Smiths adopt Carlotta, having made arrangements with some of her relatives in New Orleans, and she and John Smith grow up as brother and sister. As Smith grows from childhood into youth, he becomes increasingly enamored of his adopted sister but represses those feelings, as all good southern gentlemen do. Meanwhile, he goes off to Chapel Hill and learns difficult lessons about drinking, dueling, and courtship. His classmate dies defending John Smith in a duel and leaves behind a heartbroken sweetheart, whose affection Smith courts but in vain. After chapters of twists and turns, John and Carlotta confess their love to each other, become engaged, and marry just before he sets off to fight Yankees. It was a simple and fast wedding, though Smith reflects, "Carlotta was dearer to me, in her simple Swiss muslin, than she would have been in satin and lace; and I felt, as she looked radiantly into my face, that she was prouder of me, in my suit of gray, than if I had worn the finest cloth." Dressed in a Confederate uniform and married to the love of his life, John Smith had become a man.

Historians have spilled quite a bit of ink on the question of why southerners took up arms, and Fuller must have been aware that one of the reasons was for the defense of home and loved ones. Not surprisingly, Carlotta sends John Smith off to war; later that same love convinces him not to desert the army when he wants to care for her after the death of their mother. Her plea is compassionate and patriotic. "You know, dear John, that I love you more than all else on earth," she explains while he's home on furlough, "but if I did not love my country, too, I would be unworthy of your love, and if you were unwilling to defend her, you would be unworthy of mine. But I know your noble heart, and trust its fervid zeal."[48] Here enter some familiar tropes—manhood and honor, tied inextricably to Confederate nationalism. As Sherman marches to the sea, John learns from Carlotta that "Yankees have taken everything from us, and burned the house. Darling mother, in escaping, was struck on the head by a piece of falling timber, and is in a most critical condition." The turncoat Frank Panning—always appearing in the novel when evil befalls John Smith and his family—was one of the Union soldiers present as the Yankees plundered his family home. Ultimately, John's father dies in prison, but John returns to his wife, Carlotta.

Although the family estate is miraculously robust and money is of no concern to John and Carlotta, John begins to feel as a stranger in a foreign land upon his return home. Much of this has to do with the new racial order after emancipation. Recall the scene with which this discussion began: Smith cannot bear suffering "under the yoke of conquest." Conquest, after all, was his ancestral right, from the mythical story of the historic John Smith and Pocahontas to the moment in youth when he and his friends claim Carlotta by the "right of discovery." He fights valiantly against his enemies during war. He is not made for conquest but to conquer. John and Carlotta tried to surround themselves "with ante-bellum comforts, and to make home feel like home." Yet it does not. John checks his ambitions against his new reality. He realizes that they cannot live in a state controlled by Federal troops. He writes, "The boyish dreams I had so long cherished, of distinction in the political arena, were now vanished forever; and the practice of law, for which I had studied, under the Provisional Government was little better than a system of pettifogging, that was as undignified as it was profitless." He is, in other words, dishonored in defeat and cannot live as a full man in a southern home of Yankee design. So he leaves it all behind and sets out for Cuba with his "sea gift," the only antebellum comfort that remains. And this is how the novel concludes. The couple has moved to Cuba, but happiness is tempered by homesickness, or what nineteenth-century Americans called "nostalgia." We do not know what becomes of them once they leave the South.

Willing expatriation to Cuba may seem a bit preposterous to twenty-first-century readers, but Fuller engineered a resolution to the novel that completed deeply rooted masculine fantasies of establishing a slaveholding empire in Latin America. As Matthew Karp argues, southern politicians viewed the region as part of a broad "hemispheric defense of slavery."[49] Following British and French abolition of slavery in the West Indies, southerners wanted to reestablish slavery in the region as part of this defense. U.S. victory in the Mexican War, coupled with Manifest Destiny, inspired southerners at the forefront of foreign policy. In 1848, President Polk, a southerner, wanted to annex the Yucatán Peninsula. Robert E. May argues, "The annexation of Cuba gradually became an unofficial national policy" in the 1850s and an especially *southern* dream after the 1854 Kansas-Nebraska Act signaled hardening of antislavery politics at the federal level. In this period, Latin America captured the imaginations of young southern men through the press.[50] These themes appeared in antebellum popular culture. In particular, the image of filibusterers such as William Walker, who captured Nicaragua in 1856, intrigued ambitious young men who dreamed of steering the ship of Manifest Destiny to the Caribbean. According to Amy Greenberg, Walker "became one of the key cultural icons of the 1860s" among young men.[51] During the Civil War, the Confederacy prioritized the domestic preservation of slavery *and* its global expansion.[52] During Reconstruction, some men exiled themselves to far-off destinations in the American West, Canada, Europe, and most notably, Latin America.[53] The so-called Confederados have received considerable scholarly attention, despite the fact that so few southerners actually left the country.[54] Ideas about exile spread by word of mouth and the press by the end of the war and continued throughout Reconstruction, when a new genre of propagandistic travel literature attracted disgruntled ex-Rebels.[55] Fuller would not have missed the news. Thus he joined the chorus of men eager to leave the South but through literature rather than actual expatriation.

In 1874, the twenty-eight-year-old Edwin Wiley Fuller died of pneumonia. Before his early death, he probably heard about emigration schemes, and he most certainly reflected longingly on his "old Southern home" while establishing a new one with his real wife, Mary. To date, however, the record of his life amounts to census records, a few biographic encyclopedia entries, an obituary, and reviews of his published works. He might have kept a diary during the war, which would certainly illuminate that which is autobiographical in *Sea-Gift*, but in the absence of those documents, we probably never will know the reasons why he made the authorial decision he did, why his hero left the South for the Caribbean with his Cuban wife. Textual evidence suggests that the novel's protagonist reasonably reflects Fuller's fantasies of patriotic Confederate and southern manhood. Through the characterization of John Smith, Fuller embraced the civilizing fantasy that defined manhood in his age. Here, his classical and southern education served him well after the war by offering a means to escape, to find a unique peace, which Reconstruction could not bring but its literature could. Though he himself did not willingly expatriate to Cuba, he felt a profound sense of exile in his own land, enough to write it into a story that—Cuban sister/wife notwithstanding—paralleled his own life rather closely. Exile, in other words, could be a movement as much as a state of mind. In novels such as *Sea-Gift*, exile could become any southerner's "dreamland."

In all, this essay has emphasized historicizing men's fantasies by using cultural history and textual analysis as a way to approach both the life of a text and the life behind its construction. This is possible because Reconstruction created a reactionary intellectual event among writers who sought to make sense out of their private confederacies. Much attention has been given to organizations of the Lost Cause, especially veterans organizations. In order to dig more deeply into the inner experiences of *how* these former Confederates thought, however, we must consider how their ideas took shape. Commemorative and social organizations certainly influenced men's postwar thinking but so did literature. Of course, the masculine fantasies have and still do perpetuate violence. Thomas Dixon's *The Clansman* was at once popular and destructive in its legitimation of the Ku Klux Klan.[56] Scholarship on that work and on Klan violence reminds us of the pernicious legacy that fantasies create. Applying the tools of cultural history (analysis of genre, representation, and fantasy) to intellectual history (the history of ideas, texts, and contexts) uncovers postwar thought among those, such as Fuller, who used fiction to contemplate the South's history in the Civil War era and its futurity. In other words—and to further Schivelbusch's metaphor—fiction allows us to excavate this dreamland, to unearth its bedrock, explore its terrain, and wander along its borders. Ultimately, understanding the imaginative world of Fuller's *Sea-Gift*—in the context in which it emerged—enriches our historical perspective on the uses of myth and memory in the South's ongoing struggle to come to terms with its past.

NOTES

1. Edwin Wiley Fuller, *Sea-Gift: A Novel* (New York: E. J. Hale and Son, 1873). See also E. T. Malone Jr., "The University of North Carolina in Edwin Fuller's 1873 Novel, 'Sea-Gift,'" *North Carolina Historical Review* 53, no. 3 (July 1976): 302.

2. Michael Sistrom, "Edwin Wiley Fuller, *Sea-Gift: A Novel*," in "The North Carolina Experience," Documenting the American South, https://docsouth.unc.edu/nc/fuller/summary.html, accessed August 5, 2020.

3. The best articulation of new directions in the field of Reconstruction-era literary studies is articulated in "Reenvisioning Reconstruction," special issue, *American Literary History* 30, no. 3 (Fall 2018): 403–651; see esp. Gordon Hutner, "Reenvisioning Reconstruction: An Introduction," in that issue, pp. 403–6.

4. James J. Broomall, *Private Confederacies: The Emotional Worlds of Southern Men as Citizens and Soldiers* (Chapel Hill: University of North Carolina Press, 2019), 3.

5. Stephen William Berry, *All That Makes a Man: Love and Ambition in the Civil War South* (New York: Oxford University Press, 2003); Peter S. Carmichael, *The Last Generation: Young Virginians in Peace, War, and Reunion*, Civil War America (Chapel Hill: University of North Carolina Press, 2005); Craig Thompson Friend, "'The Crushing of Southern Manhood': War, Masculinity, and the Confederate Nation-State, 1861–1865," in *Masculinities and the Nation in the Modern World, 1800–1945*, ed. Simon Wendt and Pablo Dominguez (London: Palgrave Macmillan, 2014); Craig Thompson Friend and Lorri Glover, eds., *Southern Manhood: Perspectives on Masculinity in the Old South* (Athens: University of Georgia Press, 2004); Stephanie McCurry, *Masters of Small Worlds: Yeoman Households, Gender Relations, and the Political Culture of the Antebellum South Carolina Low Country* (New York: Oxford University Press, 1995); Christopher J. Olsen, *Political Culture and Secession in Mississippi: Masculinity, Honor, and the Antiparty Tradition, 1830–1860* (New York: Oxford University Press, 2000); Timothy J. Williams, *Intellectual Manhood: University, Self, and Society in the Antebellum South* (Chapel Hill: University of North Carolina Press, 2015); Bertram Wyatt-Brown, *Southern Honor: Ethics and Behavior in the Old South* (New York: Oxford University Press, 1982).

6. Williams, *Intellectual Manhood*, 248; Susan-Mary Grant, "The Lost Boys: Citizen-Soldiers, Disabled Veterans, and Confederate Nationalism in the Age of People's War," *Journal of the Civil War Era* 2, no. 2 (June 2012): 237.

7. Williams, *Intellectual Manhood*, 121–47.

8. Aaron Sheehan-Dean, *Why Confederates Fought: Family and Nation in Civil War Virginia* (Chapel Hill: University of North Carolina Press, 2009).

9. John C. Murray diary, January 1864–June 1865, folder 52, box 3, Civil War Collection, Manuscripts Collection 524, Louisiana Research Collection, Howard-Tilton Memorial Library, Tulane University, New Orleans, Louisiana.

10. Song quoted in Eugene C. Harter, *The Lost Colony of the Confederacy* (Jackson: University Press of Mississippi, 1985), 10.

11. Gaines M. Foster, *Ghosts of the Confederacy: Defeat, the Lost Cause, and the Emergence of the New South, 1865 to 1913* (New York: Oxford University Press, 1987), 207n20.

12. Scholarship on the Lost Cause myth is vast. See esp. David W. Blight, *Race and Reunion: The Civil War in American Memory* (Cambridge, Mass: Belknap Press of Harvard University Press, 2001); Karen L. Cox, *Dixie's Daughters: The United Daughters of the Confederacy and the Preservation of Confederate Culture*, New Perspectives on the History of the South (Gainesville: University Press of Florida, 2003); Foster, *Ghosts of the Confederacy*; Sarah E. Gardner, *Blood and Irony: Southern White Women's Narratives of the Civil War, 1861–1937* (Chapel Hill: University of North Carolina Press, 2004); and Caroline E. Janney, *Remembering the Civil War: Reunion and the Limits of Reconstruction* (Chapel Hill: University of North Carolina Press, 2013).

13. Wolfgang Schivelbusch, *The Culture of Defeat: On National Trauma, Mourning, and Recovery*, trans. Jefferson Chase (New York: Picador, 2001), 13.

14. W. J. Cash, *The Mind of the South* (New York: Knopf, 1941); William R. Taylor, *Cavalier and Yankee: The Old South and American National Character*, 2nd ed. (1961; repr., New York: Oxford University Press, 1993).

15. Coleman Hutchison, *Apples and Ashes: Literature, Nationalism, and the Confederate States of America* (Athens: University of Georgia Press, 2012), 8; Cody Marrs, "Three Theses on Reconstruction," in "Reenvisioning Reconstruction," special issue, *American Literary History*, 30 (Fall 2018): 419.

16. Marrs, "Three Theses on Reconstruction," 421; emphasis in original.

17. Berry, *All That Makes a Man*; Carmichael, *Last Generation*; Peter S. Carmichael, *The War for the Common Soldier: How Men Thought, Fought, and Survived in Civil War Armies* (Chapel Hill: University of North Carolina Press, 2018).

18. Ian Binnington, *Confederate Visions: Nationalism, Symbolism, and the Imagined South in the Civil War* (Charlottesville: University of Virginia Press, 2013); J. Matthew Gallman, *Defining Duty in the Civil War: Personal Choice, Popular Culture, and the Union Home Front* (Chapel Hill: University of North Carolina Press, 2015); Gardner, *Blood and Irony*; Hutchison, *Apples and Ashes*.

19. Michael O'Brien, *Conjectures of Order: Intellectual Life and the American South, 1810–1860* (Chapel Hill: University of North Carolina Press, 2004), 1:17.

20. Sidney Lanier, *Tiger-Lilies: A Novel* (New York: Hurd and Houghton, 1867). Lanier's novel has received more critical attention from literary scholars than *Sea-Gift* but not much and not recently. See Nathalia Wright, "The East Tennessee Background of Sidney Lanier's *Tiger-Lilies*," *American Literature* 19, no. 2 (May 1947): 127–38; John S. Mayfield, "Sidney Lanier's *Tiger-Lilies*: A Bibliographical Mystery," *Papers of the Biographical Society of America*, 54, no. 4 (1960): 265–72; and William J. Kimball, "Realism in Sidney Lanier's *Tiger-Lilies*," *South Atlantic Bulletin* 36, no. 2 (March 1971): 17–20.

21. Jones Fuller, Franklin County, North Carolina, dwelling 751, family 748, in U.S. Bureau of the Census, *1860 Census: Population of the United States* (Washington, D.C.: Government Printing Office, 1864), 89, ancestry.com.

22. Edwin Wiley Fuller, *The Angel in the Cloud*, 4th ed. (New York: E. J. Hale and Son, 1881), ii; George-Anne Willard, "Louisburg Male Academy," NCPedia, 2006, https://www.ncpedia.org/louisburg-male-academy.

23. Williams, *Intellectual Manhood*, 204–5.

24. Anna Fuller diary, April 29, 1865, quoted in "Fuller House," National Register of Historic Places Inventory Nomination Form, section 8, p. 2, U.S. Department of the Interior, National Park Service, Washington, D.C. On wartime Louisburg, see David Silkenat, "'In Good Hands, in a Safe Place': Female Academies in Confederate North Carolina," *North Carolina Historical Review* 88, no. 1 (January 2011): 40–71.

25. Fuller diary, May 7, 1865, 2.

26. Fuller diary, May 9, 1865, 3.

27. Malone, "University of North Carolina," 290.

28. Mitchel Malone, Starkville, Mississippi, dwelling 526, family 450, in U.S. Bureau of the Census, *1860 Census*, 69, ancestry.com.

29. "New Publications," *New York Times*, August 31, 1871; Fuller, *Angel in the Cloud*, vii.

30. Malone, "University of North Carolina," 291.

31. *Historical Magazine and Notes and Queries Concerning the Antiquities, History and Biography of America* 22 (1873): 187.

32. *Publishers Weekly*, 93 (October 25, 1873): 451.

33. Fuller, *The Angel in the Cloud*, xii.

34. Fuller, *Sea-Gift*, 408.

35. McCurry, *Masters of Small Worlds*; Berry, *All That Makes a Man*; Williams, *Intellectual Manhood*, esp. chap. 2.

36. Paul Quigley, *Shifting Grounds: Nationalism and the American South, 1848–1865* (New York: Oxford University Press, 2011), 145–47.

37. Fuller, *Sea-Gift*, 9.

38. Harry St. John Dixon, August 15, 1860, in Stephen William Berry, *Princes of Cotton: Four Diaries of Young Men in the South, 1848–1860* (Athens: University of Georgia Press, 2007), 162–63.

39. James Hilliard Polk, October 5, 1859, diary, folder 1, in James Hilliard Polk Diary #5259-z, Southern Historical Collection, Wilson Library, University of North Carolina at Chapel Hill.

40. Fuller, *Sea-Gift*, 9.

41. Edwin Wiley Fuller, "An Elegy, Written on the Rotunda Steps," *Virginia University Magazine*, January 1868, 60–61.

42. Fuller, *Sea-Gift*, 55, 69, 74, 72, 155.

43. Fuller, 299.

44. Berry, *All That Makes a Man*, 51–52, 55.

45. Williams, *Intellectual Manhood*, 122–23; McCurry, *Masters of Small Worlds*.

46. Fuller, *Sea-Gift*, 179.

47. Fuller, 66, 70.

48. Fuller, 337.

49. Matthew Karp, *This Vast Southern Empire: Slaveholders at the Helm of American Foreign Policy* (Cambridge, Mass.: Harvard University Press, 2016), 89.

50. Robert E. May, *The Southern Dream of a Caribbean Empire, 1854–1861*, 2nd ed. (Gainesville: University Press of Florida, 2002), 12, 18–19, 32–37.

51. Amy S. Greenberg, "A Gray-Eyed Man: Character, Appearance, and Filibustering," *Journal of the Early Republic* 20, no. 4 (Winter 2000): 674.

52. May, *Southern Dream*, 242–46. See "Constitution of the Confederate States: March 11, 1861," Avalon Project: Documents in Law, History and Diplomacy, art. 4, http://avalon.law.yale.edu/19th_century/csa_csa.asp, accessed October 18, 2019.

53. "Peace after War," *Norfolk (Va.) Post*, August 9, 1865; "Condition of the South," *New York Herald*, July 23, 1865; "Brazilian Meeting," *Opelousas (La.) Courier*, July 29, 1865.

54. Cyrus B. Dawsey and James M. Dawsey, *The Confederados: Old South Immigrants in Brazil* (Tuscaloosa: University of Alabama Press, 1995); William Clark Griggs, *The Elusive Eden: Frank Mcmullan's Confederate Colony in Brazil* (Austin: University of Texas Press, 1987); Harter, *Lost Colony*; Daniel E. Sutherland, "Exiles, Emigrants, and Sojourners: The Post–Civil War Confederate Exodus in Perspective," *Civil War History* 31, no. 3 (September 1985); Blanche Henry Clark Weaver, "Confederate Emigration to Brazil," *Journal of Southern History* 27, no. 1 (February 1961).

55. On travel writing in the postwar period, especially related to Cuba, see Edlie L. Wong, *Racial Reconstruction: Black Inclusion, Chinese Exclusion, and the Fictions of Citizenship* (New York: New York University Press, 2015), esp. 20–21, 25–26, and also 37–38, 40, 46–50, 51, 53. Popular works included James McFadden Gaston, *Hunting a Home in Brazil* (Philadelphia: King and Baird, 1867); Lansford W. Hastings, *The Emigrant's Guide to Brazil* ([Mobile, Ala.?], ca. 1867); and Ballard Smith Dunn, *Brazil, the Home for Southerners* (New York: G. B. Richardson, 1866). See also Weaver, "Confederate Emigration to Brazil," 35n6; and Beatriz E. Balanta, "Tropical Dreams: Promoting Brazil in Nineteenth-Century U.S. Media," in *Envisioning Others: Race, Color, and the Visual in Iberia and Latin America*, ed. Pamela A. Patton (Boston: Brill, 2015), 243.

56. Michele K. Gillespie and Randal L. Hall, eds., *Thomas Dixon Jr. and the Birth of Modern America* (Baton Rouge: Louisiana State University Press, 2006).

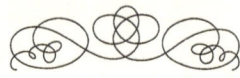

THE DISCOURSE OF CONFLICT IN THE RECONSTRUCTION SOUTH

Land, Labor, and Immigration

MITCHELL SNAY

FOR AT least two generations, historians have documented and explained the transformative effects on the nineteenth-century South wrought by Reconstruction. We now have an abundance of sophisticated studies on the emancipation of slaves, the rise of tenant farming and sharecropping, the complexity of Reconstruction politics, and changes in gender relations.[1] What we lack, however, is an understanding of the impact of Reconstruction on southern intellectual history. Part of the problem might well be the lack of material. The dean of southern intellectual historians, Michael O'Brien, once remarked that the fifty years "between Appomattox and the Southern Renaissance is the most uninviting of Southern moments, drab, impoverished, obscure, unprescient." Although some of the history and biography of the Lost Cause began to emerge during the 1860s and 1870s, there were few giant figures in literature, theology, philosophy, or science before 1880. In addition, the economic devastation and social dislocation wrought by war clearly damaged intellectual institutions such as colleges and religious seminaries. There is another explanation for the lack of post–Civil War southern intellectual history. As Leslie Butler has suggested, Reconstruction has been divorced from the momentous ideological transformations of the 1870s such as Darwinian evolution, the emergence of pragmatism, and the rise of the modern university.[2]

Southern intellectual historians might profitably turn to the vast polemical literature produced during Reconstruction for source material. In newspapers, pamphlets, and constitutional conventions, Democrats and Republicans, planters and plain folk, and former masters and former slaves set forth and debated their vision of a postwar order. Simply, these forms of printed literature provided a context for the formulation of southern social thought. In turn, these ideas could function as well as an ideology to advance certain political, economic, and social interests. Reconstruction was part of a period of partisan journalism that tolerated and even encouraged biased or exaggerated interpretations. To survive, editors had to demonstrate partisan and sectional loyalties. The polemical literature of Reconstruction laid bare conflicting assumptions regarding such issues as political economy, social relations, and race.[3]

The debate over immigration from roughly 1865 to 1880 provides a particularly promising window to explore larger economic, social, and political issues being contested in the post–Civil War era. Then, as now, immigration functioned as a code word for race, ethnicity, citizenship, labor, and property. An 1866 address to Georgia planters on German immigration was revealingly titled "The Labor Question of the South." The discourse of immigration exposes the various fault lines that made conflict so violent and frequent in the postemancipation South. A close study of the debate over immigration thus contributes to the expanding list of topics that now fit into the study of American Reconstruction. It also fits unusually well into a volume of essays organized around the theme of insider/outsider. Immigration to the postwar South potentially invited such outsiders as northerners, Europeans, and Asians to the South. And implicit in the debates over immigration was the question of who would be invited into the postwar southern body politic and who would remain outside, a question still pressing in the South and the rest of the nation.[4]

Calls for immigration resounded throughout the Reconstruction South. "Public spirited, influential, able men in all parts of the South," proclaimed the Democratic Selma *Southern Argus*, "are devising plans for the promotion of immigration." A northern newspaper correspondent in Mississippi observed that there "was never such an anxiety among the Southern people for the introduction of white immigrants." Southerners of all political persuasions joined in hailing immigration as a panacea for the social and economic dislocations resulting from the Civil War. The Honorable E. Carrington Cabell of Memphis believed that "the first and most important step to revive the prosperity of the South is to encourage the immigration of an intelligent and industrious white population into her limits." Republican politician Carl Schurz, touring the South Carolina Low Country in 1865, found that "the idea of introducing German and Irish laborers in large numbers to do the work of the negroes is seriously discussed."[5]

The support for immigration in the Reconstruction South went beyond rhetoric. Southern planters, politicians, and businessmen offered private assistance and sought government help to bring white immigrants into the former states of the Confederacy. In November 1865, a Virginia and North Carolina Land, Immigration, and Colonization Society was established. Four years later "representative planters" in Arkansas formed the Arkansas River Valley Immigration Company. There was a Free Land and Colonization Company in DeSoto County, Mississippi. Advocates of white immigrants convened in Jackson, Mississippi, in March 1868. State meetings were held in South Carolina in 1870, in Tennessee in 1873, and in Louisiana in 1876. Private businesses in search of labor supported immigration. The commercial firm of Harris and Ashby in Tennessee was contacted about foreign immigrants. Industrial entrepreneurs supported immigration for labor. The president of the Shelby Iron Company in Alabama sought immigrants for "a large and industrious population." Finally, several of the agricultural societies and journals that had been so influential in the antebellum South joined the chorus for immigration. The New Hanover Agricultural Society in North Carolina agreed that the introduction of foreign immigrants was "desirable and necessary." In October 1871, the magazine *Southern Field and Factory* urged southern landowners to break up their landholdings "and encourage industrious immigrants to come and settle upon them."[6]

During the period of Presidential Reconstruction (1865–67), southern Democratic governments lent their support to these calls for immigration. George Adair of Georgia called upon his state legislature "to grant a liberal charter to a land and immigration company." State legislatures in the early years of Reconstruction chartered land and immigration companies, permitted immigration under labor contracts, and fostered direct steamship connection with European ports. When Radical Reconstruction began in 1867, the newly founded Republican Party in the South advocated immigration in its party platforms and created immigration offices and commissioners in the new state constitutions written between 1867 and 1869. For example, article 12, section 23, of the Mississippi Constitution called for the appointment of a commissioner of immigration and agriculture. Other Republican governments sustained the immigration crusade. The first Republican legislature of Arkansas passed "An Act to Provide for the Appointment of a Commissioner of Immigration and State Lands, and Defining the Duties of that Officer." Under Republican governor Henry Clay Warmoth, Louisiana expanded its board of immigration from one to six commissioners.[7]

The immigration crusade in the Reconstruction South did net a few successes. The Arkansas River Valley Immigration Company sent Capt. J. C. Gift to China, and he returned a year later with 189 Chinese. An agent of the Panola Immigration Society in Mississippi went to Chicago in 1870 to procure immigrant labor and returned with thirty-five workers. But such stories were few and far between. When Capt. R. E. Houston of Mississippi was sent to lure Swedish and Norwegian laborers to the South, his efforts failed. In 1868, the Water Valley Manufacturing Company of Yalobusha County, Mississippi, procured over 100 immigrants from the northern part of Sweden. Soon after arriving in May, many of these Swedes became sick from the heat. The newly built factory had to be turned into a hospital.[8]

By demographic standards, the southern Reconstruction campaign for white immigrants was a failure. Simply, the post–Civil War South did not attract immigration from abroad. There were fewer immigrants in the South in 1880 than there had been in 1860. In 1868, only 564 immigrants went to Louisiana, while about 34,000 had emigrated to Illinois. The number of foreign-born in South Carolina declined between 1860 and 1880. By 1886, Mississippi abolished its Board of Immigration and Agriculture.[9]

Postbellum southerners offered several explanations for the failure to bring immigrants to the South. One acknowledged the inability of southern planters to move beyond slavery. According to one observer, employers in Virginia and Tennessee "expected them to live on the same diet on which the colored population had been accustomed to live." A Mississippi editor characteristically blamed the North, who embraced "every opportunity to represent the South in an unfavorable light." Another editor, this one from south Alabama, suggested similarly that immigrants failed to come "from a strong misapprehension of things and ignorance of the facts."[10]

The reasons for the failure of the immigration crusade are not hard to find: the lack of industry in the South, the relative difficulty of obtaining land, and the unrealistic expectation of southern whites that immigrants would become landless laborers who would replace African Americans. It should come as no surprise then that an earlier but astute student of the subject concluded that the postwar southern effort to lure northern and foreign immigrants to the South "was but a minor and futile phase of the New South."[11]

Still, the immigration crusade was ubiquitous in the post–Civil War South. One historian claims that immigration was the subject of more editorials in Reconstruction South Carolina newspapers than any other topic. What also draws our attention to the subject is its diversity. If the call for immigration was practically universal in the Reconstruction South, different groups supported it for different reasons. For landowning planters, it held a potential for an alternative labor force to freed people. Yet there were a few dissenting Democratic/Conservative voices who questioned the possibility of assimilation and the adaptability of foreign workers to a plantation system. Southern Republicans called enthusiastically for foreign and northern immigration as part of a developmental ethos to reshape the southern economy along the lines of free-labor capitalism. Not surprisingly, African American leaders—who supported the Republican Party—were wary of immigration as a source of cheap labor that would depress the wages of freed people.[12]

With the advent of Radical Reconstruction in 1867, southern Republicans launched a crusade to bring white immigrants from both Europe and the North to the postwar South. "At present," insisted the Atlanta *Daily New Era*, "the South needs immigration more than anything else." In 1868, the Little Rock *Republican* claimed that immigration was the key to progress in Arkansas. As late as 1875, with Reconstruction about to unravel in Mississippi, a leading Republican newspaper there insisted that the only thing that could save the state was immigration. One historian of Reconstruction in Arkansas called immigration "fundamental" to the Republican creed in that state.[13]

The Reconstruction immigration crusade was rooted in the Republican ideology of the 1850s. Southern Republicans presented immigration as part of a free-labor, free-soil vision of a postwar South. Drawing upon traditional notions of Republican political economy, they portrayed a New South order of small farms cultivated by independent yeomen. White immigrants from the North would help create a rural, commercial middle-class society of small farmers that would develop both socially and economically.

The first step in the Republican immigration program was the destruction of the antebellum plantation world. During Reconstruction, southern Republicans drew upon the premise developed before the Civil War that slavery was an inefficient form of labor working in the backward economic system of the plantation. If immigrants were to come to the South, the plantation had to be dislodged as the key economic institution of the South. Speaking in New York, Charles W. Godard of Florida reminded his audience that antebellum planters "liked large plantations of many thousands of acres to be worked by slaves." Their mistake, according to Republican spokesmen, was to remain wedded to a dependent labor force that would perpetuate this outmoded form of production. "The first idea of immigration among the Southern people," complained an Alabama Republican editor, "was that it would give them labor that would take the place of the negro; labor that would work for ten dollars a month, a log cabin with three pounds of pork, and a peck a meal a week." The *Weekly Mississippi Pilot*, the leading Republican journal in the state, editorialized similarly that immigration would not be successful until planters could "forever rid themselves of the delusion that in some way they can keep their immense plantations and get labor in some form that shall be a substitute for slavery, now dead and buried."[14]

The eradication of the plantation system would reclaim the ground for white immigrants. "The South must be built up on free labor," insisted a Republican editor from Mississippi. "We must have farmers instead of planters to cultivate the soil," argued the Atlanta *Daily New Era*, "and manufactories must spring up all over the state. To do this we need immigration." A correspondent from the Macon *Telegraph*, covering a meeting of the state agricultural society of Georgia, reported that "it was assumed on all sides that it [white immigrant labor] must be followed by small tenant or freehold farms, and great modifications of the present plantation system." Southern Republicans were looking for certain kinds of immigrants—independent subsistence farmers. The *Beaufort Republican* sought that class "having families and a little money; possessing also something of education and character, such as will become small proprietors rather than simple laborers." A writer to a South Carolina Republican journal, styling himself "Progress," hoped that the South could procure immigrants arriving in the United States with "sufficient capital with them to purchase their little farms of from one to two hundred acres each." It was hoped that immigrants would develop unoccupied and unfarmed land. One Mississippian argued that his state had "a vast extent of good, arable land now uncultivated." To make that land productive and contribute to the welfare of the state required immigrants: "Hard working, industrious people here who will gradually occupy and cultivate all these lands."[15]

A reconstructed society of small farms based on free labor would lead to "improvement," a core value of Republican political economy. To accomplish this, southern Republicans advocated bringing in immigrants with some material substance. "The great and pressing need of Alabama," wrote the state Republican newspaper in Montgomery, "is an extensive immigration, and the introduction of capital now lying idle for want of a remunerative investment." Immigrants with capital would hasten economic development. The *Weekly Mississippi Pilot* believed that immigration would "aid us in redeeming our neglected and devastated homes, build railroads, towns and cities, and in many ways add to our property." Advocating immigrants from France, the *Tallahassee Sentinel* wrote: "Let these people be placed in colonies along the line of our railroads, and the result in a few short years would be evident in an enormously increased carrying trade, an invigorated commerce, and life and energy infused into every branch of trade and manufacture."[16]

To create a middle-class rural order in the South, southern Republicans sought collective rather than individual immigration. "Immigration should come in colonies," explained an Alabama Republican journal, "several families managing to settle in the same neighborhood. They could thus make their own society and keep up old customs, which differ in some respects from those they will find here." The president of the Florida Improvement Company urged prospective urban immigrants from New York to "go in bodies large enough to secure you the society and social comforts and the school-houses and churches that are the most congenial to your tastes." The German Homestead Association of Cincinnati planned to purchase 30,000–40,000 acres, divide it between 150–200 families and leave ten acres for a school and a town, a movement the *Weekly Mississippi Pilot* considered to be "in the right direction."[17]

In essence, southern Republicans envisioned immigration as a means of northernizing the South. This goal had roots in the antebellum era. One land reformer in Virginia advocating the division of plantations into small farms looked to the success of the immigrant community in Fairfax established by a group of New Jersey Quakers in 1846. Another veteran of land reform supported the Free State Colony in Wood County, Virginia, and the separation of those western counties that would eventually form West Virginia in 1863. Northern Free-Soilers were eager to show the superiority of free labor. In 1856, Eli Thayer of Massachusetts planned a free-labor colony in western Virginia in what became the town of Ceredo. John C. Underwood settled dairy farmers in Clarke and Fauquier Counties in Virginia. Both Thayer and Underwood were also active in the Republican cause. An important partner in Thayer's Homestead Company was New York Free-Soiler Charles B. Hoard. These efforts to populate the slave South with free-labor experiments gained the support of leading Republican editors such as Horace Greeley and William Cullen Bryant. Another advocate for planting free-labor colonies in the South was Henry C. Carey, perhaps the most influential Republican political economist in the mid-nineteenth century.[18]

These antebellum efforts to populate the slave South with pockets of free-labor immigrants from the North anticipated the Republican immigration program of Reconstruction. A South Carolina Republican newspaper explained that "our preference is, of course, for Northern emigrants—men from the bold hills of Maine and New Hampshire, from New York, Pennsylvania and New Jersey." In endorsing immigration, the editor of the *Weekly Mississippi Pilot* explained that the South needed to "learn to follow in the footsteps of the free States of the North, and accept the means employed by them for the acquirement of population and wealth, if we expect to become like them in these attainments." The *Charleston Daily Republican* believed that northern immigrants would "cultivate our broad acres, scatter school-houses, churches and factories over the state." The role of immigration in northernizing the South was perhaps best captured in an editorial in the Republican *Houston Union*:

That Northern agriculturalists are just the kind of persons to aid us in doing this important work, is obvious. They would bring with them their labor saving machinery, their improved agricultural implements, their various late inventions, the vast amount of agricultural knowledge which they have acquired from the various books and periodicals on that subject which abound in the North; above all, they would bring to their aid the habits of industry, enterprise and perseverance, which characterize the Northern population, and which have made the North a hive of industry, and the North Western States the granaries of the United States.[19]

Republican spokesmen made clear that the next desirable immigrants were white Europeans. "We need the swart German, the stout Irishman, and the broad-hearted Scotchman," claimed the *Daily New Era* of Atlanta. A committee of the Industrial and Immigration Association of Middle Florida preferred the "Scandinavian and Tueton [*sic*]." The committee explained that "these children of Thor and Odin have that untiring patience, invisible will, and powers of endurance that will develop the resources of our beautiful and fertile lands." A Florida Republican newspaper considered French immigrants from the regions of Alsace and Lorraine to be "industrious, thrifty, and inventive." Following this praise of the European race, a Republican editor in Mississippi proclaimed that the Germans were "the most advanced people in Europe to-day in civilization."[20]

The significance of the Republican immigration campaign to our understanding of Reconstruction lies in the attempts to apply northern free-labor ideology to the southern social and economic landscape. Of course, these ideas also shaped the transition from slavery to freedom. As we have seen, southern Republican calls for immigration rested upon a particularly Republican model of social and economic development first formulated during the 1850s. According to historian Eric Foner, this free-labor ideology was "grounded in the precepts that free labor was economically and socially superior to slave labor and that the distinctive quality of Northern society was the opportunity it offered wage earners to rise to property-owning independence." Republicans in the South believed that northern and foreign immigration would help create a republic of middling-size farms under individual ownership that would form the basis for a healthy economy and civilization.[21]

A relatively shared commitment to economic and social development among southern Republicans is all the more noteworthy considering the heterogeneity of the party. Historians have long recognized that the Republican Party in the Reconstruction South was a coalition—often an uneasy one—among northern Republicans, native southern whites, and African American freedmen. The Republican Party, of course, began in the mid-1850s as a coalition of abolitionists, antislavery Democrats, former Whigs, and Know-Nothings. This diversity only increased when the party moved south after the Civil War. Its primary goal was to mobilize African American freedmen for voting across the region. Yet in states without a black majority, Republicans also had to reach out for white support. The agendas of freed people and southern whites often conflicted. The course of Reconstruction exacerbated these divisions and created new ones. Prewar antipathies between planters and yeomen persisted after the Civil War. Republicans themselves were divided over civil rights, the disfranchisement of former Confederates, federal patronage, and the Liberal Republican revolt of 1872. Programs of economic development such as railroads often reignited the dormant animosities between prodevelopmental former Whigs and Jacksonian Democrats opposed to corporations.[22]

Did these intraparty divisions shape the southern Republican campaign for immigration during Reconstruction? This question is more easily asked than answered. Most statements endorsing immigration appeared in Republican newspapers. Since establishing a viable press was one way to achieve legitimacy, the party established about 430 newspapers from 1857 to 1877. Their editors came from the ranks of both northern Republicans and native southern whites. For instance, Pierce Burton, editor of the Demopolis, Alabama, *Southern Republican* from 1869 to 1871, had been a Freedmen's Bureau agent from Massachusetts. The Atlanta *Daily New Era* was edited by Samuel Bard, a native New Yorker who had been active in Louisiana politics. A northerner also edited the Augusta *Loyal Georgian*, an important voice of Republicanism during Presidential Reconstruction. In contrast, Republican newspapers such as the *Houston Union*, *Huntsville Advocate*, and *Fort Smith New Era* were edited by native southern whites. One might expect that the free-labor ideology embodied in the immigration campaign would have emanated more from northern Republicans. Yet my study of Republican newspapers shows a notable consensus over the support for northern and foreign immigrants that elided intraparty divisions.[23]

It was the African Americans in the southern Republican Party who mounted the dissent against immigration. The editor of the *Colored American* of Augusta, Georgia, considered it "folly to talk of bringing white labor to compete with and drive out the colored." Black leaders recognized that immigration was a means to repress the freedmen. One called immigration "an inimical blow at the freedmen." The logic of black opposition to immigration was clearly set forth by the Reverend James Lynch in a speech before the Tennessee Colored Convention in

1865: "Some talk of the colored man being supplanted by the emigrant of Europe as a laborer. How absurd! Will the emigrant pick up the hoe and plow when the black man drops it, for a few cents a day, when he can go to the great West and get a homestead for a nominal fee . . . and there enjoy a climate like that to which he has been accustomed, besides his independence as a man? [No, never, never!]"[24]

Southern Democrats (often called Conservatives) during Reconstruction also supported immigration. Like Republicans, they believed that it would be instrumental in rebuilding the postwar South. In 1867, the South Carolina Bureau of Immigration declared that immigration was "one of the most vital necessities of the State and a sure means by which a portion of our farmer prospects may be soonest recovered." The editor of the Darlington *New Era* suggested that immigrant labor would "help us to build up our exhausted and desolated country." Francis W. Pickens urged South Carolina governor John Orr to buy lands "to enable us to make settlements for foreigners on a large scale, and the population itself would be the capital & resources of the State."[25]

What distinguished Democratic from Republican support for immigration was its acknowledgment of the need for labor in the Reconstruction South. "Our citizens through the country," proclaimed the *People's Press* of Mississippi as early as 1866, "have not succeeded in getting a supply of laborers, and consequently many open fields will not be cultivated this year." The *Livingston Journal*, a Democratic newspaper from Sumter County, Alabama, believed that when "our rich lands are industrially worked by intelligent labor, we will see the fairest and happiest land of the beautiful South." For Democratic planters and landowners, a new labor force would preferably be white. In South Carolina, as in most states of the Cotton South, conservative white planters wanted to replace black workers with white immigrants. One writer from Richmond insisted that "the cry is more for white labor, and honest white men are heartily welcomed whenever they come." The Macon *Telegraph* agreed that "negro labor is rapidly diminishing and must be supplanted by some other."[26]

Indeed, the diminution and devaluation of African American labor became a constant refrain in the calls of white landowners for immigration. "It is becoming more and more impressed upon the minds of thinking men among us," editorialized the *Norfolk Virginian* as early as November 1865, "that, as he has hitherto proved, the free-negro is not to be depended upon for that species of continuous labor required by the

Southern people." The editor of a Savannah newspaper explained that the "true condition of the labor question in the South" was the question of the reliance on free labor from former slaves. These attacks on black workers drew upon the long-standing and widespread belief in the racial inferiority of former slaves. For instance, the president of the Shelby Iron Company in Alabama, seeking a source for industrial labor in 1869, argued that the black worker was inferior to the white. A spokesperson for a Memphis company seeking to promote immigration to the South referred to the freedmen as "ignorant, indolent, and non-progressive 'sons of Africa.'" John W. Wagner, speaking on immigration at a mass meeting in Darlington District, South Carolina, asked rhetorically whether "our people are so satisfied with free negro labor and its prospects in the future, as to deem such effort as we suggest, unnecessary?"[27]

In Democratic/Conservative thinking, whiteness was synonymous with European immigration. One North Carolina editor believed that "our only and best plan would be to employ European laborers." J. S. Hutton, addressing the Macon Board of Trade in 1868, advised similarly that land be sold "to settlers of the better class, such as the tenant farmers of England, Scotland, Ireland, France and Germany." Some southern proponents of foreign immigration presented themselves as amateur ethnologists. For example, the *Abbeville Press* of South Carolina believed that the Scotch Irish were "steady, thrifty, [and] industrious" and had already "furnished the best blood that flows in our veins." A writer from Greensburg, Louisiana, explained this ethnic argument for European immigrants: "The greatest desire—nay *determination*—of our landed proprietors to get along with the slightest possible assistance from Sambo, was never so manifest and decided as at the present time—while the Teutonic element is even now considerably, and rapidly rising." A Savannah Conservative newspaper agreed, suggesting that "one of these German emigrants will do twice the labor of a negro plantation hand."[28]

The white conservative arguments on behalf of European immigration thus laid bare the racial assumptions of the landowning class. The advent of white immigrants would support the persistence of white supremacy. The *Keowee Courier* of South Carolina openly supported "a wall between the two races" that could only be effected "by inviting the foreigner to make his home among us." The *Montgomery Advertiser* insisted that along with other benefits, immigration "offers a speedy and final cure for negro domination." The influential Savannah *Morning News* similarly proclaimed "that only on the basis of a white population can we hope for the re-establishment of our prosperity and power." The Valdosta *South Georgia Times* agreed that the "African has proved a baleful curse to the whole country, especially our portion of it." As had been the case in the antebellum South, racial supremacy was inextricably bound up with political hegemony. Southern white conservatives recognized that white immigrants might also serve as a counterweight to a rising black politics. For instance, an editorial on immigration that appeared in the *Mobile Tribune* argued that immigrant labor would provide "security against negro domination and Radical persecution." Similarly, Democrats in Arkansas accused Radical Republicans in that state of attempting to "Africanize Arkansas" by bringing in freed people from other states as agricultural laborers.[29]

In supporting the replacement of black agricultural workers by white foreign immigrants, southern planters openly revealed their search for a tractable labor force to replace slavery. Skeptical Republicans in the Reconstruction South recognized and tried to expose this motive. The *Weekly Mississippi Pilot* believed that most southern planters "are anxious to procure laborers whom they can control somewhat after the manner of their former slaves, having them in fearful subjection and obedience, to the commands of their master." Another Republican editor believed that southern Democrats wanted foreign immigrants "not so much of free thinking independent men as of men who will do a great deal of manual labor for very small pay."[30]

Notwithstanding the strong and elaborate justifications put forth by conservative southern whites for pursuing foreign immigration, a few dissenting Democrats opposed immigration. John B. Gordon, a leading Conservative from Georgia, expressed his opposition to immigration during congressional hearings on the Ku Klux Klan. "In the Southern Cultivator, the leading agricultural journal in Georgia," Gordon claimed, "you will find article after article, from the first planters of the State, opposing the introduction of white laborers from abroad, on the ground that the negro is the proper laborer for our State, that we understand him and he understands us." In an address before the Virginia State Agricultural Society in 1866, Willoughby Newton expanded on the reasons that native black workers were preferable to foreign labor: "They understand our language, our modes of farming and crops, and can go to work at once without training, whereas the foreigner has to be taught everything." There was also opposition from southern farmers who feared that immigrants would buy and settle upon open or public land that had traditionally been used by the yeomanry to graze their livestock. A farmer from Corinth, Mississippi, for instance, worried that immigrants would buy up uncultivated land that would leave the farmer "no place for his cattle to range."[31]

The question of Chinese immigration to the post–Civil War South further illustrates the contrasting views of immigration offered by Republicans and Democrats during Reconstruction. The influential journal *De Bow's Review* acknowledged, "Opinions vary as to the character of the *Coolie*; some authorities describing him as a demoralizing blight to any community, while on the other hand travelers in *Mauritius, California* and *elsewhere* give him a very good character." The Chinese movement was a popular topic of conversation in the press, especially during the years of Presidential Reconstruction (1865–67). As historian Eric Foner has noted, southern planters followed the use of "coolie" labor in the West Indies. There were several instances of Chinese workers in the Reconstruction South. Organized in June 1869, the Arkansas River Valley Immigration Company specifically wanted Chinese laborers. One agent went to Asia and returned with 189 Chinese workers. Most often, Chinese immigrants were sought as agricultural laborers in the sugarcane fields of Louisiana. Five hundred Chinese "coolies" arrived in Natchitoches, Louisiana, in 1867. They were also employed on the Alabama & Chattanooga Railroad. Shipments of Chinese laborers arrived in New Orleans in June and July of 1870.[32]

Democratic Conservative spokesmen, representing the interests of planters and large landowners, largely endorsed Chinese immigration as a source of labor. By 1869, the *Rural Carolinian* insisted that Chinese labor on the rice and cotton plantations of the South was "a foregone conclusion." As we have seen, most southern Conservatives preferred European immigrants. But if they would not come, some planters explained, "we must take the Chinese." One South Carolinian believed that "the Coolies would suit our rice lands well as they are accustomed to cultivate rice in their own land." Once again, southern Democrats coupled the advantages of class and race. The Tuscaloosa *Independent Monitor*, for instance, welcomed "another race introduced in this country, if it can starve out the negro." Reflecting their desire to continue the slave labor regime, another Alabama editor maintained that the "natural" docility of Chinese workers would strengthen plantation discipline in a new era of free labor.[33]

Yet some Democratic voices spoke out against Chinese immigrants. One agricultural journal argued that the Chinese, who would tend to associate only in large numbers, would end up only in the large plantations. Characteristically, southern Democrats also worried that the Chinese would pose a danger should they become citizens and gain the right to vote. As one South Carolina editor worried, "They will find always a radical party ready to cooperate with them to set up Budah [*sic*] or any other god for the sake of sharing the spoils."[34]

In vivid contrast, southern Republicans shunned Chinese immigrants. They argued that planters and their Democratic spokesmen schemed for the Chinese to replace slave labor. "Ignorant as are the Chinese," wrote the *Charleston Daily Republican*, "they nevertheless know that they are invited here as a substitute for African slaves and by the late slaveholders." One writer to this same paper considered arguments on behalf of Chinese labor "puerile" and "unworthy of notice." Republican nativism surfaced quickly in editorials about immigration to the Reconstruction South. At different times, for example, the editor of the *Weekly Mississippi Pilot* spoke of the "ignorant barbarians of Asia" and "the Coolie order of human beings." For their part, black leaders also insisted that the importation of Chinese labor would hurt the black laborer. The editor of the *Arkansas Freeman*, for instance, argued that the movement to introduce Chinese immigrants to the South was motivated by "the purpose of bringing cheap labor into the State opposed to the colored labor of the country."[35]

After emancipation, southerners of all political stripes looked toward immigration as a means of implementing their vision of a postwar economic and social order. These ideals, as various as they were plenty, closely corresponded to the main fault lines in the Reconstruction South. Immigration was part of the southern Republican agenda to develop the postwar South on the basis of northern free-labor society. Black Republicans, however, opposed foreign workers as a threat to their own hopes for independent black laborers and landowners. Most Democratic and Conservative spokesmen supported European immigration as one way of removing freedmen and freedwomen from their envisioned "New South."

The discursive debate over immigration examined here can provide new insights into Reconstruction in the South. First, the inclusion of immigration lends force to the globalization of American Reconstruction. As historian Matthew Pratt Guterl has argued, "Southerners in the United States were economically, culturally and socially connected to the global experience of emancipation and labor adjustment in the Americas." According to another historian, the "best work on Reconstruction focuses on integrating Reconstruction in the South into larger national and international contexts." Since the advent of postrevisionism in the 1960s and 1970s, historians of American Reconstruction have compared emancipation in the United States to that in other New World slave societies to both show the commonalities of the transition from slavery to freedom and highlight the unique features of the American experience. The potential role of foreign immigrants as a labor force was also raised in other postemancipation societies such as Cuba, Brazil, and the Caribbean. The Chinese had been recruited as indentured laborers in British Guiana as early as 1838. During the 1840s and 1850s, Louisiana sugar planters watched as Asian workers helped the agricultural production of sugar in the British West Indies and Cuba. Recent students of Reconstruction have also turned their attention to international developments in the 1860s and 1870s. Historian Mark Smith goes so far as to argue that Reconstruction "is best understood by appreciating foreign developments and initiatives."[36]

Second, the discourse of immigration laid bare the economic, social, and racial assumptions of both Republicans and Democrats. It most obviously spoke to the very real material struggles over property and power between southern whites and freed people. Equally important, the debate over immigration reveals the contradictory and often self-destructive efforts of both southern Democrats/Conservatives and Republicans. As historian Eric Foner has suggested, southern plans for immigration reflected "the divided mind and contradictory aims of those advocating economic change." He argued further that New South reformers "clung to hopes for labor control and racial subordination that belied their rhetorical commitment to far-reaching social change." Paradoxically, Democratic calls for foreign immigration must also have at least disquieted African American laborers so essential to white planters in their quest for economic recovery in the Cotton South.[37]

Republican efforts at immigration, part of their larger developmental ethos for the Reconstruction South, might also have worked against their own success. The immigration of northern and foreign workers offered nothing to two groups essential to their success, African American freedmen and white yeoman farmers. Republican spokesmen never explicitly said that immigration would benefit the yeomanry. Although evidence on the attitudes of yeoman farmers toward immigration is scarce, there are reasons to believe that the arrival of northern and foreign immigrants would be inimical toward their interests. First, immigrants would buy and improve land and thereby raise the value of all land, perhaps making it harder for aspiring landowners to purchase farmland. More important, the southern yeomanry had traditionally depended on the availability of the public domain to graze their pigs and livestock. They had assumed certain common rights to use public land. In their eyes, the rise of homesteading and land purchases might have limited the amount of public land for grazing.[38]

For all these reasons, the debate over immigration, so prevalent in the literature of the postwar South, deserves a prominent niche in Reconstruction historiography. It provides a revealing microcosm of the larger discussion about what forms the social and political order of the New South should take. Central to Reconstruction then was the troubling and monumental question of who would remain inside and who would remain outside the New South vortex.

NOTES

1. Of course, the historical literature on Reconstruction is vast and still growing. A bibliography published in 2000 listed over 2,900 separate entries. See David A. Lincove, *Reconstruction in the United States: An Annotated Bibliography* (Westport, Conn.: Greenwood, 2000). Eric Foner, *Reconstruction, 1863–1877: America's Unfinished Revolution* (New York: Harper and Row, 1988), remains the best interpretive survey. Michael W. Fitzgerald, *Reconstruction in Alabama: From Civil War to Redemption in the Cotton South* (Baton Rouge: Louisiana State University Press, 2017), is the most recent study of a southern state during Reconstruction. Valuable for understanding more current Reconstruction historiography is John David Smith, ed., *Interpreting American History: Reconstruction* (Kent, Ohio: Kent State University Press, 2016). Another useful discussion of more current Reconstruction historiography can be found in "Historians' Forum: Reconstruction," *Civil War History* 61, no. 3 (September 2015): 281–301.

2. Michael O'Brien, *Rethinking the South: Essays in Intellectual History* (Baltimore: Johns Hopkins University Press, 1988), 131; Leslie Butler, "Reconstructions in Intellectual and Cultural Life," in *Reconstructions: New Perspectives on the Postbellum United States*, ed. Thomas J. Brown (New York: Oxford University Press, 2006), 174, 183. In fairness, I should recognize such studies as Jack P. Maddex, *The Reconstruction of Edward A. Pollard: A Rebel's Conversion to Postbellum Unionism* (Chapel Hill: University of North Carolina Press, 1974); Wayne Mixon, *Southern Writers and the New South Movement, 1865–1913* (Chapel Hill: University of North Carolina Press, 1980); and Sarah E. Gardner, *Blood and Irony: Southern White Women's Narratives of the Civil War, 1861–1937* (Chapel Hill: University of North Carolina Press, 2004).

3. The fusion of polemical literature, political ideology, and intellectual history characterizes some of the most influential historical works of the late twentieth cen-

tury. They include Marvin Meyers, *The Jacksonian Persuasion: Politics and Belief* (Stanford, Calif.: Stanford University Press, 1957); Bernard Bailyn, *The Ideological Origins of the American Revolution* (Cambridge, Mass.: Harvard University Press, 1967); Gordon S. Wood, *The Creation of the American Republic, 1776-1787* (Chapel Hill: Published for the Institute of Early American History and Culture by the University of North Carolina Press, 1969); and Eric Foner, *Free Soil, Free Labor, Free Men: The Ideology of the Republican Party before the Civil War*, 2nd ed. (1970; repr., New York: Oxford University Press, 2005).

4. Lonnie A. Burnett, *The Pen Makes a Good Sword: John Forsyth of the* Mobile Register (Tuscaloosa: University of Alabama Press, 2006), 2. For a similar point, see Richard H. Abbott, *For Free Press and Equal Rights: Republican Newspapers in the Reconstruction South*, ed. John W. Quist (Athens: University of Georgia Press, 2004), 2. See also Foner, *Free Soil, Free Labor*, lx; and Frank Schaller, *The Labor Question of the South: An Essay, with Special Reference to the Introduction of German Agriculturalists and Laborers to the State of Georgia* (n.p., 1866).

5. *Southern Argus* (Selma, Ala.), June 23, 1869; *Wilcox County (Ala.) News*, September 20, 1867; *Eufala (Ala.) Daily News*, October 14, 1865; *Wilmington (N.C.) Journal*, June 14, 1868; Robert H. Woody, "The Labor and Immigration Problem of South Carolina during Reconstruction," *Mississippi Valley Historical Review* 18 (September 1931): 195; Joseph H. Mahaffey, ed., "Carl Schurz's Letters from the South," *Georgia Historical Quarterly* 35 (September 1951): 240.

6. Rowland Berthoff, "Southern Attitudes toward Immigration, 1865-1914," *Journal of Southern History* 17, no. 3 (August 1931), 336; *Norfolk Virginian*, November 22, 1865; Thomas S. Staples, *Reconstruction in Arkansas, 1862-1874* (New York: Columbia University Press, 1923), 341; Irby C. Nichols, "Reconstruction in DeSoto County," *Publications of the Mississippi Historical Society* 11 (1910): 311; Campbell Brown to his mother, January 7, 1866, Brown-Ewell Family Papers, Filson Historical Society, Louisville, Kentucky; Frank E. Dykema, "An Effort to Attract Dutch Colonists to Alabama, 1869," *Journal of Southern History* 14, no. 2 (May 1948): 255; *Wilmington Journal*, June 14, 1868; *Southern Field and Factory*, October 1871, 337-38. For additional evidence, see also *Laurensville (S.C.) Herald*, March 1, 1867; and Robert A. Calvert, ed., "The Freedmen and Agricultural Prosperity," *Southwestern Historical Quarterly* 76 (April 1973): 463.

7. *Central Georgian* (Sandersville), May 6, 1868; Berthoff, "Southern Attitudes toward Immigration," 336; *Nationalist* (Mobile, Ala.), June 18, 1869; Claude P. Smith, "Official Efforts by the State of Mississippi to Encourage Immigration, 1868-1886," *Journal of Mississippi History* 32, no. 4 (November 1970): 327; Beverly Watkins, "Efforts to Encourage Immigration to Arkansas, 1865-1877," *Arkansas Historical Quarterly* 38 (March 1979): 44; E. Russ Williams, "Louisiana's Public and Private Immigration Endeavors: 1866-1893," *Louisiana History* 15, no. 2 (Spring 1974): 156. The most recent study of the constitutional conventions of the Reconstruction South is Richard L. Hume and Jerry B. Gough, *Blacks, Carpetbaggers, and Scalawags: The Constitutional Conventions of Radical Reconstruction* (Baton Rouge: Louisiana State University Press, 2008).

8. Staples, *Reconstruction in Arkansas*, 341; John W. Pyle, "Reconstruction in Panola County," *Publications of the Mississippi Historical Society* 12 (1912): 85; E. F.

Puckett, "Reconstruction in Monroe County," *Publications of the Mississippi Historical Society* 11 (1910): 140–42; Julia C. Brown, "Reconstruction in Yalobusha and Grenada Counties," *Publications of the Mississippi Historical Society* 12 (1912): 260–61.

9. E. Merton Coulter, *The South during Reconstruction, 1865-1877* (Baton Rouge: Louisiana State University Press, 1947), 104–5; *Southern Argus*, June 23, 1869; Foner, *Reconstruction*, 213. Eric Foner (*Reconstruction*, 420) has also noted that New South economic reformers "clung to hopes for labor control and racial subordination that belied their rhetorical commitment to far-reaching social change." Another historian makes a similar comment regarding Chinese immigrants: "More than anything, the agriculturalists who grasped at the improbable scheme to import Chinese betrayed an inability to come to terms with a free labor system in which African Americans were free to do what they wanted with their labor." Jeffrey Moran, "Chinese Labor for the New South," *Southern Studies: An Interdisciplinary Journal of the South* 3, no. 4 (1992): 283.

10. Hermann Bokum, "Address of Mr. Hermann Bokum before the Tennessee Immigration Society at the City Hall, November 19, 1867," quoted in *Nashville Union and Dispatch*, November 21, 1867; *Mississippi Index* (Columbus), July 30, 1867; *South Alabamian* (Jackson), May 15, 1869.

11. Berthoff, "Southern Attitudes toward Immigration," 343.

12. Woody, "Labor and Immigration Problem," 195.

13. *Daily New Era* (Atlanta), January 19, 1868; Watkins, "Efforts to Encourage Immigration," 43; *Weekly Mississippi Pilot* (Jackson), January 2, 1875; Staples, *Reconstruction in Arkansas*, 339–40.

14. *Tallahassee (Fla.) Sentinel*, May 6, 1871; *Southern Republican* (Demopolis, Ala.), September 29, 1869; *Weekly Mississippi Pilot*, April 9, 1870. See also *Weekly Mississippi Pilot*, March 5, 1870.

15. *Weekly Mississippi Pilot*, April 9, 1870; *Daily New Era*, January 30, 1868; *East Alabama Monitor* (Opelika, Ala.), February 19, 1869; *Beaufort (S.C.) Republican*, May 21, 1870; *Charleston (S.C.) Daily Republican*, August 19, 1869. See also *Weekly Mississippi Pilot*, March 5, 1870; and *Daily New Era*, January 19, 1868.

16. *Alabama State Journal* (Montgomery), January 16, 1869; *Weekly Mississippi Pilot*, March 5, 1870; *Tallahassee Sentinel*, April 22, 1871.

17. *Southern Republican*, March 24, 1869; *Tallahassee Sentinel*, May 6, 1871; *Weekly Mississippi Pilot*, April 16, 1870.

18. Mark A. Lause, *Young America: Land, Labor, and the Republican Community* (Urbana and Chicago: University of Illinois Press, 2005), 127; Richard H. Abbott, "Yankee Farmers in Northern Virginia, 1840–1860," *Virginia Magazine of History and Biography* 76, no. 1 (January 1968): 61, 57, 63; Otis K. Rice, "Eli Thayer and Friendly Invasion of Virginia," *Journal of Southern History* 37, no. 4 (November 1971): 591, 577; George Winston Smith, "Ante-bellum Attempts of Northern Business Interests to 'Redeem' the Upper South," *Journal of Southern History* 11, no. 2 (May 1945): 180, 193.

19. *Charleston Daily Republican*, September 10, 1869; *Weekly Mississippi Pilot*, March 5, 1870; *Houston (Tex.) Union*, January 20, 1869.

20. *Daily New Era*, January 19, 1868; *Tallahassee Sentinel*, May 6, April 22, 1871; *Weekly Mississippi Pilot*, April 9, 1870.

21. Foner, *Free Soil, Free Labor*, ix. Further explorations into northern free-labor ideology include Jonathan A. Glickstein, *Concepts of Free Labor in Antebellum America* (New Haven, Conn.: Yale University Press, 1991); and Joshua Michael Zeitz, "The Missouri Compromise Reconsidered: Antislavery Rhetoric and the Emergence of the Free Labor Synthesis," *Journal of the Early Republic* 20, no. 3 (Autumn 2000): 447-85.

22. Abbott, *For Free Press*, 26-27, 143. On Republican factionalism in general, consult Foner, *Reconstruction*, chaps. 7-8; Mark W. Summers, *Railroads, Reconstruction, and the Gospel of Prosperity: Aid under the Radical Republicans, 1865-1877* (Princeton, N.J.: Princeton University Press, 1984); and Richard H. Abbott, *The Republican Party and the South, 1855-1877: The First Southern Strategy* (Chapel Hill: University of North Carolina Press, 1986). See also Richard H. Abbott, "The Republican Party Press in Reconstruction Georgia, 1867-1874," *Journal of Southern History* 61, no. 4 (November 1995): 732.

23. Abbott, *For Free Press*, 3, 5, 53, 86. Burnett, *Pen Makes a Good Sword*, adds to our understanding of Reconstruction journalism (Democratic, in this case).

24. *Colored American* (Augusta, Ga.), October 31, 1868, March 2, 1867; James Lynch speech quoted in *Weekly Mississippi Pilot*, November 27, 1869.

25. Woody, "Labor and Immigration Problem," 195; "Circular, South Carolina Bureau of Immigration, Charleston, April 5, 1867," quoted in *Charleston (S.C.) Daily Courier*, April 8, 1867; *Keowee (S.C.) Courier*, January 20, 1866; Francis W. Pickens to James L. Orr, September 10, 1867, James L. Orr Governor's Papers, South Carolina Department of Archives and History, Columbia. For other examples of Democratic support for immigration, see *Picayune* (New Orleans), quoted in *Southern Ruralist* (Greensburg, La.), January 18, 1867; F. A. Hervey comments, *South Alabamian*, May 15, 1869; and *Montgomery (Ala.) Mail*, quoted in *Eufala Daily News*, October 14, 1865.

26. Nichols, "Reconstruction in DeSoto County," 311; *Livingston (Ala.) Journal*, May 17, 1872; Woody, "Labor and Immigration Problem," 201, quoted in *Morning News* (Savannah, Ga.), August 12, 1869. See also *Daily News and Herald* (Savannah, Ga.), September 16, 1867.

27. *Norfolk Virginian*, November 22, 1865; *Daily News and Herald*, September 16, November 30, 1867; Dykema, "Effort to Attract," 260; *Southern Field and Factory*, May 1871, 197; *Edgefield (S.C.) Advertiser*, May 29, 1867. See also *Southern Field and Factory*, August 1871, 304; *Federal Union* (Milledgeville, Ga.), quoted in *Eufala Daily News*, October 14, 1865; and *Griffin (Ga.) Tri-Weekly Star*, October 28, 1865.

28. *Southern Field and Factory*, August 1871, 304; "Address of J. S. Hutton to the Macon Board of Trade," quoted in *Daily News and Herald*, November 19, 1868, and in *Laurensville Herald*, February 1, 1867; *Southern Ruralist*, January 18, 1867; *Daily News and Herald*, December 24, 1867.

29. *Keowee Courier*, January 13, 1866; *Montgomery (Ala.) Advertiser*, June 14, 1869; *Morning News*, February 25, 1869; *Independent Monitor* (Tuscaloosa, Ala.), December 4, 1867; Staples, *Reconstruction in Arkansas*, 342. See also *Southern Factory and Field*, April 1871, 154. Revealingly, J. S. Hutton, speaking to the Macon Board of Trade, believed that white immigrants would have a "beneficial effect on the negro race—setting them an example of persevering industry which will no doubt be an incentive to many." *Daily News and Herald*, November 19, 1868.

30. *Opelika (Ala.) Era and Whig*, February 10, 1871; *Weekly Mississippi Pilot*, March 5, 1870; *Southern Republican*, March 24, 1869.

31. *Testimony Taken by the Joint Select Committee to Inquire into the Condition of Affairs in the Insurrectionary States Georgia*, vol. 6, *Georgia: Volume 1* (Washington, D.C.: Government Printing Office, 1872), 307–8; *Southern Planter*, n.s., 1 (February 1867): 30; *Memphis (Tenn.) Morning Post*, February 4, 1866. The conflict between planters and yeoman farmers over common rights for grazing became a major source of conflict in the post-Reconstruction South. See two important essays by Steven Hahn: "Common Rights and Commonwealth: The Stock-Law Struggle and the Roots of Southern Populism," in *Region, Race, and Reconstruction: Essays in Honor of C. Vann Woodward*, ed. J. Morgan Kousser and James McPherson (New York: Oxford University Press, 1982); and "Hunting, Fishing, and Foraging: Common Rights and Class Relations in the Postbellum South," *Radical History Review* 26 (1982): 37–64. For a contrary view, see Shawn Everett Kantor and J. Morgan Kousser, "Common Sense or Commonwealth? The Fence Law and Institutional Change in the Postbellum South," *Journal of Southern History* 59, no. 2 (May 1993): 201–42.

32. Stuart Creighton Miller, *The Unwelcome Immigrant: The American Image of the Chinese, 1785-1882* (Berkeley: University of California Press), 153; Eric Foner, *Nothing but Freedom: Emancipation and Its Legacy* (Baton Rouge: Louisiana State University Press, 1983), 47; Staples, *Reconstruction in Arkansas*, 341; Matthew Pratt Guterl, "After Slavery: Asian Labor, the American South, and the Age of Emancipation," *Journal of World History* 14, no. 2 (June 2003): 229–30; Coulter, *South during Reconstruction*, 105–6; Andrew Gyory, *Closing the Gate: Race, Politics, and the Chinese Exclusion Act* (Chapel Hill: University of North Carolina Press, 1998), 47.

For a long time, the major work on Chinese immigrants in the context of Reconstruction was Alexander Saxton, *The Indispensable Enemy: Labor and the Anti-Chinese Movement in California* (Berkeley: University of California Press, 1971). Reflecting the global turn of American history and the increased attention to ethnic diversity, a number of new studies have appeared: Lucy M. Cohen, *The Chinese in the Post-Civil War South: A People without History* (Baton Rouge: Louisiana State University Press, 1984); Najia Aarim-Heriot, *Chinese Immigration, African Americans, and Racial Anxiety in the United States, 1848-82* (Urbana: University of Illinois Press, 2003); Moon-Ho Jung, *Coolies and Cane: Race, Labor, and Sugar in the Age of Emancipation* (Baltimore: Johns Hopkins University Press, 2006); Edlie L. Wong, *Racial Reconstruction: Black Inclusion, Chinese Exclusion, and the Fictions of Citizenship* (New York: New York University Press, 2015); Beth Lew-Williams, *The Chinese Must Go: Violence, Exclusion, and the Making of the Alien in America* (Cambridge, Mass.: Harvard University Press, 2018); and Joshua Paddison, *American Heathens: Religion, Race, and Reconstruction in California* (Berkeley: University of California Press, 2012). On the issue of Chinese immigration to the Reconstruction South, see also Lucy M. Cohen, "George W. Gift, Chinese Labor Agent in the Post–Civil War South," *Chinese America: History & Perspectives* 1 (1995): 157–79; and Lucy M. Cohen, "Entry of Chinese to the Lower South from 1865–1870: Policy Dilemma," *Southern Studies*, n.s., 2, nos. 3–4 (1991): 281–313.

33. *Rural Carolinian*, December 1869, 129; Coulter, *South during Reconstruction*, 105; Francis Pickens to James L. Orr, September 9, 1867, James L. Orr Governor's

Papers, South Carolina Department of Archives and History, Columbia; *Selma (Ala.) Press*, April 17, 1869; Foner, *Reconstruction*, 419.

34. Coulter, *South during Reconstruction*, 106. One historian has accurately noted, "More than anything, the agriculturalists who gasped at the improbable scheme to import Chinese betrayed an inability to come to terms with a new labor system in which African-Americans were free to do what they wanted with their labor." Moran, "Chinese Labor," 283.

35. *Charleston Daily Republican*, September 10, October 13, 1869; *Weekly Mississippi Pilot*, April 9, 23, 1870; *Arkansas Freeman* (Little Rock), October 5, 1869. Moon Ho-Jung raises the important point that even discussion about the arrival of Chinese immigrants raised thorny problems of racialization in the post–Civil War South. See Jung, *Coolies and Cane*, esp. chap. 5.

36. Guterl, "After Slavery," 209; David Smith, *Interpreting American History*, 8; Jung, *Coolies and Cane*, 2, 4; Mark Smith, "The Past as a Foreign Country: Reconstruction, Inside and Out," in Thomas J. Brown, *Reconstructions*, 117. Other relevant works include Edgar T. Thompson, *Plantation Societies, Race Relations, and the South: The Regimentation of Populations* (Durham, N.C.: Duke University Press, 1975); Thomas C. Holt, "An Empire over the Mind: Emancipation, Race, and Ideology in the British West Indies and the American South," in Kousser and McPherson, *Region, Race, and Reconstruction*, 283–313; John W. Cell, *The Highest Stage of White Supremacy: The Origins of Segregation in South Africa and the American South* (New York: Cambridge University Press, 1982); Frederick Cooper, *From Slaves to Squatters: Plantation Labor and Agriculture in Zanzibar and Coastal Kenya* (New Haven, Conn.: Yale University Press, 1980); Rebecca J. Scott, *Slave Emancipation in Cuba: The Transition to Free Labor, 1860–1899* (Princeton, N.J.: Princeton University Press, 1985); Thomas C. Holt, *The Problem of Freedom: Race, Labor, and Politics in Jamaica and Britain, 1832–1938* (Baltimore: Johns Hopkins University Press, 1992); and Frederick Cooper, Thomas C. Holt, and Rebecca J. Scott, *Beyond Slavery: Explorations of Race, Labor, and Citizenship in Postemancipation Societies* (Chapel Hill: University of North Carolina Press, 2000). Finally, see the recent essays in David Prior, ed., *Reconstruction's World* (New York: Fordham University Press, 2018).

37. Foner, *Reconstruction*, 213, 520.

38. Steven Hahn, *The Roots of Southern Populism: Yeoman Farmers and the Transformation of the Southern Upcountry, 1850–1890*, updated ed. (New York: Oxford University Press, 2006), remains the best overall study of the yeomanry in the nineteenth-century South. Yeoman communities also existed in the plantation belt of the Old South. Pioneering works include Frank L. Owsley and Harriet C. Owsley, "The Economic Basis of Society in the Late Ante-bellum South," *Journal of Southern History* 6, no. 1 (February 1940): 24–45; and Frank L. Owsley, *Plain Folk of the Old South* (Baton Rouge: Louisiana State University Press, 1949). See also Eugene D. Genovese, "Yeoman Farmers in a Slaveholders' Democracy," *Agricultural History* 49, no. 2 (April 1975): 331–42; Lacy K. Ford, "Yeoman Farmers in the South Carolina Upcountry: Changing Production Patterns in the Late Antebellum Era," *Agricultural History* 60, no. 4 (Fall 1986): 17–37; and Stephanie McCurry, *Masters of Small Worlds: Yeoman Households, Gender Relations, and the Political Culture of the Antebellum South Carolina Low Country* (New York: Oxford University Press, 1995).

For a more current review of Reconstruction historiography with attention to the yeomanry, see Stephen A. West, "'A General Remodeling of Every Thing': Economy and Race in the Post-emancipation South," in Thomas J. Brown, *Reconstructions*, 10–39. More recent studies of the yeomanry include Margaret Storey, *Loyalty and Loss: Alabama's Unionists during Civil War and Reconstruction* (Baton Rouge: Louisiana State University Press, 2004); and Michael Fitzgerald, *Reconstruction in Alabama: From Civil War to Redemption in the Cotton South* (Baton Rouge: Louisiana State University Press, 2017). Perhaps unnecessary to state, W. E. B. Du Bois, *Black Reconstruction in America* (1935; repr., New York: Athenaeum, 1975), still merits careful reading by every student of the subject.

PART TWO

IDEAS ABOUT THE SOUTH

SOUTHERN LITERATURE AND THE ANTHROPOCENE

MELANIE BENSON TAYLOR

IN 2015, literary critic Zackary Vernon challenged colleagues in southern studies to, finally, engage with the Anthropocene: a conception of geological time and of a natural world shaped—indeed, ravaged by—human interventions.[1] The hesitancy is something of a paradox, given the region's long heritage of both large-scale agribusiness and ecological stewardship, and especially given its deeply rooted, passionate investments in championing or descrying development and disaster in turn. Indeed, southerners, both long before and well after the Vanderbilt Agrarians, have bemoaned the rude destruction of the South's "humane" plantation ventures and the erosion of its pristine green spaces and forests. Vernon is right to be puzzled by the lack of Anthropocenic discourse among southern scholars, outside of a handful of ecocritics, but Jon Smith is also correct to be skeptical about the form and value of those potential contributions. Ecocriticism has a tendency, as Smith puts it, "to state the obvious": "We knew about preindustrial agriculture, the ecological sublime, local foodways, and sustainable tourism before we cracked the books," Smith avers and suggests that reading authors such as Faulkner and Glasgow[2] for their environmentalist musings might ultimately be less effective than multifaceted, multidisciplinary activism on both the campus and community levels.[3] In other words, as Cherokee poet Marilou Awiakta put it memorably in the midst of a fierce debate about the Tennessee Valley Authority's Tellico Dam project that threatened to destroy sacred Cherokee places as well as the endangered snail darter: "What good is it to sling a poem at a dam?"[4]

Not much, unfortunately, at least not in the short term—or in these particular terms at all. Perhaps we have, until recently, been asking the wrong questions: at a moment when intellectual products are considered property to be mobilized for maximum applicability or gain, the utility of literary studies or of individual works of art in the wake of catastrophic global weather changes, natural disasters, extinctions, and erosions can seem feeble at best. But when we consider that the Anthropocene itself is, like any other scientific paradigm, a new narrative that simply recalibrates prevailing assumptions about geologic time—and that all stories are maps of power differentials composed of self-serving assumptions and pregnant silences—then few disciplines other than literary studies seem better suited to grapple with the imaginaries produced in the wake of anthropogenic crisis. And few regions, arguably, have as much to contribute as the South does to a productive *complication* of Anthropocene discourse—not the teleological conscriptions or the facile echolalia that Smith predicts.

"The Anthropocene" is an umbrella term, both deferred and deficient, for a storm of ancient conditions and contradictions. In the broader terrain of intellectual history, it has been a conceptually fluid container for thinkers in cultural, political, scientific, and even humanities disciplines; in southern intellectual history in particular, the conversations have been curiously absent but, arguably, uniquely applicable. A millennial concept (coined in 2000 and added officially to *The Oxford English Dictionary* in 2014) to describe the impact of human intercessions in geological and ecological time, the Anthropocene concept entails a basic paradox: Are humans its perpetrators or its casualties? If, as Bruno Latour has urged, we manage to bridge the great divide between humanism/culture and nonhumanism/nature, then who among us is doomed, and who will be saved? To better parse the complexities, a pageant of supplementary concepts has appeared—among them, Capitalocene, Chthulucene, Plantationocene, and Manthropocene, to name only a few monikers for the agents, structures, and institutions effecting catastrophic climate change and social death conjointly. The vast structural inequities in (and obscured by) the Anthropocene have been further unpacked by anthropologists, historians, geologists, and humanists such as Donna Haraway, Anna Tsing, Sylvia Wynter, Elizabeth Povinelli, Shona Jackson, Kathryn Yusoff, and others. As Yusoff puts it in *A Billion Black Anthropocenes or None* (2018), "The Anthropocene . . . is just now noticing the extinction it has chosen to continually overlook in the making of its modernity and freedom."[5] In the particular textures of southern history and thought, and their vexed relationships to "modernity" and "freedom," the Anthropocene waits to be noticed.

The South, a haunted space that insists stubbornly on its abject *placeness*, has always been a project striated by brutal evictions, stained by perverse economic investments, and enlivened by both the realities and pageantries of victimization and loss. Here, the terrors of "slow violence"—a term coined by Rob Nixon to describe the accretive, invisible effects of climate change, man-made disasters, and "natural" catastrophes on the world's poor and marginalized—have widespread applicability. As the last few decades of New Southern Studies scholarship have laid bare, in its wholesale "disrupting [of] everyone's enjoyment," as Smith boldly puts it, seemingly every southerner, regardless of skin color or social status, nourishes some private narrative of dispossession and perceived assault.[6] All may inhabit the Anthropocene, but the scenery looks quite different—and, somewhat unexpectedly, dizzyingly congruous—for a conservative white property owner, an African American child, and an Indigenous casino employee. In the startling interplay among these polarized but analogous groups, the real complexities and challenges of the Anthropocene, and the future of southern thought, may well lie.

Southern literature has always been apocalyptic. Particularly in the decades following Civil War defeat and the incursions of Reconstruction, white southern writers mourned their shattered, occupied worlds; most famously, the Vanderbilt Agrarians grieved the colonial-capitalist dismantling of the South's plantation economies and idyllic social formations, erecting a mythical plantation pastoral in righteous retrospect.[7] As the region reluctantly shuttled into modernity, its most famous writers grieved the decimation of its rural ecologies; the mechanization of its agricultural enterprises; the spread of mass railway systems; the anonymity and seductions of material culture in the marketplace; and with it all, the depleted and "doomed wilderness whose edges were being constantly and punily gnawed at by men with plows and axes," as Faulkner's

Isaac McCaslin puts it memorably in "The Bear." The rise and fall of the southern self, broadly construed, is predicated on the flourishing of its "natural" spaces and orders, variously imagined and undermined. But as Lumbee anthropologist David Shane Lowry reminds us, Anthropocene discourse tends to essentialize the conflict—man versus nature—and thus erroneously assumes "we *all* had/have *equitable* opportunities to affect, craft, and enact policies regarding human vulnerability," a hierarchy that smooths out the functional differences between white policy makers, elite landowners, and marginalized minorities. In the taxonomies of blame and reparations, where do we place the "South" writ large, a region where the dissembling experience of defeat and dispossession has, as C. Vann Woodward put it, always set it apart from the rest of the United States and its triumphalist narratives? How do we parse the complicated webs of appropriation and exceptionalism—old southern narratives, to be sure—being quietly revivified and complicated by the new crises of the twenty-first century?[8]

Anthropogenic critique gives us new ways to intervene in contemporary culture's increasingly compartmentalized discussions of human disposability. Patrick Wolfe has deemed settler colonialism a zero-sum operation contingent on "the elimination of Native alternatives" and the consequent "social death of Nativeness." Similarly but diametrically, Afro-pessimist logic, laid out forcefully by Frank B. Wilderson III, holds that black people were "meant to be accumulated and die" from the start and essentially classes all nonblack agents as inherently "*anti*-black."[9] Concomitantly, settler colonial studies declares that all non-Indigenous actors are de facto settlers, including African Americans. Scholars Iyko Day and Glen Sean Couthard encourage a more complex, dialectical model for the growth of the American nation-state, where land and labor are the linked, paradigmatic grounds for the genocidal subsuming of *both* Indigenous and African elements. While America's Natives suffered a policy based on eradication, and its slaves on (paradoxically) increase, nonetheless, these experiences together serve a unitary agenda of supporting and making coherent white proprietorship. Yet the distinction here is not even close to being simply racial: it fails to account for the extraracial (e.g., cultural, relational, juridical) sources for Indigenous sovereignty. As Judith Butler argues in her concept of the "throwaway body," echoed by Patricia Yaeger in her now canonical *Dirt and Desire*, women's bodies regardless of color suffer uniquely under regional, hegemonic controls. The biopolitical vulnerability of the body is a gigantic phenomenon that demands a wide-angle lens, but too often its contemporary applicability in the South is artificially delimited, tagged as a post-Katrina or post–Black Lives Matter artifact. As Christopher Lloyd puts it, "Focusing on displaced or disposable bodies after Katrina can illuminate the multitudinous ways in which southern life is regulated by historically racialized forces: what I call the South's corporeal legacies."[10] Too often, though, those histories are flattened and simplified in ways that mask the complexities of internal assaults and erasures, unnatural disasters and extirpations, and brutal cycles of internecine wounding. And this is just the human layer: other scholars—chiefly, Elizabeth Povinelli, Eric Santner, Colleen Glenney Boggs, Cary Wolfe, Pieter Vermeulen, and Virginia Richter—have argued in various ways for ontological recalibrations that shatter the tenuous borders between human, animal, and seemingly "inanimate" life forms.

While scholars such as Nixon have done an exemplary job of merging postcolonial analysis with environmentalism—illuminating the cultural and economic dimensions of ecological crises—the application of such critical frames founders in the densities of the U.S. southern context. In Daniel Spoth's pathbreaking essay on the representation of "slow violence" in several southern texts, he makes the compelling counterclaim that such narratives epitomize not embeddedness and stasis but rather unruly, satirical, and even parodic relationships to ecological attachment.[11] What Spoth's analysis uncovers along the way, but ultimately leaves unexamined, is the pointed use of the Indigenous in each of these texts—by white and black, male and female, northern and southern artists—as flat templates for loss and alterity. How do we apply Nixon's concept of the "environmentalism of the poor"—the latter an intentionally "compendious category" fracturing along "the multiple fault lines of ethnicity, gender, race, class, region, religion, and generation"—to a context in which deprivation is a state of mind and a rhetorical strategy as well as a real, felt experience within the broad textures of U.S. economic hierarchies?[12]

Most scholars have remained uncertain about how to suture the discourses of environmental and settler apocalypse in more than snapshot or episodic ways—that is, in "case studies" such as Katrina, which gave way to an eruption of critical and creative texts witnessing the entrenched vulnerabilities of black Americans in coastal communities. These include a surfeit of narrative nonfiction by Dave Eggers, Douglas Brinkley, Shari Fink, Dan Baum, Chris Rose, and Jed Horne; poetry by Natasha Trethewey; and fiction by James Lee Burke, Tom Piazza, and Jesmyn Ward, whose celebrated novel *Salvage the Bones* received the 2011 National Book Award for Fiction. Stories about the event have flooded other genres, including graphic novels, visual and plastic arts, and film. These narratives are, like Spike Lee's 2006 documentary *When the Levees Broke*, aimed at exposing the contingent failures of both New Orleans's levee system and a multigenerational legacy of governmental intervention and neglect that formed the twin engines of disaster for the ghettoized poor.

One of the most critically attended post-Katrina narratives, Benh Zeitlin's 2012 film *Beasts of the Southern Wild* offers an affecting story about a young African American girl and her flawed, ailing father struggling to maintain their detritus-ridden home in an island community called "The Bathtub," about to be deluged by an approaching hurricane. Most critics have interpreted Zeitlin's narrative, based on a stage play by Lucy Alibar, as a dramatization of the collision of "natural" disasters stoked by both gross governmental manipulation and neglect of the marginalized poor. Zeitlin's focus is on the heroic, even mythicized African American child. As Veronica Barnsley notes, the film's odd infusions of magical realism remind us that disasters inaugurate new narrative forms, and that art in particular "has a vital function in revealing and re-imagining, sometimes in contradictory ways, the crisis-driven reflexes of late capitalism" and "relies upon a familiarity with historical relations of displacement, colonization, and economic control that have contributed to environmental destruction."[13] As Barnsley further observes, the trope of the postcolonial child has become a recognizable feature of much postdisaster fiction, a handy device for knitting together the collisions of trauma, hope, vulnerability, and futurity demanded by our incessantly utilitarian cultural narratives. (Delia Owens's recent, arresting debut *Where the Crawdads Sing* functions similarly but with a young white heroine.) Even as the motley cast of the Bathtub presents a deliberately multiracial face—and the film's own creator is a white, Jewish man from Brooklyn—the film's telescopic elevation of the child protagonist, Hushpuppy, allows us to bracket the rude complexities of postsettler marginality, including the curiously underdiscussed fact that *Beasts'* location is based on the real Isle de Jean Charles, populated almost exclusively by the Biloxi-Chitimacha tribe who waged their own fruitless battles for recognition and levee protection.

Disaster narratives are obvious opportunities for artistic experimentation, but they can also be uncanny vehicles for depositing new mythologies and essentialisms in their wake. Perhaps more noteworthy are the many contemporary texts that lay bare the erosions of Anthropocenic time as influential but unseen elements of the everyday, their very obscurity a map of sorts to the tangle of postsettler exclusions and divisions. As Jay Watson suggests, "current efforts to rehabilitate nostalgia, utopia, apocalypticism, and other discourses of temporal alterity as bases for environmental activism and critique can guide southern studies scholars to a deeper consideration of which pasts to claim and which forms of change to interrogate or contest in the field's ongoing work of negotiating tradition"; he, too, calls upon Nixon's concept of "slow violence" as a revelatory framework for exposing the "unspectacular, incremental forms of micro- and macro-level harm that are often the broadest, bitterest legacy of hyperdevelopment, underdevelopment, warfare, and other modes of environmental injustice."[14] In these spaces, Watson suggests, southern studies scholars might best "extend and clarify Patricia Yaeger's call for closer attention to the quotidian forms of injury and exploitation that attend southern living in the register of 'the non-epic everyday.'"[15]

Indeed, while there is plenty of provocative new literary work to examine in what we might term a postapocalyptic southern imaginary—e.g., Cormac McCarthy's *The Road* and Jeff VanderMeer's *Southern Reach* trilogy—and rather more still in the wide net of southern-focused "ecological" or "environmental" writing by authors such as Wendell Berry, Janisse Ray, and Rick Bass, perhaps the least touched and most promising archive lies in the province of the quotidian or, at the very least, in works that filter ecological concerns through these thicker, contorting matrices of economic, racial, political, and cultural dynamics.[16] Ursula Heise knits together these vectors of inquiry, challenging us to ask, "What stories do we tell about the relationship between colonialism, the oppression of humans, and the endangerment of animals and plants? How do these stories respond to the theoretical questions and ethical dilemmas that arise in the confrontation with the immiseration of humans and nonhumans? What dimensions do they highlight, which ones do they hide, and why?"[17] Indeed, like the occluded Indians in *Beasts*, which features *do* they hide, and why?

Repeatedly, it seems, in a cultural moment intent on recovering deep pasts and lessons that predate and somehow endure Anthropocenic time with fantastical immunity, southern texts are often keen to hide the insupportable *absence* of such histories and alternatives. Writing before the current explosion of Anthropocene discourse, essayists such as Berry and Ray were already trafficking in unapologetic assumptions of autochthony. "I was born from people who were born from people who were born from people who were born here," Ray tells us at the start of her eco-autobiography, *Ecology of a Cracker Childhood* (1999): "The Crackers crossed the wide Altamaha into what had been Creek territory and settled the vast, fire-loving uplands of the coastal plains of southeast Georgia, surrounded by a singing forest of tall and widely spaced pines whose history they did not know, whose stories were untold. The memory of what they entered is scrawled on my bones, so that I carry the landscape inside like an ache. The story of who I am cannot be severed from the story of the flatwoods."[18] Ray's genealogical reiterations unravel here to both assert and undercut her family's long tenure in Baxley, Georgia; while the repetitions of being "born here" have a functional limit—that is, she does not pretend that the "Crackers" were actually Indigenous—she does posit a new narrative of beginnings (the Crackers were from nowhere remarkable before they were "here") over the Creeks' unremarkable finale. She loops back to and embellishes this origin story later, but the second delivery is just as neutral: the Creeks "ceded the land to Georgia," and that was that. "We have been here for a hundred and eighty years," she claims.[19] The first-person plural smartly elides the history of place with the imaginary deep time of the postsettler condition, one that is brilliantly painful and apparently inseverable.

Ray's smooth subsuming of the Creek narrative is not a hostile gesture; much to the contrary, she repeats an autochthonizing exercise that the Agrarians had perfected decades earlier, one in which the Indigenous erasure is a foregone conclusion and Native commemoration and kinship a matter of little question or debate. Throughout *I'll Take My Stand* (1930), the twelve southern eco-intellectuals in fact ally themselves with Native Americans as a group similarly victimized by the nation's material aggressions. Many style themselves explicitly as "natives," and the northern carpetbaggers as "invaders"; nearly all profess a nativist kinship with a preindustrial world and a commitment to preserving both a landscape and a culture under siege.[20] The twentieth-century southern literary "renaissance" emerged directly from this crisis of dislocation and alienation and continued its tradition of Indigenous appropriation: in works by writers such as Stark Young, Allen Tate, Eudora Welty, Caroline Gordon, and William Faulkner, Indians figured increasingly as noble allies whose humanist, anticommercial values opposed the industrial incursions and exploitation of southern resources and production.[21] More disturbing, the Indigenous ally has occasionally been styled to serve a white nationalist cause, most plainly in the counterfeit autobiography *The Education of Little Tree* (1976), in which Alabama segregationist Forrest "Asa" Carter reinvents himself as a Cherokee youth. The book charmed and fooled readers for nearly two decades, when it was discovered to be a hoax; but its reclassification as fiction did not prevent it from being read, taught, and celebrated for some time after. As Michael Marker suggests, the story's appeal—despite its fraudulent origins—lies in its ability "to provide simplistic answers to troubling and intricate questions."[22] To be sure, the crises of the Anthropocene have redoubled the allure of the Indian as a facile figure of salvation, one that might both deliver and redeem an ecologically minded and exploited rural South.

By now, the deployment of an Indigenous comrade in ecological straits—particularly among those writers such as Ray who bloom beside junkyards rather than on the front porches of neoplantations—seems ordinary and perhaps even logical. Thus, we are unlikely to find in contemporary nature writing the truly complex, challenging engagements with deep pasts and potential futurities demanded by southern colonial-capitalist ecologies. In his essay "A Native Hill," Wendell Berry briefly acknowledges the "painfully divided" condition of loving his Kentucky home despite the knowledge of awful settler colonial violence enabling his own "nativeness." He romanticizes the land's original inhabitants as exemplars of stewardship and spirituality—unreal beings incapable of defiling the sacred earth—thus stoking fictions that are ultimately as harmful as more plain racialism. Still, the strategy seems compulsory in the white southerner's efforts to "return home again" to ancestral lands overridden by both colonial and industrial advances. In the end, Berry views modern man as ruined by his failure to properly respect the earth as the Indians did. By destroying its abundance, settlers ensured that they would never truly possess it: "And so there is a sense in which *we are still not here*," he laments. "Surely there could be a more indigenous life than we have."[23] To be emphatically "here," as Ray insists via her own family's Athena-like eruption from the land, one would have to wrest "a more indigenous life"—an antidote to the affronts of modernity and the white southerner's own double consciousness, at once the victim and perpetrator of settler colonial histories.

And yet, these maneuvers have the odd effect of both sanitizing removal and sidestepping the chattel economy yoked to its execution.

The temptation to privilege Native American voices as vestiges of primordial keepers of the past and of the land would be to fundamentally misinterpret the lessons of colonial history and, also, to distract from the disturbing coil of Indigenous and plantation histories, where Indians were not always and simply victims. In cultural discourse more broadly, Indians' primitive belief systems are regularly summoned as the "placeless place," the absent "there where I am not" of modernity, and especially as a nourishing antidote to the instabilities bred by capitalism. Philosopher Scott Pratt, for instance, proposes that we view Native American thought "as a way to answer the problem of origin. By tracing the career of the central commitments of pragmatism beginning in Native American thought, through their use in resisting exclusion, racism, and sexism, to their emergence in the work of the classical pragmatists, these ways of understanding and acting in the world can become renewed resources."[24] Pratt is a philosopher, but his ecocritical metaphor here echoes what has become an emerging trend in discussions of the Anthropocene/Capitalocene, which often explicitly posit Indians as custodians of renewal, magically unbedeviled by all of the isms of modernity. At their most dangerously idealistic, such positions assert that, as Alan Trachtenberg once put it, paraphrasing a 1934 statement by Oglala Lakota chief Standing Bear, "America can be revived, rejuvenated, by recognizing a native school of thought. *The Indian can save America.*"[25]

The dense interweavings of Indigenous, African American, and white settler narratives in the South complicate this fantasy beyond legibility or recovery. Indeed, African Americans have claimed Indigenous genealogies as fervently, and sometimes fraudulently, as have their white neighbors and enemies. While the demographic of the "Black Indian" was born in the long history of the circum-Caribbean plantation complex, the merging of bloodlines often exceeds the biological or cultural.[26] In Patrick Minges's curation of numerous Works Progress Administration interviews with former slaves, African Native heritage and kinship is frequently asserted.[27] Even as recently as 2000, African American scholar Willard Johnson attests, "the majority of African American families I know, or that I have come into contact with and have worked with, claim to have an Indian connection. A majority, by far." Johnson cites scholarship suggesting that two-thirds to three-quarters of black Americans have "some Native blood tie." Few African Americans acknowledge that this mixture is a by-product of slavery and of blacks serving as chattel for Indian masters. These connections are often untraceable and "fuzzy," or wholly invented and romanticized, and for an important reason: "The only forty acres blacks ever got came from the Indians."[28] The bequest is spiritual rather than material: the postemancipated black worker might thus reclaim tenancy within poisoned landscapes and economies that effected what Orlando Patterson, Frank Wilderson, and others have deemed the slave's permanent "social death."

In the evictions and extinctions of coiled southern and Anthropocenic histories, these are, finally, generative moves rather than appropriative ones. In the closing lines to her poem "News from the Imaginary Front," Alabama Creek poet Janet McAdams encourages a forthright plundering of history for the ways that even its most terrible legacies might nourish the present: "I'm licking salt from the long wound of history," she writes. "The blood is sweet and my mouth's full of it. / I'm milking this body for everything it's worth."[29] The image is consonant with much of McAdams's poetry, in which she corporealizes the concept of Indigenous and southern histories—her purposefully, inextricably intertwined landscapes—and creates in the process an almost eroticized relationship to the ravages of history. It is a curious kind of magnetism, she avers, that draws the contemporary subject toward the source of trauma; the collision is a conscious, hungry devouring and recycling of history into image and expression. She revisits the concept of history's generative wound in "Dreaming, the Book of," published in her collection *Feral* (2007), where her speaker imagines "the dream where water calls to water / tugging the body toward / lake river ocean / the salt water that will scrub a wound from its history."[30] Here, the human body and the body of water—any body of water—are indistinguishable and intimate, communicative. The earlier poem's sweet salt *extracted* from the wound here returns to it, mutated into the very agent of cleansing. But what does it mean to "scrub a wound from its history"? The grammar inverts our expectation—normally, we would "scrub history from its wound" in the way that the earlier speaker "lick[ed] salt from the long wound of history," but here physical contact seems to actively reinflict the wound even as it satisfies the speaker. Indeed, the process is as rich with desire as it was in the earlier poem: "Skin / in love with water / will crease and fold to drink in more, / each cell opening / its dry, dry throat." The human body, depleted, craves contact with the natural resources and the histories suppressed within it—one composite body, slaked and haunted.

The rest of *Feral* reinforces this theme with staggering density and nuance. Taken together, the collection's poems echo one another across vast geographies and temporalities, converging repeatedly on the porous interface between the human and the wild. In "Polar Journeys," a poem about Arctic exploration and whaling, her alienated, unhomely speaker wonders, "Which of us knows his body anymore?" The proclivity for measuring and knowing has been cathected onto the sextants and "foolish" instruments that catalog the unfathomable world. "This is history," the poem concludes, "that every world grows smaller."[31] Known, circumscribed, gutted—"history" is a gigantic container for the iterative operations of assault, seizure, and undoing in the name of discovery (another layered operative for the confiscations of land and liberty that signify settler modernity), and it is the thing that paradoxically collapses distinctions between the world and the body. "Knowing" the body thus depends vitally for McAdams on navigating the textures of the world and of history in all their tangled, painful guises. Her poems are constantly attuned to the slender margins that separate bodies from environments: "Skin / the poorest fence between the cold world and my body," one speaker muses.[32] An insistent question posed variously throughout is "What if the world came back? / Even in miniature or scarred." What if, indeed—and what world would it be, after all? It wouldn't matter, she suggests, so long as it were "strong enough" to remove the barriers between self and planet, "to sweep the dust from stone, / uncover bone or story. / What if your stone heart turned to salt? / What if it turned to water / and roared through your body like an ocean?"[33]

Two seemingly opposed motifs appear twinned throughout McAdams's work: the desiccation of bodies ruined and buried by imperial processes, and the flowing water of oceans and rivers that mimics and restores humanity's lifeblood. Of the two, the latter is decidedly the more sanguine model for recuperation; indeed McAdams's frequent turn to oceanic horizons anticipates a broader movement within American studies, where scholars are now urging a "decontinentalization" of U.S. space that would invert the hierarchical maps of hemisphere and rim, mainland and island, and earth and ocean in order to mobilize instead an "archipelagic" imaginary that is not peripheral but in fact central to America's self-conception. In their introduction to the seminal *Archipelagic American Studies* (2017), Brian Russell Roberts and Michelle Ann Stephens call for a new praxis centered on a broader geography of islands, shorelines, coasts, and oceanic currents—a wider, relational conception of American space constituting an "archipelagic nissology," guided by "such notions as the anti-explorer, the infinite island, the insular-real, the mise en abyme, and the catachrestic."³⁴ Such a methodology promises to upend the continental bias of much American studies scholarship: privileging alternative, often Indigenous knowledge systems that reject positivist, Euclidean, and hierarchical laws in favor of the untidy, the uncanny, and the unknowable. While the micrologic and ur-regionalism of the archipelagic turn may threaten to reverse what Wai Chee Dimock and others have termed the "planetary" scales of much new Americanist scholarship, Roberts and Stephens suggest again that a generative dialectic between seeming counterimpulses might emerge, and Paul Giles likewise suggests that such approaches may be accretive rather than displacing.³⁵

The influence of the archipelagic on southern literary critical thought is not necessarily new; it is, to be sure, disruptive in all the right ways, providing reminders of the Atlantic slave trade that ripple the smooth promise of Indigenous alterity. The postcolonial poetics of Antonio Benítez-Rojo and Édouard Glissant were in fact fundamental to much of the New Southern Studies' engagement with circum-Caribbean histories; reciprocally, Glissant's *Faulkner, Mississippi* (2000) affirmed the unseen continuities between the fractal, untidy logic of the island and the dark knowledge embedded in southern plantation sites. The basis for much of southern studies' own global and transatlantic turns hinged on deepening knowledge of the southern slaveholders' pivotal role in a triangular economy that ran from the Deep South to the Caribbean and yoked together human chattel and global capital. As Martyn Bone puts it, "The centrality of slave labor to both the South's earlier 'globality' and the development of its own more local economy and identity can hardly be understated."³⁶ And yet, the region's plantation economy is precisely what compelled its formation as a region and cemented its idiosyncratic position as a closed society, prompting the compulsory exodus of its Indigenous populations and the xenophobic nationalism that discouraged new immigration.³⁷ Most compelling for southern studies, perhaps, would be the intercessions of the nissological "precisely when one encounters the unknowable and the unfamiliar, that is, phenomena in the Real, that uncanny Lacanian space of a reality that cannot be measured and has not been integrated into the symbolic orders of language and knowledge"—giving birth, perhaps, to a more freshly realized, embodied "Real" beyond the South's typical, deceptive coordinates.³⁸

To be sure, a sturdy application of such reorientations—ocean and land, island and mainland, slave and Indigenous—would reveal the field's own self-deceptions: rather than a celebratory, carnivalesque unshackling of the South's perversions, we would instead confront and interrogate the material logic by which such fantasies originate and persist. The logic of the archipelago thus encompasses, for southern writers, a seductive contagion: the vital promise of insurgency and community metered by the brutal consequences of such movement and connectedness. In McAdams's poetry, then, oceans and islands are often the province of dreams and desires rather than sustainable futures. What lingers and haunts are the skeletal remains of history and of people torn viscerally from the umbilicus of earth; in the final stanzas of *Feral*'s closing poem, her speaker mourns, "The land they took us from, the mothers' milk dried up, / every womb a dried-up / crackle of flesh. Earth my body / is trying to remember." The sour "milk" of history's wound from her earlier work is all that is left to the suckling orphan, the Indigenous exile from a long-forgotten earth. The compressed grammar here collapses "Earth" and "my body" so that they are not simply estranged—the body "trying to remember" its earth—but rather linked: "Earth" and "my body" enjambed in appositivistic alignment, sutured together and trying to remember. But what, exactly? That is always the haunting question in McAdams's poetry and throughout so much southern and Indigenous literature: When the coiled operations of colonial capitalism hammer bodies from their homeplaces, what memories are left to return to? McAdams refuses to indulge the easy vision quests of much Indigenous literature, which often stake a proprietary claim on both transcendent pasts and meteoric futures in unmapped terrains of alterity. To the barren womb (and wound) of her people's history, she advises, "Child-That-Was, don't try to remember, but lean back / into this place outside history," an admittedly mythical place where "we / were more than meat, more / than a handful of carbon. // We were cell and stone and field, the sky: / Stars pulled down from their wandering."[39]

McAdams's poetry habitually toes this fragile line between exorcising history and dwelling forthrightly within it. It is a haunted in-betweenness that typifies advanced modernity and, importantly, not simply for Indians—who are rarely catalogued as such in her work—but for her motley casts of "wandering" survivors. In the aptly named "Ghost Ranch," the penultimate poem in *Feral*, she prepares us for that excursus "outside history" by sending her speaker and a presumed lover on a hike: "Land for miles and miles— / so much land. You find a pile of bones // and hold the pelvis up to frame a ragged disc / of sky. Not the real sky, I thought that day, / but blue enough to tell this story." As the final poem will tell us, these once-children know autonomically that their origins are celestial, but the immense earth and its exhumed casualties proffer only a sublime, partial glimpse of alternative pasts. None of it is real, she reminds us, and all of it is simply story. But what is "this" story in particular? The poem brilliantly elides a parable of postsettler exhumation, an unburying of brutal remainders, and a private drama between the hiking couple who struggled for intimacy after some unspoken rift:

> We touch and circle and touch and circle
> until we only circle: cloth against cloth, skin
> not quite meeting, the way fences touch at the corners
> of nations. Last night you slept so quietly,
> I put a hand to your back to make sure
> you were breathing, the other over your shoulder
> and flat against the skin between nipple
> and solar plexus: because breath may not be
> a sure enough measure. We hover
> over the animal that carved itself
> this place to rest, past molecule, atom,
> the stinging energy that drums the universe
> into being. Don't say you never felt it.
> Even the stone was pulsing. Take my hand
> if you can bear it, but let the other story go.

The wounded, lost children in so many works of southern literature become wounded, lost adults who strain to connect. The project of escaping modernity's profound isolations is a compound task, sited simultaneously in bedrooms and in vast landscapes: the "pulsing" energy of the entombed past, the disinterred "animal" that closes in on the human drama—here, now, in "this place." McAdams's speaker issues a challenge to the dumb insensibility of modern actors—"Don't say you never felt it"—even as she knows that the "other story" needs to be settled and silenced before peace will reign.

It turns out, over and over again, that living "outside history" really means inhabiting it with an intrepid poise between immersion and immunity—between devouring and abstaining. Quietly managing the difficult embodiments of the contemporary quotidian. McAdams's is a powerful voice in the new work of the southern Anthropocene because its reach is inestimably vast, almost overwhelmingly so, explicitly transcending regional and racial experiences while allowing for their unexorcisable residence in our bodies. She might well be consciously toying with philosopher Quentin Meillassoux's paradigmatic concept of the "arche-fossil," which suggests "the existence of an ancestral reality or event; one that is anterior to terrestrial life."[40] But McAdams would urge us to recognize, as have Bruno Latour and Elizabeth Povinelli, the final inextricability of nature from culture, of the object from the human, the human from the animal—the fossil from the hand. As Povinelli suggests, "On the one hand, the fossil seems to be composed of something before what the hand is composed of and able to endure beyond the hand's span of life and all human hands' lifespans. On the other hand, the fossil is nowhere but there in the hand. It is not in a different time, nor is it enduring over time. It is changing as it moves across material and discursive substrates. *There is no difference between the fossil and the hand* unless we abstract each out of the ongoingness of their material becoming."[41] Like Povinelli, McAdams tunes her poetry to an awareness of this dynamism, a constant state of "material becoming," that allows—indeed requires—Indigenous survival above and beyond traditional, delimited, exclusionary vocabularies of loss.

A startling new panorama of difficult contingencies and fraught endurance would emerge, I think, if we began to read southern writers who similarly reorient us in the wake of natural disasters and excavations, intent on witnessing the long endurance of the human and the wild twined together in the resting places they "choose."[42] Such new works thrum with energy and agency in ways that suggest optimism beyond the usual guises of activism. As Florida author Karen Russell puts it, writing about her choice of a remote Irish island as the setting for a story that could well be about her native Everglades, poised perpetually on the brink of encounter and apocalypse: "Here is an island where the raised bogs are threatened by industrial harvesters, where nobody quite remembers the old stories. . . . But the landscape itself still retains this oneiric power, and a humming autonomy—that's the sublimity of places like swamps and bogs, I think, and also of mountains and ocean trenches, landscapes that resize you, landscapes that are uncanny reminders of the brevity of a human lifespan and the vastness of geologic time."[43] Russell's writing navigates this immensity via the snapshots of humanity cresting the rim of the iceberg, as it were, in a relentlessly weird fictional world peopled by lost and searching tribes that exist just out of view of mainstream culture. Throughout, her fiction haunts the fluid borders between life and death, history and the present, fantasy and reality, island and mainland, human and animal. Her protagonists are, once again, often young people navigating uncharted terrain or spectral encounters, usually without adult supervision—a viewpoint that contributes to her stories' uncanny wonder. But while these narrative perspectives are disarmingly smart and frequently comic, the settings and journeys they survey are the real subject of the fiction: "oneiric" spaces with deep histories and "autonomy," bequeathing lessons as old and as vast as the earth itself, that repeatedly ask, *What does it mean to be human?*

For Russell and others, the answers are elusive: they involve searches for memory and truth across immense landscapes of time, geography, and cultures, and more often than not, they testify to the failures of such quests under the tyranny of the suffocating present. Yet her characters remain haunted by their desires and stubbornly refuse to admit defeat. Often, they inhabit island or coastal communities where oceans and swamps guard tantalizing, freshly wounding mysteries. And always, they are yearning to connect more deeply and failing to do so, adrift at the edges of histories that have literally blown them apart. Nowhere is this phenomenon more achingly demonstrated than in her debut novel, *Swamplandia!*, short-listed for the Pulitzer Prize in 2012, about a family who, in the unapologetic guise of fake Indians, runs a decaying alligator-wrestling theme park in the Florida Everglades. The tribe is falling apart—the mother lost to cancer; the father moonlighting at a casino to earn money; one daughter dating and attempting to elope with ghosts; a brother defected to the mainland and their encroaching competitor, the mega-theme park World of Darkness; and the final, youngest daughter, our ingenuous narrator, raped by a mysterious Bird Man who dupes her with his quasi-Indigenous wisdom and takes advantage of her desperate desire for human contact. The Everglades, close to Russell's own native Miami, offer just the right space for this microcosmic drama—a swampy pocket of national history that might otherwise be forgotten to mainstream culture. Often deemed America's last frontier, wild and untouched well after the closing of the western front, the Everglades is now a "tattered battlefield": half is "gone"; the other half "is an ecological mess."[44] Russell once told an interviewer that "this book grew out of my sense that I had arrived a little late for the party, that a few generations ago . . . the Everglades was a wonderland. I grew up in a time when there was an increased consciousness of phosphor solution and development . . . [a] reckoning with the past twenty years of development and its consequences. So I think it must always be the case that you are in the shadow of an Eden that was more spectacular than your own."[45]

What better tour of the Anthropocene and its fictions than these fantastical, sobering dives into the Edenic regional fantasies that always, at bottom, conceal a knotty web of colonial-capitalist processes underwriting and undermining the South's Child-That-Was and the pastoral-that-was-not. As North Carolina Cherokee poet MariJo Moore puts it in a poem about her Appalachian home, "Memories unfold from around these / glorious ancestral mountains / . . . close enough to smell / but not close enough to touch / just close enough to taste / but never close enough to touch."[46] Barely interred histories somehow become intangible—simultaneously present and absent and pleading for nuanced reconstitution. In Virginia writer Belle Boggs's masterful collection of short stories *Mattaponi Queen* (2010), winner of the prestigious Bread Loaf Writers' Conference Bakeless Prize, we find ourselves in just this kind of watershed: somewhere between the Mattaponi Indian reservation and the Mattaponi River itself—formed by the mingling of three separate streams—Boggs's stories enact the fluid, turbulent cohesion of the red, black, and white communities that have long lived together in rural Virginia. Her vision is neither Romantic nor apocalyptic but simply and palpably keen to circumvent the easy, fossilized narratives about race and region that we think we know.

The collection's opening vignette sets out the challenge—a call to arms for both southern writers and its critics, facing down the challenges of Anthropocenic time in a haunted geography of stupendous, striated loss. An art teacher has composed objects for a still life assignment, all items unearthed from her own backyard: "A beautiful little hand-blown glass bottle, an arrowhead, a Confederate belt buckle, a bone toothbrush without any bristles. How did you find those things anyway? her husband wanted to know. I dug around a little, she said, remembering descending the sloping sides into the hole's cooler air, brushing away the layers and layers of leaves and scraping the damp clay walls with her fingers. Next time you'll likely find a copperhead, he said."[47] Preserved by "layers and layers" of the earth's debris are reminders of the region's abutments—a Confederate artifact and a Native weapon entombed coevally. It is, finally, the artist's task to brave the snakes and reassemble the remains, which, placed just above the heating vents in the classroom, "bend and waver in the warm, billowing air . . . mysterious and wavering and fragile-looking."[48] So much opportunity for representation and misrepresentation, so much mystery and fragility and warped ways of looking and knowing. But today's finest southern writers continue to dig and deliver—to, as Janet McAdams urges, "let that other story go" and compose brave new worlds from the inexhaustible, inestimably old.

NOTES

1. Zackary Vernon, "The Anthropocene and the Future of Southern Studies," in "Emerging Scholars Roundtable," ed. Zackary Vernon et al., special issue, *Mississippi Quarterly* 68, nos. 1-2 (Winter/Spring 2015): 5-57, 32-34.

2. William Faulkner is well known to most scholars in and out of southern studies; Ellen Glasgow, a newer addition to the canon, wrote over twenty influential, early feminist novels as well as short stories attuned to the domestic, racial, and ecological crises of the postplantation South, such as *Barren Ground* (1925) and *This Is Our Life* (1941; winner of the Pulitzer Prize for the Novel in 1942).

3. Jon Smith, "Response to Emerging Scholars Roundtable," *Mississippi Quarterly* 68, nos. 1-2 (Winter/Spring 2015): 46.

4. Marilou Awiakta, *Selu: Seeking the Corn-Mother's Wisdom* (Golden, Colo.: Fulcrum, 1993), 43.

5. Kathryn Yusoff, *A Billion Black Anthropocenes or None* (Minneapolis: University of Minnesota Press, 2018), xiii.

6. Jon Smith, *Finding Purple America: The South and the Future of American Cultural Studies* (Athens: University of Georgia Press, 2013).

7. Collectively known as the Twelve Southerners, the Vanderbilt Agrarians collaborated on a collection of essays: Twelve Southerners, *I'll Take My Stand: The South and the Agrarian Tradition* (1930; repr., Baton Rouge: Louisiana State University Press, 1977).

8. David Shane Lowry, "AGU: My concern with the Anthropocene," February 8, 2018, https://anthrodendum.org/2018/02/08/agu-my-concern-with-the-anthropocene, accessed December 12, 2020. See, for example, C. Vann Woodward, "The Irony of Southern History," *Journal of Southern History* 19, no. 1 (February 1953): 3-19

9. Wolfe and Wilderson quoted in Iyko Day, "Being or Nothingness: Indigeneity, Antiblackness, and Settler Colonial Critique," *Critical Ethnic Studies* 1, no. 2 (Fall 2015): 102.

10. Christopher Lloyd, "Creaturely, Throwaway Life after Katrina: *Salvage the Bones* and *Beasts of the Southern Wild*," *South* 48, no. 2 (Spring 2016): 246-64, 247.

11. Daniel Spoth, "Slow Violence and the (Post)Southern Disaster Narrative in Hurston, Faulkner, and *Beasts of the Southern Wild*," *Mississippi Quarterly* 68, nos. 1-2 (Winter-Spring 2015): 145-66.

12. Rob Nixon, *Slow Violence and the Environmentalism of the Poor* (Cambridge, Mass.: Harvard University Press, 2011), 4.

13. Veronica Barnsley, "The Postcolonial Child in Benh Zeitlin's *Beasts of the Southern Wild*," *Journal of Commonwealth Literature* 51, no. 2 (June 2016): 240-55; quote on 242.

14. Jay Watson, "The Other Matter of the South," *PMLA* 131, no. 1 (January 2016): 159. See Lawrence Buell, *The Environmental Imagination: Thoreau, Nature Writing, and the Formation of American Culture* (Cambridge, Mass.: Harvard University Press, 1996), 280–309; and Rob Nixon, *Slow Violence*.

15. Watson, "Other Matter," 159.

16. See, e.g., Wendell Berry's eight novels and more than fifty short stories based in his fictional Port William, Kentucky, as well as his ecologically minded poems and essays such as those collected in *Home Economics* (San Francisco: North Point, 1987) and *The Art of the Commonplace* (Berkeley, Calif.: Counterpoint, 2002); Janisse Ray, *Ecology of a Cracker Childhood* (Minneapolis: University of Minnesota Press, 1999); and Rick Bass's numerous works of fiction and nonfiction including *All the Land That Holds Us* (New York: Houghton Mifflin Harcourt, 2013).

17. Ursula Heise, *Imagining Extinction: The Cultural Meanings of Endangered Species* (Chicago: University of Chicago Press, 2016), 166.

18. Ray, *Ecology of a Cracker Childhood*, 4.

19. Ray, 83.

20. John Crowe Ransom, "Reconstructed but Unregenerate," and Herman Clarence Nixon, "Whither Southern Economy?," both in Twelve Southerners, *I'll Take My Stand*, 23, 193.

21. See Young's best-selling 1934 novel, *So Red the Rose*, which was adapted into a Hollywood film the following year; Lytle's *At the Moon's Inn* (1941) and *Alchemy* (1942) (Young and Lytle were also members of the Vanderbilt Agrarian group that collaborated on *I'll Take My Stand*); Gordon's frontier fiction, such as "The Captive" (1941) and *Green Centuries* (1941); and Faulkner's so-called "Indian stories," written mostly in the 1930s—"Red Leaves" (1930), "A Justice" (1931), "Lo!" (1934), "Mountain Victory" (1932), "A Bear Hunt" (1934), and "A Courtship" (1948)—as well as *Go Down, Moses* (1942), the ex post facto appendix to *The Sound and the Fury* (written in 1945 on the occasion of Malcolm Cowley's compilation of *The Portable Faulkner*), *Requiem for a Nun* (1951), and a 1954 essay, "Mississippi."

22. Michael Marker, "The Education of Little Tree: What It Really Reveals about the Public Schools," *Phi Delta Kappan* 74, no. 3 (November 1992): 226–27.

23. Wendell Berry, "A Native Hill," *Hudson Review* 21, no. 4 (Winter 1968–69): 628; emphasis added.

24. Scott L. Pratt, *Native Pragmatism: Rethinking the Roots of American Philosophy* (Bloomington: Indiana University Press, 2002), 9.

25. Alan Trachtenberg, *Shades of Hiawatha: Staging Indians, Making Americans, 1880–1930* (New York: Hill and Wang, 2004), 307; emphasis added. Trachtenberg is invoking a 1934 text by Oglala Lakota chief Standing Bear.

26. The history of slavery among southeastern Native American tribes and individuals is relatively new but voluminous. The most recent and influential works include Robbie Ethridge and Sheri M. Shuck-Hall, eds., *Mapping the Mississippian Shatter Zone: The Colonial Indian Slave Trade and Regional Instability in the American South* (Lincoln: University of Nebraska Press, 2009); Barbara Krauthamer, *Black Slaves, Indian Masters: Slavery, Emancipation, and Citizenship in the Native American South* (Chapel Hill: University of North Carolina Press, 2013); Tiya Miles, *Ties That Bind: The Story of an Afro-Cherokee Family in Slavery and Freedom* (Berkeley:

University of California Press, 2016); Tiya Miles, *The House on Diamond Hill: A Cherokee Plantation Story* (Chapel Hill: University of North Carolina Press, 2010); Celia Naylor, *African Cherokees in Indian Territory: From Chattel to Citizens* (Chapel Hill: University of North Carolina Press, 2008); Claudio Saunt, *Black, White, and Indian: Race and the Unmaking of an American Family* (New York: Oxford University Press, 2005); and Christina Snyder, *Slavery in Indian Country: The Changing Face of Captivity in Early America* (Cambridge, Mass.: Harvard University Press, 2010).

27. Patrick Minges, ed., *Black Indian Slave Narratives* (Winston-Salem, N.C.: John F. Blair, 2004).

28. Wilma Mankiller, Willard R. Johnson, Daniel F. Littlefield Jr., Patrick Minges, Deborah Tucker, and David Wilkins, "Exploring the Legacy and Future of Black/Indian Relations" (breakout discussion, National Congress of American Indians 57th Annual Session, St. Paul, Minn., November 14, 2000), http://web.mit.edu/wjohnson/www/kiaanafh/NCAI_pdf_Transcript.pdf.

29. Janet McAdams, "News from the Imaginary Front," in *The Island of Lost Luggage* (Tucson: University of Arizona Press, 2000), 14.

30. Janet McAdams, "Dreaming, the Book of," in *Feral* (Cambridge, UK: Salt, 2007), 47.

31. Janet McAdams, "Polar Journeys," in *Feral*, 16–17.

32. Janet McAdams, "Ghazal of the Body," in *Feral*, 49.

33. Janet McAdams, "The Way the World Comes Back," in *Feral*, 52.

34. Brian Russell Roberts and Michelle Ann Stephens, eds., *Archipelagic American Studies* (Durham, N.C.: Duke University Press, 2017), 19.

35. Paul Giles, afterword to Roberts and Stephens, *Archipelagic American Studies*, 427–35.

36. Martyn Bone, *Where the New World Is: Literature about the U.S. South at Global Scales* (Athens: University of Georgia Press, 2018), 4.

37. Bone, 4–5.

38. Bone, 24.

39. Janet McAdams, "Earth My Body Is Trying to Remember," in *Feral*, 76.

40. Quentin Meillassoux, *After Finitude: An Essay on the Necessity of Contingency* (London: Bloomsbury Books, 2008), 5.

41. Elizabeth A. Povinelli, "An Interview with Elizabeth Povinelli: Geontopower, Biopolitics and the Anthropocene," interview by Mathew Coleman and Kathryn Yusoff, in "Geosocial Formations and the Anthropocene," special issue, *Theory, Culture and Society* 34, no. 2–3 (May 2017): 169–85; quotes on 177–78, 182.

42. See, e.g., work by other Indigenous poets such as Karenne Wood (Virginia Monacan), MariJo Moore (North Carolina Cherokee), and Alison Adelle Hedge-Coke (mixed heritage, including southeastern Cherokee, Huron, and Metis); and fiction by African American and Cherokee author Alice Walker.

43. Willing Davidson, "This Week in Fiction: Karen Russell on Balancing Humor and Horror," *New Yorker*, June 13, 2016, http://www.newyorker.com/books/page-turner/fiction-this-week-karen-russell-2016-06-20.

44. Michael Grunwald, *The Swamp: The Everglades, Florida, and the Politics of Paradise* (New York: Simon and Schuster, 2007), 3–6.

45. Karen Russell, "Karen Russell on *Swamplandia!*," interview by Nicole Rudick,

Daily (blog), *Paris Review*, February 3, 2011, https://www.theparisreview.org/blog/2011/02/03/karen-russell-on-swamplandia.

46. MariJo Moore, "In These Mountains," in *The People Who Stayed: Southeastern Indian Writing after Removal*, ed. Geary Hobson, Janet McAdams, and Kathryn Walkiewicz (Norman: University of Oklahoma Press, 2010), 177.

47. Belle Boggs, *Mattaponi Queen* (Minneapolis: Graywolf, 2010), 5.

48. Boggs, 6.

THE WRECKING CREW

Willie Morris, Larry L. King, Marshall Frady, and the Southern Turn in American Literary Journalism

JOHN GRAMMER

ON MARCH 1, 1971, Willie Morris, editor in chief of *Harper's Magazine*, wrote the magazine's owner, John Cowles Jr., to offer his resignation. It was a bluff; he merely wanted Cowles to stop second-guessing editorial decisions and pinching pennies. He was reasonably sure the offer wouldn't be accepted. True, the two men had often disagreed about the direction of the magazine, and true, they could hardly have been more different personally: the hard-drinking, risk-taking editor from Mississippi and the cautious, buttoned-up publishing heir from Minnesota. But Morris knew, and assumed Cowles knew, that in his four years as editor he had transformed *Harper's* from one of the dullest publications in the country into what Norman Mailer called "the most adventurous of all magazines."[1] What Morris had accomplished was remarkable. *Harper's* on his watch had published the first excerpt of William Styron's *The Confessions of Nat Turner*; it had devoted nearly an entire issue to Mailer's "On the Steps of the Pentagon," which in book form became *The Armies of the Night*, one of the most acclaimed nonfiction works of the twentieth century. Morris had published Seymour Hersh's devastating exposé of the My Lai massacre in Vietnam and portions of David Halberstam's *The Best and the*

Brightest. By 1971, as associate editor Midge Decter recalled later, *Harper's* was "a hot book," the kind of magazine "to which already established writers are pleased to contribute and which . . . has the power to confer success on the as-yet unknown."[2] The critic Louis Menand recalls that he and his roommate at the time, intellectually pretentious "eighteen-year-old experts on life," found *Harper's* such a repository of transgressive cool that they spent their last pennies on the March 1971 issue so they could read Mailer's "A Prisoner of Sex."[3] A hot book indeed; no wonder Morris thought the magazine's owner would meet him halfway.

Thus it came as a shock to him when, returning to the office the next day, he was greeted by a secretary expressing regret at his imminent departure. Cowles had accepted his resignation, and one of the most remarkable interludes in American magazine journalism came to an abrupt end. At the heart of it, as I will argue here, was a significant chapter in the intellectual and literary history of the South.

That is not merely because Morris was a southerner, raised in Yazoo City, Mississippi, or because he actively solicited work from the most distinguished southern writers of the time: under his editorship it was a rare issue that didn't contain something by Styron, or Walker Percy, or Robert Penn Warren, or any of several other anthology-worthy southerners: Arna Bontemps, James Dickey, Elizabeth Hardwick, Albert Murray, C. Vann Woodward. Nor was it simply that his bullpen of regular writers—"Morris's Wrecking Crew," as Cowles called them, not affectionately—was dominated by brash, talented young southerners of his own generation, especially Larry L. King and Marshall Frady. It was that Morris and his most important contributors, in the pages of *Harper's* and elsewhere, significantly extended and revised the literary tradition of their region. Marrying the techniques of fiction to the form of carefully reported journalism, they tried to make the literary resources of the South respond to the moral challenge of the civil rights movement.

Such ambition was not unreasonable for Morris, whose literary career to date had been nothing less than stunning. As fellow editor Norman Podhoretz noted, Morris's talent and ambition had "carried him from Yazoo City to the 'red-hot center' of the New York literary world in record time"—with brief stops at the University of Texas (where he won national fame as the crusading editor of the college paper), Oxford University (for a Rhodes Scholarship), and the *Texas Observer*, a tiny but influential liberal weekly.[4] He came to New York as the heir apparent to *Harper's* editor John Fischer in 1963 and became editor in chief—the youngest in the magazine's long history—in 1967, the same year he published his first book, the highly praised memoir *North Toward Home*. In 1971 he was at the peak of his fame and influence.

Neither Larry L. King nor Marshall Frady claimed quite such an impressive résumé. Born in tiny Putnam, Texas, and educated at Texas Tech, King had come up through a series of small-town papers in his region, published a novel (*The One-Eyed Man*, 1966), and worked for a couple of Texas congressmen in Washington before becoming one of Morris's most consistent contributors. Frady was from Augusta, Georgia, the son of a Baptist preacher. After graduating from Furman University, he went to work at *Newsweek* and wrote a classic book about Alabama governor George Wallace, all before publishing his first article in *Harper's* in 1969. But they and Morris had more in common than just southern birth. Born within a decade of one another, all had begun their working lives as reporters in Georgia, Mississippi, and Texas. They were all aware of the distinguished literary tradition they inherited as southerners, and like many bookish southerners of their generation, they all wanted to write novels. Reading Faulkner, as Frady remarked, is "an experience that a lot of Southern boys spend their lives trying to recover from."[5] But, though two of the three did manage to publish novels, Morris, Frady, and King all did their best work, and made their strongest claims on literary stature, as journalists, with feature-length or book-length reported pieces. All three writers might have confessed, as Frady did in so many words, to being "forestalled, unbegotten novelist[s] left with journalism to do it all in."[6]

But they were doing it, fortuitously, at a time when journalism was being practiced at an unprecedentedly high level, by some accounts challenging the novel's supremacy as a literary form. Since the early 1960s, in magazines such as *Esquire*, the *New Yorker*, and *New York*, writers such as Jimmy Breslin, Hunter Thompson, Gay Talese, Joan Didion, and Terry Southern had been writing features that read almost like short stories. The enterprise came to be called the New Journalism, the title another practitioner, Tom Wolfe, gave to a 1973 anthology of this writing. He defined it as simply "accurate non-fiction with techniques usually associated with novels and short stories"—specifically "scene-by-scene construction, point of view, dialogue, and the detailing of status life." The first was most important, because for New Journalists "the basic reporting unit is no longer the datum, the piece of information, but the scene, since most of the sophisticated strategies of prose depend upon scene."[7]

The New Journalists' original purpose, Wolfe claimed, was merely to transcend the boredom of most magazine writing, whose tone was that of "a radio announcer at a tennis match."[8] None of them meant their improvised, bastard form to "wipe out the novel as literature's main event," but according to Wolfe, it had done just that.[9]

One last aspect of New Journalism deserves mention: its habit of accounting for itself in terms of the failure of some other kind of reporting. Wolfe's own first effort in the new form came when, hopelessly blocked and up against *Esquire*'s deadline for a story about a car show, he gave up and submitted his notes to the mercies of a rewrite man. Instead they were published verbatim as "There Goes (Varoom! Varoom!) That Kandy-Kolored (Thphhhhhh!) Tangerine-Flake Streamline Baby (Rahghhh!) Around the Bend (Brummmmmmmmmmmmmmm . . .)."[10] Hunter Thompson had a similar experience when *Sports Illustrated* sent him to Las Vegas to cover a dune-buggy race. When the dune buggies disappeared into a cloud of sand within a few seconds of the starting gun, Thompson was left with his expense account, rented convertible, and drug stash but nothing to cover; the result, of course, was the classic *Fear and Loathing in Las Vegas*. Possibly the most famous example is Gay Talese's attempted profile of Frank Sinatra for *Esquire*. His subject, grumpy and under the weather, kept refusing to be interviewed, so Talese narrated his own frustration and produced another classic, "Frank Sinatra Has a Cold." All of them had their version of Michael Herr's recognition, recorded in his Vietnam book, *Dispatches*: "Conventional journalism could no more reveal this war than conventional firepower could win it."[11]

Morris, Frady, and King shared a number of literary characteristics with the New Journalists Wolfe canonized in his 1973 anthology—Talese, Thompson, Herr, Didion, and others. The best Wrecking Crew writing was boldly novelistic, relying on dialogue more than exposition, patiently constructing scenes to reveal character, experimenting with point of view. Like Wolfe and his fellows, they showed no sign of wanting to start a literary revolution; they seem to have evolved their method haphazardly. But what was the precipitating failure—the equivalent of Frank Sinatra's cold—that sent them down their experimental path, away from both fiction and conventional journalism? I suspect the answer begins with one shared biographical circumstance, one that all three wrote about in detail. This was their exposure, as young reporters, to what Frady called "the Damascus Road event in more lives than mine": the civil rights movement in the South.[12]

In 1954 King was covering sports and general news for the Odessa, Texas, *American*, when he learned that a black army veteran planned to enroll in the local junior college. "Willie Byrd," as King calls him in his memoir, *Confessions of a White Racist*, knew that the recent decision by "the big court" gave him the right to enroll and assumed his white neighbors would be "level-headed" and obey the law.[13] But when King's article made the front page, the local police began harassing Byrd relentlessly, repeatedly arresting him on doubtful charges, finally including attempted rape. King followed up for a time, but at last his editors told him they wanted no more articles about Byrd's troubles. By this time neither did Byrd, who abandoned his plans and left town. King wasn't far behind him, heading to Washington for a job on a congressman's staff. When he reentered journalism ten years later, he began by sending a long, novelistic piece about Texas politics to Morris at *Harper's*.

At about the same time that King met Byrd, young Willie Morris was editorializing in the student newspaper at the University of Texas in support of the *Brown v. Board of Education* decision, while warning that "only a patient and comradely approach to the problem can be of permanent good."[14] A few months later the issues at stake became more personal. Returning home to Yazoo City during the summer of 1955, Morris found a crisis brewing: a number of black citizens had signed a petition calling for the immediate desegregation of the local schools, and the white community responded by organizing a chapter of the White Citizens Council. Along with nearly every trusted adult of his childhood, Morris attended the group's introductory meeting and watched in dismay as they planned revenge on their black neighbors: firings, evictions, and boycotts against all who had signed the petition. As he would recall twelve years later in his memoir, one neighbor tried to argue—"Gentlemen, all this is *unconstitutional*, it's against the Consti . . ."—but was shouted down with boos and catcalls that "might have wilted Judge Earl Warren himself."

> For a brief moment I was tempted to stand up and support my neighbor, but I lacked the elemental courage to go against that mob. For it *was* a mob, and I was not the same person I had been three years before. In the pit of my stomach I felt a strange and terrible disgust. I looked back and saw my father, sitting still and gazing straight ahead; on the stage my friends' fathers nodded their heads and talked among

themselves. I felt an urge to get out of there. *Who are these people?* I asked myself.

He returned to Austin as quickly as he could, assumed the editorship of the *Daily Texan*, and started climbing the ladder whose pinnacle was *Harper's*.[15]

In 1965, just out of college, Frady was dispatched by the Atlanta bureau of *Newsweek* to cover the manslaughter trial of Tom Coleman, the Alabama deputy who killed civil rights worker Jonathan Daniels and wounded another, Richard Morrisroe. The article he contributed, "A Death in Lowndes County," was an astonishingly precocious example of what he later called the "unchurched coupling between the novel and journalism."[16] In the introduction to his book *Southerners*, a collection of magazine articles, he recalls being "lobbed abruptly into the tumults and mighty theatre of the Movement in the South," one of those "climactic moments of truth when everything—past and present, inward and outward—suddenly glares into a resolution larger and more urgent than its ordinary aspect." It was then that he came to realize that his literary ambitions could best be fulfilled in journalism.[17]

I don't mean to oversimplify these careers. Of the three, only Frady seems to have emerged from his encounter with the movement already prepared to write innovative, experimental journalism, and he came along late enough to have gotten some hints from other practitioners. Morris and King moved more slowly toward their versions of New Journalism. That is why Frady's account is most suggestive, offering a rough diagram of the careers of all three writers: first a fateful encounter with the civil rights movement; then a recognition of one's vocation—journalism in search of "climactic moments of truth"; and finally the discovery of a path forward, offered by the new intimacy between the novel and journalism. But what connected the three vocational phases? What, specifically, did civil rights have to do with experimental journalism?

The Damascus Road experience of another reporter, never identified as a New Journalist, sheds some light here. In 1961 Pat Watters, a thirty-four-year-old writer for Atlanta's afternoon paper, was dispatched to the south Georgia town of Albany to cover a local civil rights group's attempt to desegregate the lunch counter at the Trailways bus depot. As he would explain in his memoir *Down to Now*, published ten years later, he attended a meeting at Shiloh Baptist Church, where he found himself unexpectedly moved by the preaching and the hymns, sensing "something I had not known before, yet had always known ... something powerfully alive within me as well as these few brave singers in the cold little church building." Later he repaired to his motel room to write the story:

> And that night, sitting at a portable typewriter in the motel room's air-conditioned cigarette smoke, I couldn't begin to convey it. This was not the normal frustration at newspapering's well-nigh insuperable challenge, all its limitations of space and scope and constricting conventionalities. I sensed even then that I was into something more basic than the limitations of newspapering or my own incoherence, and I have since come to feel that the most important, or most useful truth to be discovered from the experience of the southern movement has to do with a continuing difficulty of Americans to tell about or to perceive the full of what was afoot.[18]

The problem, Watters concludes, was that the movement of which he had just caught his first glimpse was *unprecedented*, such a radical interruption in the moral history of the South and the United States that journalism had no language for it. His memoir is, among other things, a long meditation on journalism's failure to reveal the truth of the movement.

The failure was owed, Watters thought, not to the personal biases of the reporters, though they may have been present, but to the intrinsic limitations of standard journalistic practice. Covering, for example, a lunch-counter sit-in, standard journalism would place any violence (or lacking that, any threat of violence) right after the lede. The motives of the participants would be treated only in late paragraphs that might well be cut by editors. And the great salient fact of *nonviolence* wouldn't be reported at all, since newspapers rarely have room to report on things that didn't happen. Thus, Watters concludes, conventional journalism was required by its own procedural canons to miss the real story.

In *The Race Beat: The Press, the Civil Rights Struggle, and the Awakening of a Nation*, Gene Roberts and Hank Klibanoff offer this example of the kind of flawed reporting Watters describes:

> Greensboro, N.C. (AP)—A group of Negro students—at one time numbering up to 27 men and four women—sat down at a 5- and 10-cent store lunch counter Tuesday in an attempt to obtain service and break racial barriers.
> They failed.

But one of the students said the group "is prepared to keep coming back for two years if we have to."[19]

But they go on to identify one reporter, covering the same event, who found a way out of the trap. Albert L. Rozier, writing for the college paper at North Carolina A&T, revealed the situation with elegant clarity:

> BLAIR: I'd like a cup of coffee.
> WAITRESS: I'm sorry. We don't serve colored here.
> BLAIR: I beg to disagree with you. You just finished serving me at a counter only two feet from here.[20]

Rozier, that is, had stumbled across the same truth that Tom Wolfe would recognize a decade later: that when journalism reached beyond the limits of who-what-when-where, the basic reporting unit must be the scene. Not long after their encounters with the movement, Frady, Morris, and King came to the same recognition.

By the time Wolfe created the first canon of New Journalism, Morris, King, and Frady had been working in a similar form for several years. It is interesting, and possibly revealing, that Wolfe never acknowledged them, apparently noting some fateful difference between Wrecking Crew journalism and his own. Asking what that was can help us recognize what was distinctive about the journalism produced by these ambitious southerners.

Their exclusion from Wolfe's canon was not a matter of regional bias; Wolfe himself was a southerner, born and raised in Virginia, and he made room in his anthology for Hunter Thompson of Kentucky and Rex Reed and Terry Southern from Texas. But none of these writers showed any special interest in his region. All were thoroughly cosmopolitan, Wolfe, Reed, and Southern fully assimilated to Manhattan, Thompson to California. Even when an assignment took them back south, they tended to adopt the stance of outsiders, insulated from emotional engagement by a highly developed capacity for irony. Consider a "southern" piece that Wolfe chose for his anthology, "Twirling at Ole Miss" by Terry Southern. The author traveled to Oxford, Mississippi, in 1962 to report on a remarkable local institution, the Dixie National Baton Twirling Institute. With wide-eyed amazement Southern watches hundreds of adolescent girls twirling and gyrating among the elms in the university grove. He interviews them and their instructors, then places them all—with exquisitely maintained deadpan—within the larger story of "the development of American baton twirling."[21] Only in passing does he mention that all this foolishness is taking place the day after William Faulkner's funeral, on a campus already bracing for the expected enrollment of its first black student, James Meredith.

It is easy to imagine what Frady or Morris or King would have made of such a convergence, of a single episode in which the death of the South's greatest novelist—the anguished analyst of its racial tragedy—coincided with the epochal transformation and moral challenge symbolized by Meredith's brave gesture. What would Faulkner say? And what must the journalist himself say, the inheritor of Faulkner's vocation? None of the Wrecking Crew could have resisted such thematic riches.

But Southern dismisses the convergence as a "grotesque coincidence."[22] As for Meredith and the challenge he would soon pose, the journalist recounts his brief discussion of the topic with two law students, duly noting their affable manners and tasteful summer suits, then quotes without comment the song they sang to him, to the tune of "John Brown's Body": *"Oh we'll bury all the niggers in the Mississippi mud . . ."*[23] As for his own southern background, he merely hopes that "reverting to the Texas twang and callousness of my youth" will allow him to mingle safely with the natives. "Howdy," he says to the first people he meets. "Whar the school?"[24] At one point he wanders over to the library, picks up a copy of *Light in August*, and opens it to find the words "nigger lover" scrawled on the flyleaf. "I decided I must be having a run of bad luck," he mildly comments.[25] Depressed, he decides to have a drink, then turns his attention once more to the twirlers.

If Southern's coolly maintained irony (not much different from Thompson's, funnier than Didion's); if his refusal to rise, rhetorically, to a moral occasion, indeed even to acknowledge it; if his insistence on sticking—despite the temptations of personal engagement—to the discrete job of social analysis before him; if all of that represented Wolfe's journalistic aesthetic, it is no wonder he found little use for the likes of Frady, King, and Morris. To see the difference, consider two relatively typical pieces of Wrecking Crew journalism. In King's "What Ever Happened to Brother Dave?" the writer tracks down Brother Dave Gardner, a comedian of the early 1960s who emerged suddenly from Tennessee obscurity into fame on *The Tonight Show*, then sold out college auditoriums and nightclubs for a few years, embodying what seemed an impossible merger of hipster and redneck identities: imagine a chain-smoking Andy Griffith with Lenny Bruce's irreverence and Mort Sahl's material. Then he disappeared. King—himself a hip redneck with a knack for irreverence—finds himself listening again to Gardner's old records and is unable to decide whether the comedian had been an offensive bigot or a visionary genius. He decides to track him down.

The Gardner he finds, performing for a small, rough-looking crowd at a club near Charlotte in the spring of 1970, is as irreverent, as freely improvisational, as adept with dialect and wild sound effects as ever. He still calls the audience "dear hearts" and punctuates his remarks with an occasional "*Glory!*"; he still jokes about acid and reefer. But Dave is now a Nixon man, with kind words for the police and the military, scornful ones for hippies and war protesters. So far, we might be in a Terry Southern article, a wry look at an odd, vaguely disappointing corner of America.

But then Gardner lets loose a line—out of nowhere, like many of his lines—that shocks even this rough crowd: "God, wasn't that a clean hit on Doctor Junior?"[26] A few of the true hardnoses cheer, but a quip about the murder of Martin Luther King is too much for most, who gasp and head for the exits. But the author does not leave, nor can he let the moment pass unremarked, as Southern did the law students' offensive song. Instead he forces his attempted celebrity profile into a dizzying turn, swerving into a dark corner of late '60s political life and confronting the disturbingly permeable line between genius and madness. Brother Dave, it transpires, has spent the last several years immersed in a bizarre world of right-wing radicalism, some of it under the tutelage of Texas millionaire H. L. Hunt, and is now keeping some very alarming company. In this scene, the long-haired, bearded King (he's "the visitor") is introduced to one of Gardner's friends:

> A small, dark-haired man wearing a sly country grin sat in an easy chair, not bothering to rise for handshakes. "This is J. Robert Jones," Brother Dave said. The visitor's mental equipment whirred and clicked: *J Robert Jones . . . North Carolinian . . . Grand Dragon and Holy Terror of the United Klans of America . . . convicted of contempt of Congress . . . recently released from federal prison.*
>
> Mister, the bejeweled toy watchdog, was growling and snapping, another irritating concert at the visitor's heels. . . .
>
> "Maybe he don't like hippies." Though the Holy Terror smiled, his

eyes seemed to calculate how much bearded beef might dress out by the pound.

"Well, I'd hoped my accent might help."

"Yeah, Bob," Brother Dave said. "He's from Texas."

"Everybody got to be from *somewhere*," the Holy Terror said.[27]

Before long, thanks to detectives paid by H. L. Hunt, King is exposed as the left-winger his hair and beard would suggest. Gardner sends him away but betrays no hard feelings, still somehow seeing King as a kindred soul.

> "Look, man, if you ever get your head about half straightened out and decide you want to know where it's really at, politically, get in touch. I'll be your teacher. There's not much time left to save America." . . .
>
> At the door [Gardner] pursed his lips thickly, gave the clenched fist of the black power salute, and shouted, "Power to the people." Laughing, dear hearts. Laughing.[28]

A similar example of the Wrecking Crew method is Frady's 1971 article "The Judgment of Jesse Hill Ford." Ford was a briefly prominent southern novelist who was tried for murder after he shot and killed a black trespasser on his Tennessee property. He was a racial progressive, whose most famous book, the civil rights novel *The Liberation of Lord Byron Jones*, brought him and his family hostility and threats from their neighbors in Humboldt, Tennessee. Late one night, seeing a strange car parked in the driveway where his son would soon arrive, the spooked Ford loaded his rifle and approached. When the car lurched forward, Ford fired into the darkness, killing Michael Doaks, a black GI, who had been making out with his girlfriend. Ford's indictment drew the attention of more than one journalist eager to plumb the regional and racial ironies. Frady wasn't sure he wanted to join them, but he traveled to Humboldt and met Ford, free on bail and awaiting trial, who kept him up drinking late into the night:

> "Hell," Ford cried, "we grew up in another culture, where those *old* reflexes of the human heart still govern." . . . Soon some primal yawping joy seemed loosed about them in the night, a skirling of bagpipes in the heart, celebrating the South's mad and haggard honor, its

unflagging passionate follies. Ford suddenly said, "And by God, when we're faced with a threat to our *home*, to our own *family*, we answer with the same reflexes—look now, if you thought somebody was out there to waylay your son, you know you would have done exactly the same thing." . . . The journalist, momentarily tasting some old half-forgotten brine of unreckoning fierceness, quickly replied, "Yes. You're damned right. Of course I would have." And in that instant, he knew at last that he would write it. Because the act was in him too.[29]

Frady decided to take on the story only when he realized that he was personally implicated in it and it in him: he condemns Ford's violent impulse, but the story comes to life for him, and for the reader, when he recognizes the same impulse dormant in himself. King was drawn to Gardner for the same reason: like the mad comedian, King is a working-class southerner with a quick wit, an eye for absurdity, and a willingness to push boundaries. The power in both pieces arises from the fact that they are compellingly narrated, meticulously reported, and above all deeply personal. No prophylactic layer of irony intrudes between the writer (and therefore the reader) and his disturbing subject.

This last quality may explain why Wolfe makes no room in *The New Journalism* for Frady, King, or Morris, all of whom tended toward the same deeply personal engagement in the material. The truth is that, though Wolfe's cohort and the Wrecking Crew were alike in claiming novelists as literary ancestors, they had been reading very different novels. For Wolfe, the New Journalism owed its debts mainly to social realists such as Balzac, Dickens, and Howells, analysts of the complex interactions of social class, money, love, envy, and desire. Modernists such as Faulkner, whose subject, he said, was simply "the human heart in conflict with itself," mattered little to Wolfe's New Journalists.[30] But for Morris, King, and Frady, the works of Faulkner were the unquestioned touchstone by which narrative prose could be judged. Faulkner's contemporaries Thomas Wolfe and Robert Penn Warren were nearly as important, *Look Homeward, Angel* an early and indelible influence and *All the King's Men* the ultimate book on southern politics. The analytical distance of the realist and the dry irony of the satirist were not for them; in Wrecking Crew journalism, as in the great novels of the southern renascence that inspired it, the moral stakes were the highest imaginable, and the issues were deeply personal. Tom Wolfe and his friends were drawn to extravagant examples of American weirdness—Haight-Ashbury, the Hell's Angels, Ken Kesey's acid-tripping Merry Pranksters—and wrote about them with a cool (in Thompson's case, a stoned) dispassion. The material ranged from funny to sad to horrifying, and the writing was precise, lively, and sometimes wildly inventive, but it maintained a tight emotional range. Not surprisingly, a New Journalist in search of material was most likely to head for California. Morris actually spent a year in Palo Alto just before assuming his post at *Harper's*. He found it unendurably boring. His imagination, like those of his friends King and Frady, kept turning back to Mississippi, Texas, and kindred regions. They sought out not weird topics but weighty ones that lent themselves to Faulknerian intensity. Was the human heart in conflict with itself in Los Angeles? No doubt it was, but the hearts there seemed small and weightless to writers whose heroes had wrestled with Thomas Sutpen and Willie Stark.

There was, of course, an element of opportunism in these writers' journalistic engagements with the South and its racial crisis. No doubt the events they covered were personally compelling in all the ways King, Frady, and Morris said they were, but they were also exactly the material writers with their particular ambitions needed. They emerged as writers, after all, at the moment when American literature was *looking* for the younger writers who could succeed Faulkner, Warren, Thomas Wolfe, and the other great southerners of their generation. A generation of southern novelists—writers such as William Humphrey, Madison Jones, the aforementioned Jesse Hill Ford, and most prominently William Styron—were already being mentioned as solutions to the problem of Faulknerian succession. But the Wrecking Crew bet their ambitions on the claim circulated by Tom Wolfe and others: that the novel had lost its old authority and that its work must now be done by reporters of imagination and vision. The moral crisis of the civil rights moment offered the Crew exactly the subject they needed to test their consciences, their imaginations, and their prose against.

Of course any reporter who lucks into a major story—a war, a natural disaster, a sensational crime—may seem cold-blooded in seizing a career-advancing opportunity. But for the Crew—problematically, given their political and moral commitments—there was also an undeniable element of racial privilege in their positions: the privilege of seeing the struggle for black equality as—among other things—*material*. The Wrecking Crew themselves seemed aware of this problem and, taking advantage of the personal dimension in their reporting, often tried to question their own privileged positions (though rarely their pure motives): see, for example, King's 1971 memoir, *Confessions of a White Racist*. But there is no denying the essential whiteness of the Wrecking Crew project (or its essential maleness: the Crew invariably portrayed themselves as high-living, hard-drinking rowdies, overgrown boys who had somehow gotten hold of expense accounts and excellent prose styles). To see what experimental, first-person journalism about the South might look like in the hands of a black southern writer, see Albert Murray's *South to a Very Old Place* (1971), much of which actually appeared first in Morris's *Harper's*. You'll meet a writer whose freewheeling improvisations make Hunter S. Thompson look like Walter Lippmann. Murray may have been the Newest Journalist of them all, but his contributions must be a subject for another day.

As for the Wrecking Crew, what might be considered the defining document of their project was published in 1970, just a few months before John Cowles took Morris's magazine away from him and effectively broke up the team. Appropriately it appeared in *Harper's* and, even more appropriately, was written by Willie Morris himself. This was his long, carefully reported, highly personal article about the desegregation of the public schools in his Mississippi hometown. After appearing in *Harper's*, it was extended to become his second book, *Yazoo: Integration in a Deep-Southern Town* (1971). It may represent the fullest development of the Wrecking Crew method, combining traditional reporting with novelistic and deeply personal writing in order to tell an elusive story. Here the reporter becomes not just an observer or peripheral participant but a central character in the story being reported. A close look at it will make an appropriate conclusion to this discussion.

The occasion of the article and book was Yazoo City's attempt to cooperate with the Supreme Court's decision in *Alexander v. Holmes County Board of Education* (1969), which required a number of Deep South school districts to comply at last with the fifteen-year-old *Brown* decision—the decision that had prompted the angry meeting Morris observed as a young man and then described in *North Toward Home*. "Who are these people?" he had asked himself in dismay. In *Yazoo* he answers the question, returning home to see them finally face the crisis they had hoped to frighten away in 1955.

Morris arrives in Yazoo shortly before the schools open on January 7, 1970, the first day of integrated education. He is struck by how little has changed since his boyhood: familiar people are everywhere, old names and faces come flooding back, and Morris is briefly awash in nostalgia. The mood is only interrupted by the sour thought of his now-estranged wife, "who hated this place, hated the town and its people with a terrible and disparaging contempt"—and who, unforgivably, had once written "a graduate-school treatise calling William Faulkner a second-rater."[31] She is the first of several unsympathetic outsiders whose responses to Yazoo will help Morris clarify his own.

He is not the only reporter present on January 7. Because of Yazoo's proximity to the Memphis airport, "the Nationals"—*New York Times, Washington Post, Boston Globe, Chicago Sun-Times*—have all chosen Morris's hometown as their vantage point on the implementation of *Alexander*. In *Yazoo*, "the Nationals" function both as outsiders, incapable of a full understanding of the life of Yazoo City, and as embodiments of conventional reporting, unequipped to reveal the real story. All of them have the same questions, the ones conventional journalism always asked: Will there be violence? Other forms of white resistance? Or will the town somehow rise to the occasion and make integration work? These are Morris's questions too, and we see him pursuing them like a good reporter, interviewing white and black leaders and students of both races and investigating the segregated private school that has been improvised as an alternative. The record he discovers is a mixed one: there is no violence, relatively little attrition of white students, relatively little public protest. On the other hand, the high school, disappointingly, remains segregated by classroom. All this Morris learns, as do the Nationals.

But it develops that Morris, though carrying the same press pass, is not quite one of the Nationals, as we are reminded in his account of opening day. He is standing with his colleagues near the high school auditorium when a booming voice calls out, "Winkie!" It was his childhood nickname, now being shouted by a school administrator.[32] Throughout the narrative, "Winkie" has access to an understanding of Yazoo that eludes more conventional reporters, and Morris the writer is able to reveal them through vivid, sympathetic characters and carefully developed scenes. Harold Kelley, the school superintendent, offers bland words of optimism, which the Nationals also hear—but Morris gives those words a deeper resonance by remembering the harried administrator as "Hardwood" Kelley, the young basketball coach who once dazzled Morris with his dribbling and whose innovative "floating defense" neutralized Bolivar County's big man in the conference finals. We encounter Rudy Shields, the local NAACP leader, who talks tough and carries a pistol but who, in an extended scene, is finally revealed as "one of the few black radicals left who believe in integration."[33] Jeppie Barbour, another childhood acquaintance, is now the far-from-enlightened mayor, dismayed by the demands of his black constituents, alarmed by Rudy Shields, and impatient with the black police officers he has been forced to hire, but even Jeppie finally confides to his old schoolmate, "We're gonna make the most of this."[34]

In *Yazoo* these locals, fully audible only to "Winkie," form a chorus that speaks in hopeful tones. But we also hear rumors from the world beyond Yazoo, uttered in different accents. The Nixon administration, cynically cultivating white southern votes, advocates delay in implementing *Alexander*, as though integration were unimportant. An equally alien and faceless body, the young radicals of both races, have declared that integration is undesirable, black separatism being the wave of the future. Indeed "the very word [integration] seemed archaic and worn out, a little flighty and frivolous. . . . Who cared about it now?"[35] Nobody but struggling ordinary people, black and white, in places such as Yazoo City.

The real contest, *Yazoo* suggests, is not between integrationists and segregationists, or even between blacks and whites, but between two more essential factions: those who care what happens to Mississippi—which is "one of the frontiers of our strivings as a people"—and those who do not.[36] On one side are the confused, inarticulately humane Yazooans of both races, who are trying to make integration work; on the other side is a motley coalition of nihilistic outsiders: cynical Republicans, fashionable radicals, Yankee intellectuals, intolerant ex-wives who don't get Faulkner.

And where does Winkie stand? At the outset Morris represents himself as ambivalent. He tells us he would have preferred not to return to Yazoo at all during its moment of crisis, so painful are many of his memories, but "I would have been ashamed of myself if I had not."[37] This allows Morris to structure his book around two parallel narratives: the public drama of Yazoo's accommodation to the new order and a private one, that of Willie Morris's reaccommodation to Yazoo.

The crisis of this latter story comes in a late chapter, set in the second year of integrated schooling. The Nationals have long since lost interest in Yazoo, but Morris is back in town, the story not yet concluded from his point of view. He visits the cemetery as usual, remembering his late father and other absent figures from his childhood, then falls to musing on his own existence: he has become "a member of the New York literati" but has lost his marriage, his New York apartment, his books, his dog (I. H. Crane, a retriever whose virtues are extolled at length)—all *"lost!"*[38] It was Thomas Wolfe's favorite word, the essential lament of the alienated modern. Where does this bereft soul belong?

In this gloomy state, he finds himself passing the high school, sees some black students heading home at the end of the day, laughing and shoving, and slows down to stare. One of the kids notices and shouts, "Hey, man. What you think you *lookin'* at?" It's a moment of recognition for the protagonist: "My God, they aren't what they used to be. What have they done to my old school? Too much of my past welled up within me from this isolated delta town where they once were *ours*, existing at our whims and mercies; too much of my growing up was still with me."[39] It's a complicated moment. In it, Morris learns nothing new about school desegregation but something essential about himself and his hometown. He is, it turns out, as conflicted and confused, as torn between good intentions and dread of change, as his old friends and neighbors are. *Who are these people?* They are me, Morris discovers at last.

This is, in effect, the conclusion of Morris's report. After his moment of self-recognition he dutifully records a few recent developments, most notably that some students are trying to open an integrated coffeehouse, but must leave the situation essentially unresolved. Will Yazoo prove equal to its moral crisis or not? No reportable fact can answer the question definitively; maybe the Nationals were right to have moved on to other stories long ago. But in *Yazoo* Morris has tried to reveal something they were bound to miss in any case, the kind of thing, as Pat Watters argued in *Down to Now*, that ordinary journalists always missed in their search for dramatic events, for data, for winners and losers: the unarticulated essence of a moral situation. By immersing himself in Yazoo—and discovering Yazoo in himself—Morris offers his readers a steady look at a community trying to find the will to face its moral crisis.

The last few pages of *Yazoo*, a kind of coda, follow Morris out of his hometown, back into the "America" that has seemed so indifferent to the town's crisis. He goes on a college speaking tour—"'to keep in touch,' I told myself; to help pay New York alimony, I knew"—and is shocked by the nihilism and ferocious intolerance that surrounds him, contrasting sharply with the moral aspiration he has discovered in Yazoo. After a few weeks of the tour, he reports:

I had *had a crock* . . . with the illiterate posturers, the fashionable young nihilists who told the . . . faculties that what they taught amounted to nothing, and the faculties agreed. *Had a crock* with all of them who erupted in spasms of irritated self-righteousness when they said that the South was all evil and could be written off, that black separatism was the wave of the future, that the Panthers should burn down every city in sight, that revolution was the hope of survival, that literature was useless because it no longer mattered to our condition. All this, and much more, would be spoken in the name of idealism.[40]

In other words, *"Who are these people?"* Of course, they are the enlightened sophisticates for whom he once abandoned his hometown. But by the end of *Yazoo*, the struggling, tragic South has become, improbably, a locus of humane values, of imagination and hope, besieged and outnumbered by a cynical, Philistine, Faulkner-denying northern horde.

The ending of Morris's second book reads, in retrospect, like foreshadowing of the fateful clash that awaited him when he finally returned to that other locus of humane values, the magazine he had transformed during his four years as editor. He and his Wrecking Crew comrades interpreted his doomed struggle with the wealthy northern owners as another parable about the fate of the humane imagination, gallant but outgunned by a hostile enemy, its inevitable defeat a virtual Appomattox of the literary imagination. Morris himself, in a hastily composed press release, explained: "I am resigning because of severe disagreements with the business management over the purpose, the existence, and the survival of *Harper's Magazine*. . . . My mandate as its 8th editor in 120 years has been to maintain its excellence and its courage. With the contribution of many of the country's finest writers, journalists, poets and critics, I think we have succeeded. It all boiled down to the money men and the literary men. And, as always, the money men won."[41] The victorious John Cowles summoned the magazine's remaining writers to a meeting so he could notify them that they were—in King's paraphrase—"a conquered people."[42] They quit in protest and swore never to write for *Harper's* again, an oath they all kept. Meanwhile the suddenly unemployed Morris retreated to a cottage on Long Island, where he spent days on end listening to the same two records on the stereo: "An album of Mahalia Jackson spirituals, and someone reading Robert E. Lee's farewell address to the

Confederate army."⁴³ The last act of the Wrecking Crew declared, maybe more emphatically than anything they had done, their solidarity with the southern literary tradition. What story have southerners told more often than the one of noble defeat?

NOTES

1. Larry L. King, *In Search of Willie Morris: The Mercurial Life of a Legendary Author and Editor* (New York: Public Affairs, 2006), 152.
2. Midge Decter, "Southern Comforts," *Commentary*, July 1998, 26–33.
3. Louis Menand, "Willie's Version," *New Yorker*, September 20, 1993, 121–26.
4. Norman Podhoretz, *Breaking Ranks* (New York: Harper and Row, 1979), 152.
5. Marshall Frady, *Southerners: A Journalist's Odyssey* (New York: New American Library, 1980), xxiv.
6. Frady, 6.
7. Tom Wolfe, "The New Journalism," in *The New Journalism*, ed. Tom Wolfe and E. W. Johnson (New York: Harper and Row, 1973), 15, 30.
8. Wolfe, 17.
9. Wolfe, 9.
10. Tom Wolfe, *The Kandy-Kolored Tangerine Flake Streamline Baby* (New York: Picador, 2009), xiv.
11. Michael Herr, *Dispatches* (New York: Knopf, 1977), 218.
12. Frady, *Southerners*, xxv.
13. Larry L. King, *Confessions of a White Racist* (New York: Viking, 1971), 83.
14. Teresa Nicolas, *Willie: The Life of Willie Morris* (Jackson: University Press of Mississippi, 2016), 38.
15. Willie Morris, *North Toward Home* (Boston: Houghton Mifflin, 1967), 179–80.
16. Frady, *Southerners*, xxvii.
17. Frady, xxiv.
18. Pat Watters, *Down to Now: Reflections on the Southern Civil Rights Movement* (New York: Pantheon, 1971), 4.
19. Gene Roberts and Hank Klibanoff, *The Race Beat: The Press, the Civil Rights Struggle, and the Awakening of a Nation* (New York: Vintage, 2007), 223.
20. Roberts and Klibanoff, 223.
21. Terry Southern, "Twirling at Ole Miss," in Wolfe and Johnson, *New Journalism*, 164.
22. Southern, 162.
23. Southern, 168.
24. Southern, 162.
25. Southern, 169.
26. Larry L. King, "What Ever Happened to Brother Dave?," in *The Old Man and Lesser Mortals* (New York: Viking, 1974), 66.
27. King, 70.

28. King, 80.

29. Marshall Frady, "The Judgment of Jesse Hill Ford," in *Southerners*, 198.

30. William Faulkner, "Address upon Receiving the Nobel Prize for Literature," in *The Portable Faulkner*, ed. Malcolm Cowley, rev. ed. (New York: Viking, 1967), 723.

31. Willie Morris, *Yazoo: Integration in a Deep-Southern Town* (New York: Harper's Magazine Press, 1971), 26.

32. Morris, 40.

33. Morris, 63.

34. Morris, 79.

35. Morris, 169.

36. Morris, 120.

37. Morris, 13.

38. Morris, 153.

39. Morris, 154–55.

40. Morris, 171–72.

41. King, *In Search*, 140.

42. Larry L. King, "Looking Back on the Crime, or, Rememberin' Willie and Them," in *Old Man and Lesser Mortals*, 298.

43. Michael Schnayerson, "He'll Always Have Elaine's," *Vanity Fair*, October 1993, 140.

IDENTITY AS DEBATE

The Subintellectual History of Edward A. Pollard's True Southerners

SCOTT ROMINE

"MUCH OF the history of the Southern mind," Michael O'Brien once wrote, "is such a debate: not how many angels may dance upon the head of a pin but how many and what manner of men may crowd upon the word *South*." It is an offhand comment, meant to evince the peculiar nature of a South that was not, as many had supposed, a *community* grounded in the "concrete" (scare quotes O'Brien's) but rather a "metaphysical construct, born of the interaction of an intellectual tradition, historicist Romanticism, with social and political history."[1]

To someone who is not a historian, much less an intellectual one, this passage raises more than a few questions. What is meant by the "southern mind"? It seems inclined to questions of metaphysics, but wasn't H. L. Mencken right to say that such minds were rare as oboe players in the southern states? Certainly the mind seems different from W. J. Cash's version, which seems to avoid thinking altogether. And what of history? Is the southern mind its subject or object—the thing debating or the thing being debated?

Despite the questions it posed when I came across it some two decades ago, the passage makes two claims that struck me as intuitively persuasive. First, to an assistant professor of English, O'Brien's derision toward the southern "concrete" seemed well deserved. I had been hearing about the southern concrete for a while but hadn't managed to come up with any evidence that it referred to anything in particular. It was just something people said, like "sense of place." Second, I was persuaded that "community" and "South" were both constructs, if not necessarily metaphysical ones. The question of who counts—or who crowds—as a southerner perplexed me as well, as did the question of why it still seemed to matter. But then, why "South"—a division of space, not persons or peoples—as the word determining insiderhood? Why not "southerner"?

I hope the answer to that question does not appear too self-evident. I don't think it did to O'Brien, who imagined (rightly) that a brain could inhabit the U.S. South (and perhaps even be born there) without having a southern *mind* or without crowding upon the word "South." Even without actual tar and feathers, many a mind has been ridden out of Dixie on a figurative rail, and the "no true southerner" test has exiled many, from antebellum abolitionists to, in our own time, consumers of mayonnaise other than Duke's. In 2007, O'Brien suggested that southern identity was indeed optional, as "the idea of the South has always been only one of the synthesizing ideas available to those people who have lived in the southeastern United States since about 1820, to accept and use if they wished, to refuse if they wished."[2] This seemed decidedly less deterministic than the idea as it appeared in his first book, where, as "centrally an intellectual perception," it "served to comprehend and weld an unintegrated social reality."[3]

Whatever the status of the southern idea—as option, postulate, or "conjecture of order . . . used to make sense of the whole business"—O'Brien's assumptions about southern identity bear the traces of his own identity as an intellectual historian.[4] Perhaps all disciplines practice a version of the saying that to a hammer, everything looks like a nail. For O'Brien, this meant looking to the idea as what nailed identity to the South, and to intellectuals as those performing the carpentry. Speaking on behalf of intellectual historians in 1988, he stated plainly that "the debate over Southern identity is the social discourse of intellectuals in the South, to be appraised as such." Intended as a corrective or supplement to "the positivist historian, unskeptical about the South and sectional identity," the claim seems nonetheless wildly wrong.[5]

Of intellectual history, O'Brien observes that "the cold truth is that its subject matter is clever people who once expressed themselves in complicated patterns, which other clever people have taken seriously."[6] Surely, though, complicated patterns and the perennial shortage of clever people pose barriers to the transmission—and thus, to some significant degree—the *influence* of ideas. Surely intellectuals have not locked down the debate over southern identity or the idea of the South; the unclever, too—the demagogue, the advertiser, the old-timer waxing nostalgic about the good old days—have had their say. As evidence, we might consider that the default rumination on southern identity today is likely to be neither clever nor complicated. Consider Rick Bragg, Tracy Thompson's *New Mind of the South* ("tradition in the South is like beachfront property in an era of global warming"), or any one of those endless lists on the internet ("How to tell you're truly southern"; "Southern women know everybody's first name: Honey, Darlin' or Shugah").[7] Identitarian fashionings of this sort bear, perhaps, faint traces of cultural romanticism, but one suspects that Herder and Schlegel have not been consulted.

And yet insiderhood is defined relative to something called "the South" and for that reason must bear some relation to the "the debate over Southern identity." If so, southern intellectual history will need to range rather far afield from intellectuals and formal thought to account for the intersection of ideas and southern insiderhood. What I wish to consider, then, as a literary scholar to whom everything looks like a *text* or a *discourse*, is how intellectual history might be supplemented by something like subintellectual history: the history of ideas that are not quite complicated, as articulated by southerners who are not quite clever.

Here, I should declare my skepticism that identities primarily, or even significantly, *derive* from ideas. Understood as a mediator between region and identity—as a conception of what the region *is* that determines or confirms insiderhood—the idea is ostensibly mimetic and ontological in nature. O'Brien, I think, understood it this way, defining "the Southern idea" as the "dialectic product" of the interaction between "social reality" and "perception" filtered through the "intellectual structures of Romanticism and modernism." Of this rather-too-neat dialectic (social reality → perception → myth), he conceded that "the interchange between these three levels was complicated and devious."[8] But the language he typically used to describe the work of ideation, which *synthesized, organized, welded, distilled, comprehended,* or *conjectured into order* a recalcitrant or inchoate reality, repeated the ground-up model of his dialectic: first social reality, then the idea that considered and explained it. This mimetic bias, in which the idea responds to and represents a prior reality, repeats itself as the idea becomes bound up with the identity, which, for O'Brien, was also explanatory. Thus, even as he voiced doubt that "a majority of those people [living in the South] ever accepted 'Southern' as the social identity most explanatory of their lives," he assumes that identity's primary function is to explain. Indeed, he speculated, southern identity "might perish, not with a bang but a whimper, because it has ceased to explain enough."[9] My suspicion is that O'Brien believed that the *quality* of ideas—their complexity, their synthesizing and explanatory power, the legitimacy of the "intellectual structures" used to produced them—bore some significant relation to their identitarian value.

I proceed from a different set of premises, beginning with the assumption that most ideas of the South have less to do with the region itself than with the question of who crowds on the word "southerner." Rather than viewing the southern idea as primarily referential or explanatory, I view it is discursive and argumentative. I approach "South," then, as a term (to borrow the language of Bruno Latour) "used to summarize the set of elements that appear to be tied to a claim that is in dispute." According to Latour, terms such as "culture" and "society" "always have a very vague definition because it is only *when* there is a dispute, *as long as it lasts*, and *depending* on the strength exerted by dissenters that such words . . . may receive a precise meaning. In other words, no one lives in a 'culture,' shares a 'paradigm,' or belongs to a 'society' *before* he or she clashes with others."[10]

From this perspective, the "metaphysical construct" appears as a rhetorical one, a body of ostensibly authoritative evidence cited in support of the motion at hand. As ideated, "South" becomes less conclusive, less the dialectical end product and more the dynamic, shape-shifting effect of contingent discursive requirements. Put another way, "Solid Souths" derive not from relatively stable social realities but from relatively stable arguments. Descriptions of a southern people become legible as appeals to a public not yet persuaded to accept and use the southern idea (as presently configured)—or, if already persuaded, to use that idea in some novel way. Although this reorientation risks, perhaps, transforming intellectual history into a kind of postintellectual history unchecked by reality, it avoids the embarrassing implication that identities succeed to the extent that they correspond to reality.[11] What Latour calls the "firm ground" of relativism offers an additional advantage: we need not adjudicate the "correctness" of identitarian claims (e.g., "we southerners value the concrete") and thus avoid policing southernness on the basis of its relationship to the (actual) South, which would surely result in mass incarceration.[12] Further, understanding "the debate over Southern identity" to *produce* (not haggle over existing) southern identities (now understood as plural and contingent) allows a richer understanding of how ideas of the South return, messily, to the region: as in-the-moment, tactical coercions disguised as truths self-evident since time immemorial. Of his "devious" dialectical interchange, O'Brien calls for the historian to intervene "for sanity's sake . . . to still this Bacchanalian whirl."[13] This need not preclude other, more happily bacchanalian, interventions.

Between his 1866 publication of *The Lost Cause: A New Southern History of the War of the Confederates* and his death in 1872, Edward A. Pollard inhabited the bacchanalian whirl. Readers of his most famous book may be surprised to learn that little of its elegiac Romanticism survived as Pollard emerged periodically to provide wildly contradictory ideas of a South to which he and all true southerners belonged. Far from embarrassed by his lack of consistency, Pollard presented each new South as the discovery or revelation of core principles and realities amounting to an essence. What he said *about* the South was rarely complicated or original, amounting at times to recitations of commonplaces or what today we would call talking points. Despite his University of Virginia education, he was an intellectual only in Latour's sense: a spokesperson who "'speak[s] for' the group existence . . . defining who they are, what they should be, what they have been."[14] But Pollard was skilled at assembling arguments out of the materials at hand and clever at inventing Souths that would support his conclusions. He was, to borrow Ralph Ellison's term, a thinker-tinker, with an emphasis on the tinkering.

In *The Lost Cause*, Pollard extended a tradition of southern defensiveness. For all the confidence exuded by proslavery writers, the fact is that defenses of the institution were, by the 1830s, entirely necessary in response not only to northern opinion but to international opinion as well. Various strategies were employed: slavery was biblically sanctioned and thus moral (Thomas Roderick Dew); slavery should be considered as a practical question, not a moral one (James Henry Hammond); slavery should be considered as an economic question, not a racial one (George Fitzhugh). The constant in these defenses was necessity. A decent respect to the opinions of mankind meant justifying an institution increasingly marked as peculiar.

Abolition, not slavery, made the South defensive, and defensiveness made the South the South. For John C. Calhoun, who did not belong "to the school which holds that aggression is to be met by concession," this meant that slavery must be a "positive good."[15] In time, the South would follow suit and for an obvious reason: if slavery was a necessary evil, then the South, being solely encumbered with it, would necessarily be impeded by it. Moving the South from the back foot to the front most often involved what O'Brien calls the "Romantic historicism of nationality": the idea, mostly German in origin, that "nations earned their place in this system by their social reality, their claim to being distinct."[16] As Johann Gottlieb Fichte explained to the German nation in 1806, a nation comprises "individuals joined together by a multitude of invisible bonds by nature herself. . . . They belong together and are by nature one and an inseparable whole. Only as each of these peoples, left to itself and in accordance with its own peculiar quality . . . is the appearance of divinity reflected in its proper mirror, as it should be."[17] Southern applications of the intellectual template required modification. There was no distinctive language, so crucial to nationalist movements elsewhere, and no primordial folk tradition to be catalogued by southern Grimms. Indeed, there was no primordial anything. Developing a Romantic nationalism in the space of a few decades meant patching together a past from disparate sources. Memories of Cavalier ancestors in merry old England, jousting festivals at county fairs (among other Walter Scottisms), slaves named Pompey, and random architectural citations by the cotton rich all spoke to the deficiency. Even so, the invention of tradition differed only in degree from other national pasts, which often relied on Ossian and other fraudulent ancestry. Sometimes nature was cited on behalf of the southern people. Examining "the conflicting characters of two great sections," William Henry Trescot would "discover that nature herself has drawn deeply the sectional lines." He was not alone in discovering this, although it provoked mirth elsewhere.[18] Above all, there was slavery to clinch the deal—slavery not only as a superior (and potentially exportable) system of labor but as the cause of the southern nation's distinctive social reality. In this configuration, slavery required no defense; it had produced a superior civilization.

This was a stronger argument, but it concealed another source of defensiveness. For all its purported superiority, an older South—not quite yet "the South"—had held a place of national prominence that had been lost in the interim. For all its civilizational superiority, the decline was apparent by the time Romantic nationalism began to gain traction. Population and economic power had trended northward such that tradition appears from the beginning as a reaction, tinged with grievance, to lost ground in national politics. This meant that the southern protonation was often expressed as the recovery of some lost not-yet-South; put another way, "southerners" appear precisely when they perceive themselves be on the back foot. As Edward Ayers shrewdly observes, "From its very beginning, people have believed that the South defined against an earlier South that was somehow more authentic, more real, more unified and distinct, was not only disappearing but declining."[19] For antebellum intellectuals, that decline could be reversed; the whole point of Romantic nationalism was to reverse it. As O'Brien observes, this task required self-confidence, at times inflated to world-historical levels. For writers such as Fitzhugh and Hammond, the South "might solve the problem of modernity" by acting as "the safeguard of the world's orderly progress." "With this," O'Brien adds, "went the idea that the South's racial and class structure provided it with an insulation against the ideological instability of modernity."[20]

This was the strongest argument of all, although it bore little relation to reality: modernity wasn't looking southward for solutions. Whether this level of confidence ever extended beyond a few books remains unclear, but the Romantic idea underwrote, at least, the possibility of a nation-state cleansed of scheming Yankees with their tariffs and abolition.

Pollard emerges as a group spokesman when the political side of the Romantic cause is lost. The difference between defensiveness and defeat is palpable, even as *The Lost Cause* draws heavily from the Romantic tradition, elaborating early, often, and with no measurable degree of originality a theory of "two nations of opposite civilizations."[21] "The distinction of North and South," he writes, "apparently founded on slavery and traced by lines of climate, really went deeper to the very elements of the civilization of each."[22] The North was puritan, and its "traits of character" (intolerance, "painful thrift," "external" piety, "lack of the sentimentalism which makes up the half of modern civilization") remained "yet visible in their descendants."[23] Conversely, "the colonists of Virginia and the Carolinas were from the first distinguished for their polite manners, their fine sentiments, their attachment to a sort of feudal life, their landed gentry, their love of field-sports and dangerous adventure, and the prodigal and improvident aristocracy that dispensed its stores in constant rounds of hospitality and gaiety."[24] To this primordial distinction, slavery confers additional value, "establish[ing] in the South a peculiar and noble type of civilization."[25] The institution "inculcated notions of chivalry, polished the manners and produced many noble and generous virtues"; it relieved the "demands of physical labor" and thus "afforded opportunity for extraordinary culture, elevated the standards of scholarship in the South, enlarged and emancipated social intercourse, and established schools of individual refinement."[26] Here is, more or less intact, the litany of southern tradition—manners, refinement, feudalism, hospitality, chivalry, and so forth—that had evolved over decades and survives to the present.

Although it remains constant—as does the litany of northern vice (coarse, materialistic, ostentatious, garish, superficial, and crude)—the causal role of slavery does not. Was southern distinctiveness "*apparently* founded on slavery," or did slavery actually "*establish*" a "peculiar and noble type of civilization"? Well, both. Paradoxically, slavery establishes the "deeper" virtues already present in the southern colonies. This causal ambivalence is necessary so that Pollard can mount an additional argument: the North, having "naturally found or imagined in slavery the leading cause of the distinctive civilization of the South," "revenged itself on the cause, diverted its envy in an attack upon slavery, and defamed the institution as the relic of barbarism."[27] Thus framed, the *moral* question of slavery is entirely beside the point, a mere pretense for Yankee revenge. Slavery thus functions as a partial, and lost, cause of a superior civilization that, having preceded the institution, might conceivably survive its loss. This made sense because the North had, in fact, eliminated what it thought made the South superior. For Pollard, southern superiority would survive but only if properly maintained. "It would be immeasurably the worst consequence of defeat in this war," he writes, "that the South should lose its moral and intellectual distinctiveness as a people, and cease to assert its well-known superiourity in civilization. . . . That superiourity the war has not conquered or lowered; and the South will do right to claim and cherish it."[28]

Pollard's history of the southern people thus shifts into an overtly rhetorical mode. The war having settled the questions of slavery and secession, Romantic nationalism would have to proceed within a government dominated by the alien people. This meant that the conflict must continue as a "war of ideas," although the ideas were thin gruel indeed—"something more," Pollard hopes, "than the shadow of State Rights" that might protect against the "dogma of Consolidation."[29] Lest a "war of ideas" sound too "formidable," Pollard adds that, "after all, it is a harmless figure of rhetoric."[30] Probably this was a fair assessment. No longer secured by slavery or political destiny, the notional South hovers in the balance and with little to do. Where a war of armies promised a state housing the southern nation, the war of ideas depends on *claims* and *assertions* of superiority, the cessation of which would lead, by Pollard's own logic, to a loss of "moral and intellectual distinctiveness." Like a defeated Greece, the South might "experience the extinction of [its] literature, the decay of mind, and the loss of [its] distinctive forms of thought."[31] Worse, the South might "bring in Northern capital and labour; to build mills and factories and hotels and gilded caravansies; and to make themselves rivals in the clattering and garish enterprise of the North."[32]

Such, for Allen Tate, would prove the fate of the South, where a feudal society had developed, remarkably, from the "capitalistic enterprise" of Jamestown. Possessing a "special secular system," but lacking a feudal religion, the South proved, in Tate's estimation, unable to "take hold of Tradition" and thus succumbed to the garish enterprise of the North.[33] But for Tate, as for Tracy Thompson, lost or threatened traditions could be assumed as a central theme of a continuous southern identity.[34] In 1866, however, it was not apparent that the Lost Cause would remain causal—that it would continue to produce "distinctive forms of thought" that would define the southern people. Pollard need not have worried, of course; the war, as the greatest of all southern reverses, would excite the most powerful regret and "memory of past joys." Imagined after the fact, the Old South would prove "more authentic, more real, more unified and distinct" than any of its predecessors, and southerners have not since stinted in asserting their "well-known superiority in civilization" (although they would eventually call it "culture"). But that could not be known in 1866. The "war of ideas" might fare no better than the war of the Confederates, and the southern people might perish from the earth.

It may seem curious, then, that Pollard did not tend the garden of southern memory.[35] In fact, that garden would not flourish until the emergence of the plantation school in the 1880s and its subsequent integration into an emerging consumer economy. By then, the antebellum South conjured in moonlit hues was not only an Old South but a Dead South. Thomas Nelson Page enters the national literary scene observing the plantation ruins of a people for whom the "outer world strode by them as they dreamed"; only *after* the world strides by does the memory seem permissible.[36] Strictly suppressed within these cultural forms was the South an existential threat to the U.S. nation-state, even if that threat had catalyzed new, more consolidated forms of national assembly. As a lost cause in this decidedly unromantic sense, the South was subjected to multiple strategies by which it was reimagined as nontraumatic, or at least manageably so.

In short, the time was not yet ripe for the compensatory fantasies of Lost Cause veneration. For Pollard, more pressing issues were at hand, and this meant radically revising the South. Perhaps sensing that his earlier Lost Cause was truly lost, he reenvisioned the war of the Confederates, which he would now call "the rebellion," as a victory. In 1868, he published *The Lost Cause Regained*, which argued that "the true cause fought for in the late war has not been 'lost' immeasurably or irrevocably, but is yet in a condition to be 'regained' by the South on ultimate issues of the political contest."[37] Those issues, newly conceived, involved "the supremacy of the white race, and along with it the preservation of the political traditions of the country."[38] As he cannily surmised, "In contesting this cause the South is far stronger than in any former contest"; "the true cause of the war," retroactively defined, might indeed result in triumph.[39] "'WHITE' is the winning word," he affirms, "and let us never be done repeating it."[40] There are several losing words, "South" and "civilization" prominent among them. There is no longer a southern civilization; "southern people" now refers merely to persons living in the South. *The people* and *our* people refer to a U.S. public predisposed to resist Radical rule. "The people," he writes, are "still able to act," and "public opinion may operate with unlimited effect"—always, Pollard imagines, in opposition to Radical Republicans, whose "design [is] . . . to keep public opinion diffuse and disorganized."[41] A people possesses an identity; a public does not. Pollard's project is to persuade the American public to become a white people.

This meant foreclosing the possibility of a southern people. Although Pollard continues to advocate a doctrine of states' rights to combat the "party of consolidation," consolidation now means division. "Before the war," Pollard observes, Radicals "were great sticklers for homogeneousness, North and South."[42] Now they propose "a terrible sacrifice of the homogeneousness and identity of the nation."[43] Subjected by unconstitutional dictate to Negro rule, the South stands segregated from the nation of which it is rightly a part; tragically, "the homogeneousness of the nation is gone."[44] Predictably, Pollard's exposure of hypocrisy conceals his own: Hadn't he argued just two years before that the United States comprises "two nations of opposite civilizations"? Having justified a war on this basis, is it fair to complain that the South is treated as a "conquered country"?[45] In 1866, "extravagant adulation" of the Union was declared "simply absurd," a garish conceit of "Yankee orators who established the Fourth-of-July school of rhetoric, exalted the American eagle, and spoke of the Union as the last, best gift to man."[46] Now, Pollard presents "veneration for the Union" as "something peculiarly glorious and sacred."[47] Appealing to a union indivisible, "like a holy unity of art," Pollard predicts Ernest Renan in opposing national memory and history.[48] "There may be an extravagance in these appeals," he writes, "when brought to severe tests of logic; but no nation is expected to measure its patriotic memories by the cold and exact rules of history."[49] The concession, keyed to the word "extravagance," is significant. Pollard's Romantic nationalism hadn't followed cold and exact rules, either, but he had not owned up to the fact.

Where *The Lost Cause* presents patriotic memories as history, *The Lost Cause Regained* is, from start to finish, a war of words designed to transform an inchoate but powerful public into a people, lest the white cause be lost. The point is made explicit in the book's conclusion: "The 'Lost Cause' needs no war to regain it. We have taken up new hopes, new arms, new methods—'By winning words to conquer willing hearts, And make persuasion do the work of fear.'"[50]

"White" being the winning word, rhetorical conquest means two things: persuading southerners to become Americans and persuading Americans to become white. Because whiteness need, in this scenario, be causal, Pollard redeploys its causality to the past. Considering slavery from the present vantage, Pollard now recognizes that the "permanent, natural inferiourity of the Negro was the true and only defense of Slavery."[51] How strangely, he observes, had "the Southern mind wandered in its defenses of Slavery," dwelling on "narrow and infamously mean" constitutional questions.[52] Meandering from best defense, the southern mind was "content to point to [slavery's] effects" and to "its evidence of benevolence"—precisely, we should note, as Pollard had done in *Black Diamonds Gathered in the Darkey Homes of the South*, his 1859 collection of sketches "illustrating very happily the patriarchal relation which subsists between the races of the South."[53] Understood properly (as Pollard now understands it), the slavery question was a moral one—a question of "right or wrong"—and slavery was wrong if "the Negro was really the equivalent of the white man enveloped in a black skin."[54] That not being the case, the moral case for slavery might have been "maintained on an impregnable principle of natural law."[55]

Pollard's retroactive apologetics shape what might be considered the first neo-Confederate project. In redefining the meaning of the war, Jack P. Maddex argues, Pollard "devised an illusion of continuity to make acceptance of the enemy's system palatable." Rhetorically, this continuity enables an appeal to a continuous southern identity, albeit one that fails every test of reason. But in offering what Maddex calls a "glowing vision of the Union's future, fusing the causes of the Union and the Confederacy in a single blurred image," Pollard grounds his project in racial animus that was hardly imaginary.[56] By 1868, white supremacist feeling was amply evident as public opinion there to be mobilized, although it had rarely appeared in proslavery apologetics.[57]

It is no mystery why, as Pollard correctly observed, proslavery writers generally avoided the topic of racial hierarchy. For one thing, it was not in dispute, and preserving the South as a "white man's country" did not require the perpetuation of slavery. Colonization would do just as well. More to the point, white supremacy made a poor defense of the South's special identity. Pollard argues in *The Lost Cause Regained* that "there is an instinct of humanity, a great unwritten law of nations, that one race only ought to have political power in the same country, each race in its own."[58] This was inconvenient to the "two civilizations" argument underlying defenses of slavery and southern nationalism: both Puritans and Cavaliers had been white. Racist feeling had been there all along, but it did not lend itself to arguments in defense of the southern people. Only after Romantic nationalism had collapsed could a collective whiteness serve a tactical purpose.

Moreover, white supremacist arguments could be mobilized against slavery, as had been evident since Jefferson's *Notes on the State of Virginia*. Slavery, in turn, could be critiqued for fracturing white solidarity. In *The Impending Crisis* (1857), for example, Hinton Rowan Helper argued that "the lords of the lash are not only absolute masters of the blacks, who are bought and sold, and driven about like so many cattle, but they are also the oracles and arbiters of all nonslaveholding whites, whose freedom is merely nominal." Abolition, for Helper, meant "the liberation of five millions of 'poor white trash' from the second degree of slavery."[59] Outside the South as well, abolitionists had argued against the "slave oligarchy" or "slave power" in terms that appealed to lower-class whites. Even the Republican Party, as Larry Gara argues, hoped "to appeal to non-slaveholders in the South as well as to northern voters if they presented the question properly as 'a question of the white man against the Ethiopian.'"[60]

Pollard's innovation was to attach white identity not simply to the reconstituted nation-state but to the history of slavery itself. Instead of establishing southern civilization, slavery now established the solidarity of the white race, on behalf of which southerners spoke with special authority. For Pollard, the "Negro Slavery of the South became the instructor of white republicanism" by eliminating the importance of "those inferior distinctions made by society in mere classes and conditions of life," thus leading the South to "clearer perceptions of the natural equality of their own species and race."[61] If Helper had argued just the opposite, defeat in the war aligned his thinking with Pollard's and with new "evidence" borrowed from science to underwrite white supremacy.[62]

This raises the possibility that Pollard is merely (or tactically) nationalizing what had been, all along, the true cardinal test of a southerner. This is the position argued by Ulrich B. Phillips, for whom the proposition that the "south is a white man's country" constituted a continuous test of southern insiderhood. Unlike Pollard, who wonders why proslavery writers had failed to make the "true and only" defense, Phillips argues that, covertly, they had. Slavery, he writes, was defended "with vigor and vehemence as a guarantee of white supremacy and civilization. Its defenders did not always take pains to say that this is what they chiefly meant, but it may nearly always be read between their lines, and their hearers and readers understood it without overt expression."[63] The problem with this reasoning is that it follows Pollard in backdating an unexpressed argument in order to establish continuity. Rather than assuming a stable group identity, such that southerners are revealed as having "really" been white supremacists all along, Pollard recodes the slavery question in terms that speak to his own historical moment. But recognizing the "illusion of continuity" also means, I suggest, rejecting Maddex's view that Pollard renders "palatable" the "enemy's system." This presupposes the very categories of enemy and ally that Pollard is attempting to dissolve and reconstitute. On a broader level, what might appear as group betrayal, inconsistency, or shoddy thinking is often better understood as signaling what's at stake in historically specific debates. Letting group spokesmen speak for themselves means recognizing that group identities are always under construction and always subject to revision.

For the Satan of *Paradise Lost*, "the mind is its own place, and in itself can make a heaven of hell." Pollard's revision, I suggest, was not merely this sort of thing—what Maddex calls a "collective falsification of memory" as "defense mechanism."[64] It was also an offense mechanism, a discursive intervention that helped to reassemble a nation. If this meant redefining a war fought on behalf of southern civilization as a war to keep the United States a white man's country, Pollard was willing to alter the terms of engagement. When Albion Tourgée lamented in 1884 that "the South surrendered at Appomattox, and the North has been surrendering ever since," he signaled an acceptance of Pollard's terms: the Confederacy, as Pollard redefined it, had triumphed.[65] National opposition to "negro rule" had emerged as a powerful political force, even among former abolitionists. In *The Prostrate State* (1874), for example, James Shepherd Pike glosses "Negro Government" as "barbarism overwhelming civilization by physical force." South Carolina, Pike writes, would avoid becoming "Africanized" only if it "remains an integral part" of a federal union "incontestably white at the centre" and "well abreast of all modern progress in ideas and improvements."[66]

Had he lived two years longer, Pollard would have partially disagreed with Pike's verdict. On the one hand, modern progress and improvements would have met his full approval. In 1870, Pollard published *The Virginia Tourist*, a guidebook presented as a "great patriotic contribution to the State of Virginia."[67] Mainly, however, it poor-mouths the "barren picture" presented by the state and its "memorials of 'improvement' under the past system of slavery."[68] In his latest revision of the war (now simply "the Civil War"), Pollard announces that its happiest outcome was the "discovery of Virginia and the Southern States by the Yankees," who, "discovering a new world of beauty," also discovered "new kingdoms of commerce and industry."[69] In *The Lost Cause*, he had inveighed against the "garish enterprise" and "gilded caravansies of the North"; now he apologizes for the "defective hotel establishment" of his native state. Northern readers, he hoped, would cure the defect by bringing enterprise, capital, "better management," and the "art of advertising."[70]

Pike's white supremacy, conversely, ran counter to Pollard's final iteration of the racialized South to which he—and now, at least partially, the freedman—belonged. In "The Negro in the South," published in *Lippincott's* in 1870, Pollard announces (again) "a discovery!" His "former views of the negro were wrong," and the "black man promises to become a true follower of the highest civilization . . . and an exemplary citizen of the South."[71] Presented as a rigorously empirical counter to the theories, speculations, hypotheses, and "unproved, reckless assertions" attending emancipation, Pollard's account of the formerly despised race glows with warmth. The "evidence of my own eyes" proves to Pollard that the freedman is industrious, sober, free from crime ("excepting the offence of larceny"), eager for education, peaceful, and ambitious.[72] "His ambition," Pollard is careful to add, "does not run in the line of social equality, nor yet even in that of political preferment."[73] Because the Negro lacks "desire of social place or of political influence in the community," it is imperative that he "be respected in [his] new estate" and that "his white countrymen . . . give him the word of acknowledgement and encouragement that he deserves."[74] Meeting this obligation, in various ways, are "every white gentleman in the South," the "brave man in the South," the "reflecting and good white citizen," "the more intelligent and respectable citizens of the South," "the just and thoughtful white people of the South," the "really respectable native white man of the South," the "decent and honorable white men in the South," and "the just and intelligent white men in the South."[75] Failing to meet this obligation, in various ways, are "lazy white persons in the South," "a low and unmannerly class of whites," "certain classes in the South," and "the lowest class of whites."[76] "The white man in the South who would insult the negro," Pollard concludes, "is a dirty enemy."[77] Pollard thus fractures white solidarity, a premise of his three previous books, in order to assemble an interracial alliance that leaves enemy whites in the dirt.

Revisiting the chivalry motif of *The Lost Cause*, he writes, "The opportunity is to build up a true school of chivalry in the South founded on the black man—one of ingenuous and brave spirits; and to indicate in the cause of the rights and progress of the colored people of the South an honorable and Romantic championship, raised far above the strife of mere political parties, and exalted to a great and knightly cause and contest in the affairs of this century."[78] There's a catch: in order to benefit from this "great and knightly cause," the Negro must abandon "his false friendships with the North, and his hopes there in the selfish and fleeting policy of an alien party." Romantic championship doesn't rise above mere politics after all, and the Republican Party, which "force[s] the negro into prominence in the political administration of the country," remains in place as Pollard's most reliable antagonist.[79]

Edward A. Pollard never wrote about the same South twice. But he never wrote about any South without repeating himself. Chivalry might define the (white) southern people of *The Lost Cause*, but it could also forge an alliance between the "good white citizen" and the "exemplary [black] citizen." That bond recalls the "affectionate respect for the old slaves on the plantation" in *Black Diamonds*.[80] But *Black Diamonds* also voices "revulsion" at the slave out of his place, a feeling scaled up to the national level in *The Lost Cause Regained*, which extends the defense of states' rights in *The Lost Cause* and offers a similar critique of the North's unchivalrous conduct in the war.

Clearly, though, Pollard's "discoveries" are more significant than his few consistencies. In what amounts to a kind of identitarian ad hoccery, he continually redrew the boundaries of a South to which southerners belonged. Merely living there was never enough; to be *in the South* was not necessarily to be *of the South*. Even in *The Lost Cause Regained*, where (white) identity transcends region, it is *southerners* who must realize "the true hope of the South" by "enter[ing] bravely with new allies and new auspices." Only in this "contest" could the Civil War, as revised and updated, be won.[81] The constant in Pollard's writing is a conception of "all true southerners," even if the true southerner in question never survived the next publication cycle. As he cycled through conceptions, he recycled topoi from earlier arguments and refashioned them in ways that would survive his own. Henry Grady's New South project, for example, would combine the boosterism of *The Virginia Tourist* with the elegiac Romanticism of *The Lost Cause*. *The Lost Cause Regained* predicts the white supremacist political alliance that would either leave Reconstruction unfinished or lead to the birth of a reconstructed (white) nation. Looking back to the old paternalism of slavery, "The Negro in the South" envisions an emergent paternalism in which recognition and respect would consolidate racial hierarchies. As James McBride Dabbs would later decode the strategy, "We like [the Negro] for staying in his place. The liking is a bonus for his staying there."[82]

Pollard's cleverness lay in assembling group identities by telling southerners what they should do under the guise of telling them who they were.

Crowding men off or upon the word "South" was thus essential to his work. Because he wrote in a time of great stress, it is tempting to view Pollard as driven by history to the modernist project of what Wallace Stevens would call "the act of the mind in finding what will suffice."[83] Certainly he found that different acts of the mind sufficed for different purposes, as did different Souths. In that sense, he proves that "no true southerner" is, indeed, a fallacy, because it is unfalsifiable. But it is less clear that southern identity has ever functioned in any other way.

NOTES

1. Michael O'Brien, *Rethinking the South: Essays in Intellectual History* (Baltimore: Johns Hopkins University Press, 1988), 165–66.
2. Michael O'Brien, *Placing the South* (Jackson: University Press of Mississippi, 2007), 19.
3. Michael O'Brien, *The Idea of the American South, 1920–1941* (Baltimore: Johns Hopkins University Press, 1979), xiv.
4. Michael O'Brien, *Conjectures of Order: Intellectual Life and the American South, 1810–1860* (Chapel Hill: University of North Carolina Press, 2004), 16.
5. O'Brien, *Rethinking the South*, 217.
6. O'Brien, *Conjectures of Order*, 16.
7. Tracy Thompson, *The New Mind of the South* (New York: Free Press, 2013), 11.
8. O'Brien, *Idea*, 216. He uses similar language in *Rethinking the South*, writing that the intellectual historian, in "studying the history of the Southern intelligentsia," would be "of use in teasing out the boundaries and dialectics of perception and discrete realities" (217).
9. O'Brien, *Placing the South*, 19. At times, especially later in his career, O'Brien edged toward considering the southern idea as it existed outside the formal thought of an intellectual class. In 2005, for example, he argued that defeat in the Civil War required in the South a "reassessment" more "emotional" than "intellectual" in nature; see Michael O'Brien, *Henry Adams and the Southern Question* (Athens: University of Georgia Press, 2005), 149. More pointedly, he observed in his preface to *An Evening When Alone* that "intellectual historians like myself are well and advised, now and again, to step beyond their customary discipline" to (among other things) be "reminded that thoughts exist in more than books, [and] that there are more thinkers than those who claim the title." Here, too, an emotional idiom appears, as reading women's diaries allowed him, he writes, "to sympathize with their lives, and to feel their predicaments." See Michael O'Brien, ed., *An Evening When Alone: Four Journals of Single Women in the South, 1827–1867* (Charlottesville: University Press of Virginia, 1993), xv, xvi.
10. Bruno Latour, *Science in Action: How to Follow Scientists and Engineers through Society* (Cambridge, Mass.: Harvard University Press, 1987), 201.
11. As I hope will be clear, this approach bears no relation to the conservative

defense of the southern "rhetorical mode." As articulated by Allen Tate, Richard Weaver, M. E. Bradford, Eugene Genovese, and others, this line of thought associates southern civilization with a preference for rhetoric over dialectic. This simply assumes a self-evident or axiomatic "civilization" out of which the rhetoric organically emerges.

12. Bruno Latour, *Reassembling the Social: An Introduction to Actor-Network-Theory* (Oxford: Oxford University Press, 2005), 24.

13. O'Brien, *Idea*, 216.

14. Latour, *Reassembling the Social*, 31.

15. John C. Calhoun, "Speech on the Reception of Abolition Petitions, February 6, 1837," in *The Works of John C. Calhoun*, ed. Richard K. Crallé (New York: D. Appleton, 1883), 2:626, 631.

16. O'Brien, *Conjectures of Order*, 1180.

17. Johann Gottlieb Fichte, *Fichte: Addresses to the German Nation*, ed. Gregory Moore (Cambridge: Cambridge University Press, 2008), 172.

18. William Henry Trescot, *The Position and Course of the South* (Charleston: Steam Power-Press of Walker and James, 1850), 8. A reviewer in *De Bow's* wrote, "Would not any one smile to think of the Ohio River and the Potomac, being such grand national barriers as must . . . constitute of necessity the nations on either side of them . . . and yet Mr. Trescott [*sic*], with great profoundness, announces this discovery." See review of *The Position and Course of the South*, by William Henry Trescott, *De Bow's Review*, February 1851, 231.

19. Edward L. Ayers, "What We Talk about When We Talk about the South," in *All over the Map: Rethinking American Regions*, ed. Edward L. Ayers, Patricia Nelson Limerick, Stephen Nissenbaum, and Peter S. Onuf (Baltimore: Johns Hopkins University Press, 1996), 69.

20. O'Brien, *Conjectures of Order*, 957–58. O'Brien here refers specifically to the work of Hammond and Fitzhugh.

21. Edward A. Pollard, *The Lost Cause: A New Southern History of the War of the Confederates* (New York: E. B. Treat, 1866), 47.

22. Pollard, 47.

23. Pollard, 50.

24. Pollard, 50.

25. Pollard, 50.

26. Pollard, 50, 51.

27. Pollard, 48.

28. Pollard, 751–52.

29. Pollard, 750.

30. Pollard, 750.

31. Pollard, 750–51.

32. Pollard, 751.

33. Allen Tate, "Some Remarks on the Southern Religion," in Twelve Southerners, *I'll Take My Stand: The South and the Agrarian Tradition* (Baton Rouge: Louisiana State University Press, 1977), 167, 168, 169.

34. Interestingly, Pollard uses the word "tradition" only twice, both times citing an unnamed southern senator to the effect that "it is a tradition of the colonies that the

South had been the seat of wealth and happiness, of power and opulence." Affirming that "this tradition was not without similitude to the reality," the senator observes a societal decline perceptible "enough to constitute a reverse, and make a contrast, and to excite the regrets which the memory of past joys never fails to awaken." See Pollard, *Lost Cause*, 60.

35. As did, longer and more faithfully, his brother H. Rives Pollard, who edited the *Richmond Examiner* until his murder in 1869.

36. Thomas Nelson Page, *In Ole Virginia: or, Marse Chan and Other Stories* (1887; repr., Chapel Hill: University of North Carolina Press, 1969), 2.

37. Edward A. Pollard, *The Lost Cause Regained* (New York: G. W. Carleton, 1868), 13.

38. Pollard, 14.

39. Pollard, 14.

40. Pollard, 165.

41. Pollard, 212–13.

42. Pollard, 132.

43. Pollard, 135.

44. Pollard, 134.

45. Pollard, 92.

46. Pollard, 51–52.

47. Pollard, 210.

48. Pollard, 199. In his 1882 "What Is a Nation?" Renan claims that "the act of forgetting, I would even say, historical error, is an essential factor in the creation of a nation, which is why progress in historical studies often constitutes a danger for nationality. Indeed, historical enquiry brings back to light the deeds of violence that took place at the origin of all political formations, even those whose consequences have been the most beneficial." See Ernest Renan, *What Is a Nation? And other Political Writings*, ed. and trans. M. F. N. Giglioli (New York: Columbia University Press, 2018), 251. Renan's immediate reference is, fittingly enough, to the unification of northern France and southern France.

49. Pollard, *Lost Cause Regained*, 210.

50. Pollard, 214.

51. Pollard, 115.

52. Pollard, 115, 117.

53. Pollard, 115. The second quotation comes from a *De Bow's* review cited in the front matter of the second edition of the book. See Edward A. Pollard, *Black Diamonds Gathered in the Darkey Homes of the South*, 2nd ed. (New York: Pudney and Russell, 1860), [xi].

54. Pollard, *Lost Cause Regained*, 117.

55. Pollard, 115.

56. Jack P. Maddex Jr., "Pollard's *The Lost Cause Regained*: A Mask for Southern Accommodation," *Journal of Southern History* 40, no. 4 (November 1974), 595, 607. As Pollard notes, seven northern states voted against black suffrage between 1865 and 1867. Pollard, *Lost Cause Regained*, 133–34.

57. Although proslavery writing generally avoided antagonistic racial feeling as a feature of slavery, it did predict such feeling as an effect of abolition. In *The Proslav-*

ery Argument (1853), for example, William Harper argues that, given the franchise, "the blacks will be tempted to avenge themselves by oppression and proscription of the white race, for their long superiority. Thus matters will go on, until universal anarchy, or kakistocracy, the government of the worst, is fully established." See Chancellor Harper, Governor Hammond, Dr. Simms, and Professor Dew, *The Proslavery Argument, as Maintained by the Most Distinguished Writers of the Southern States* (Philadelphia: Lippincott, Grambo, 1853), 90–91. In *Black Diamonds*, Pollard admits to "the most repulsive feelings toward negro gentlemen. When I see a slave above his condition, or hear him talk insultingly of even the lowest white man in the land, I am strongly tempted to knock him down." See Pollard, *Black Diamonds*, 56.

58. Pollard, *Lost Cause Regained*, 138–39.

59. Hinton Rowan Helper, *The Impending Crisis of the South: How to Meet It* (New York: Burdick Brothers, 1857), 43, 32–33.

60. Larry Gara, "Slavery and the Slave Power: A Crucial Distinction," in *Abolition and American Politics and Government*, ed. John R. McKivigan (New York: Garland, 1999), 214. Gara cites an 1859 letter from H. C. Trinne to Lyman Trumbull.

61. Pollard, *Lost Cause Regained*, 115.

62. Helper's *Nojoque*, published the year before *The Lost Cause Regained*, was more sophisticated in this regard, citing a litany of scientific experts in support of racial hierarchy. See Hinton Rowan Helper, *Nojoque: A Question for a Continent* (New York: George W. Carleton, 1867), esp. 11–80, where Helper cites extensively from the work of Georges Cuvier, Hermann Burmeister, Louis Agassiz, Charles Lyell, Josiah Clark Nott, and other scientists. Although Pollard's reference to "species and race" gestures to science, he offers a confused hodgepodge of naturalistic, biblical, and historical arguments. Helper and Pollard cite differently Jefferson's insistence on the colonization of emancipated slaves. For Helper, all "non-whites" would be banished to Mexico or "colonized in a State or Territory by themselves" (15). For Pollard, Jefferson had argued only that the two races could not "live in state of equal freedom under the same government." This raises the possibility, which Pollard leaves unexplored, of some system by which emancipated slaves might remain within the United States but be "withdrawn from competition with the white man." Pollard, *Lost Cause Regained*, 116.

63. Ulrich B. Phillips, "The Central Theme of Southern History," *American Historical Review* 34 (October 1928): 31.

64. Maddex, "Pollard's *The Lost Cause Regained*," 612.

65. Albion Tourgée, "The Apotheosis of the Kuklux Klan," *Continent* 6, no. 129 (July 1884): 153.

66. James S. Pike, *The Prostrate State: South Carolina under Negro Government* (New York: D. Appleton, 1874), 12, 22.

67. Edward A. Pollard, *The Virginia Tourist: Sketches of the Springs and Mountains of Virginia* (Philadelphia: J. B. Lippincott, 1870), 4.

68. Pollard, 18.

69. Pollard, 24.

70. Pollard, 28, 29.

71. Edward A. Pollard, "The Negro in the South," *Lippincott's Magazine of Literature, Science, and Education*, April 1870, 383.

72. Pollard, 384, 387.
73. Pollard, 389.
74. Pollard, 391.
75. Pollard, 388, 390, 391.
76. Pollard, 385, 391.
77. Pollard, 391.
78. Pollard, 391.
79. Pollard, 391.
80. Pollard, *Black Diamonds*, 49.
81. Pollard, *Lost Cause Regained*, 165.
82. James McBride Dabbs, *The Southern Heritage* (New York: Knopf, 1958), 177.
83. Wallace Stevens, "Of Modern Poetry," Poetry Foundation, https://www.poetryfoundation.org/poems/43435/of-modern-poetry, accessed August 11, 2020.

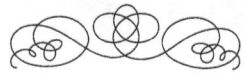

FASHIONING INSIDERS AND OUTSIDERS

Race and Gender in the Making of
The Library of Southern Literature, *1900–1920*

JONATHAN DANIEL WELLS

AT THE turn of the twentieth century, three leading men of letters, Joel Chandler Harris, Edwin Alderman, and Charles W. Kent, began planning what would become the massive, thirteen-volume *Library of Southern Literature (LSL)*, the largest printed collection of works by southern authors that had ever been published. Comprising biographies of hundreds of authors together with thousands of poems, short stories, and excerpts from novels, as well as personal letters and political speeches, the collection was a mammoth and ambitious undertaking, and when it was published in 1909, readers and reviewers recognized the collection as a landmark event in the intellectual history of the region. While southern partisans had edited several collections throughout the late nineteenth and early twentieth centuries, public opinion appeared to agree with unanimity that the *LSL* constituted a major development in the region's literary history, though readers would differ dramatically on the merits of the final product. While contemporaries almost universally granted that the publication was historically significant, few modern scholars have seen the *LSL* as a watershed moment in the mind of the South. Surprisingly, though long recognized for its attempt to offer readers a comprehensive corpus from the history of southern literary culture, the publication of *The Library of Southern Literature* has received little scholarly attention.

Given the paucity of modern analyses of the library series, fundamental questions about this seminal collection remain unanswered. Why has such a massive set of original works by southern authors gone largely without comment for so long? Is the collection to be doomed for its choice of included writers? Can the collection tell us anything valuable or instructive about race and gender ideologies in southern literary history? This essay will seek to answer several questions about the choice of authors and subjects that comprised the final publication of the *LSL*. Why the proposed publication met with widespread acclaim, and why modern literary critics see the *LSL* as little more than a footnote, is attributable to a few key factors.

One reason why the collection made only a minor splash when first released can be traced to the complaints of partisanship that emerged in contemporary reviews. Despite the grand aspirations of the editors, almost as soon as it was published the collection became a lightning rod for controversy. When planning and producing the library, Harris, Alderman, and Kent claimed that no "sinister sectionalism" lay behind the effort. On the contrary, in their introduction to the compilation, the editors explicitly stated that they were not motivated by any desire to promote literary parochialisms or to divide a nation that had only relatively recently begun to reconstruct the union. The primary motive behind the publication, the editors claimed, was "national enrichment, not sectional glorification."[1] *The Library of Southern Literature*, however, belies this claim of impartiality, a fact most clearly demonstrated in the selection of authors and works.

A chief reason why the *LSL* has not garnered attention from modern scholars lies in the gender and racial ideologies current in the nineteenth- and early twentieth-century South. Scholars of literary history have pointed to this period as a crucial moment not just in southern intellectual culture but in national literature as well. Virtually every aspect of literary culture expanded and deepened, from the number of readers to the expansion of publishing houses. Indeed, a national dialogue about literature, manifested by the fact that northern critics read and extensively commented on works by southern writers, helped to define what southern literature meant. As Sarah E. Gardner, Michael Winship, Bill Hardwig, and others have shown, periodicals such as *Harper's* and the *Atlantic Monthly* were widely distributed across the country at the same time that large publishing houses advertised the latest works by favorite authors. The emergence of a national distribution network for books and periodicals, a network that had already begun to develop before the Civil War, became one of the defining features of the late 1800s and early 1900s, providing the basis for a common dialogue about the meaning of regional differences within a national context.[2]

While scholars have revealed the ways in which national networks of literary critics shaped the evolution of southern literature, they have also embarked on a concerted campaign to recover the lost voices of the region's writers. A much greater appreciation for the contributions of women writers such as Mary Edwards Bryan and authors of color such as Anna Julia Cooper has dramatically altered our understanding of southern literary culture. Though modern southern historians and literary scholars have turned to periodicals and archives in search of black authors, such writers are basically absent in the series. The purpose of the *LSL* was to enshrine the mind of the South for future generations, but that mind was white. Almost no attention is paid to authors of color, despite the rich and important works published by southern black authors from the early nineteenth century onward. The editors elected not to include African American authors, though there were many from which to choose. Kent in particular wanted to promote the "Teutonic" vision of southern history, one that relied heavily on writing southern African Americans out of the region's intellectual past.[3]

While discounting African American contributions to regional literature, however, the editors openly welcomed white women as both subjects and contributors, and herein lies the most surprising feature of the library. The *LSL* reveals one of the starkest and most puzzling truisms about nineteenth-century southern intellectual life. Soon after the nation won independence, white women were included in the literary and cultural life of the region to an extent that might seem startling to modern observers. The days of painting the white young woman as a superficial belle are long over thanks to the important work of scholars such as Michael O'Brien, Giselle Roberts, Elizabeth Varon, Thavolia Glymph, and many others. We now know that white women were far more politically active, engaged in the public world of editing and publishing, and more directly involved in the management of the household than the trope of the southern belle would have us believe.[4] In recent years, historians have revealed the impressively deep ranks of white literary women who earned regional fame. Before the Civil War, political radicals such as Anne Royall and bold editors such as Mary Chase Barney and Mary Edwards Bryan have received long-overdue scholarly attention. In examining the making of the *LSL*, the volumes reveal much about the region's racial and gender politics as well as its intellectual life. Like other contemporary publications, such as Mildred Lewis Rutherford's *The South in History and Literature*, the library included a number of leading southern women writers such as Mary E. Johnston, Caroline Gilman, and Augusta Jane Evans. The collection also recognized the literary contributions of dozens of lesser-known white women, despite the conservative gender conventions in virtually every other aspect of the region's society, politics, and economy.

Far from putting together an objectively chosen collection of work by southern writers, the editors clearly had multiple political and social motives in mind when selecting which authors would earn the honor of inclusion. In fact, the editors followed the same path that had guided southern intellectual life throughout the nineteenth century: it was a culture surprisingly open to literary contributions from white women while remaining steadfastly opposed to recognizing black authors of either gender. As scholars have shown, even as the region countenanced no public discussions of abolitionism or racial equality, it simultaneously opened the door for white women to participate actively and vigorously in print culture.[5] White women edited their own newspapers and magazines, penned outspoken and vituperative attacks on gender-based discrimination, and carved out important roles as public critics. This is not to say, of course, that the nineteenth-century South could boast of gender equality; women were barred from virtually every professional career, except for journalism and literature. In large part because literary pursuits seemed to coincide with gender expectations, that poetry and fiction were associated in the southern mind with femininity, the region offered leading positions for white literary women.

This characteristic of the South before and after slavery is reflected in *The Library of Southern Literature*. White women were welcomed into its pages, making up almost 20 percent of the authors. Indeed, even if Alderman, Kent, and Harris were predisposed to elevate male writers, the editors could hardly ignore the fact that in the late 1800s women such as Augusta Jane Evans and Mary E. Johnston were selling novels by the tens of thousands. Furthermore, the inclusion of white women did not stop at the collection's publication. Throughout the early twentieth century, publisher Martin and Hoyt Company of Atlanta promoted the library to southern women, even sponsoring essay-writing contests with the United Daughters of the Confederacy (UDC).

A region that remained unexpectedly accessible to literary white women stood firmly against the mere recognition of black authors. In fact, the *LSL* appeared just as the region stayed fixed in the midst of a racist retrenchment so eloquently analyzed by scholars such as Tera Hunter and Nan Elizabeth Woodruff. It should not surprise us that the period between 1900 and 1920, when the *LSL* was collected, published, and reviewed throughout the South, coincided with the erection of Confederate monuments across the region. The *LSL* is itself a kind of Confederate memorial, though the collection included authors from the colonial era to the late 1800s. Despite claims of nationalistic sentiment underlying the project, the editors from the very beginning stages wanted to promote the region's literary and intellectual accomplishments, a desire that emanated from a sectionalist impulse to counteract a perceived bias in American literature in favor of northeastern writers. In fact, the final volume consists of hundreds of pages of suggestions for courses of study in southern literature. Readers and reviewers saw behind the mask and noted the limits as well as the achievements of the set. In the final analysis, then, *The Library of Southern Literature* reflected the prejudices and revealed the motives of its editors, and in revisiting the process of fashioning the collection, we learn much about the problems and the promises of the intellectual culture in which the library was created. In simultaneously granting a prominent place for women in shaping the mind of the South even as it closed off opportunities to recognize authors of color, the library mirrored the complicated history of southern intellectual life more generally, creating a stark division between those considered "insiders" and those to be left out of literature's sacred circle.

Even before the *LSL* appeared in 1909, several works had already been published that tried mightily to demonstrate the contributions of southern writers to the national literature, responding to Thomas Nelson Page's complaint, one commonly heard among post–Civil War southern intellectuals, that the region "has been left behind in the race for literary honors." This refrain was repeated often in the wake of the Confederacy's defeat and Republican claims that the Old South had been doomed by slavery to mental lassitude. In part to combat the postwar battles over the meaning and legacy of the war, white southern writers published a number of anthologies intended to bolster intellectual support for the Lost Cause.[6]

Emblematic of these paper monuments is Mildred Lewis Rutherford's substantial one-volume *The South in History and Literature*, which appeared just a few years before the *LSL* and undoubtedly provided a model for the larger compilation. As head of the Lucy Cobb Institute for girls in Athens, Georgia, and as "historian general" of the UDC, Rutherford was well placed to offer southern partisans a detailed and comprehensive regional literary history. As would soon prove true of the *LSL*, Rutherford's volume included works and biographies of hundreds of white southern women without reference to a single black poet or novelist. African Americans do appear as subjects, of course, particularly in reference to Joel Harris's *Uncle Remus* stories, but none of the nineteenth-century South's black authors warranted even a passing reference in Rutherford's mind. But while Rutherford closed the pages of her volume to authors of color, she opened them to even the most obscure white southern women, not only crediting them for contributions to poetry and novel writing but also highlighting their work as essayists, opinion makers, and orators. Even long-forgotten antebellum southern writers such as Kentucky's Amelia Welby are featured in Rutherford's selections, as well as later nineteenth-century women such as Mississippi's Sherwood Bonner. In concert with her own status as a leading southern woman of letters, Rutherford helped to set the tone for the basic approach taken by the editors of the *LSL*: white female authors were to be given every opportunity for respect and literary glory, but the mind of the South was for whites only.[7]

Yet even Rutherford could rely on a long history of one-volume compilations of works by southern writers that were similarly intended to provide evidence for the region's supposed literary greatness. James Wood Davidson, a southern teacher who had served in Lee's army during the war, published his *Living Writers of the South* in 1869, an encyclopedic collection of nineteenth-century authors that would set the tone for future anthologies of southern literature. Organized alphabetically, and with short biographies attached to writing excerpts, Davidson's collection included a few editorial notices of slavery and enslaved people but no black writers. Unsurprisingly, the volume includes scores of poems written during the short life of the Confederacy, and part of Davidson's intention was to begin memorializing the writers of the Lost Cause. Davidson did, however, publish works by southern women, though the collection relied heavily on male writers.

Perhaps in response to the paucity of women in *Living Writers*, just a few years after the appearance of Davidson's anthology, Mary T. Tardy published *Living Female Writers of the South* (1872), a massive collection of works by hundreds of white southern women. About a decade before Rutherford's collection appeared, Louise Manly (daughter of the University of Alabama president and granddaughter of the famous Southern Baptist Basil Manly Sr.) published a widely used 500-page volume that covered regional literature from John Smith to Sidney Lanier. Manly included white women poets such as Octavia Le Vert and Margaret J. Preston as well as political essayists such as South Carolina's Louisa McCord.

Tardy's comprehensive examination of white southern women influenced later anthologies, since editors could no longer claim that the region lacked notable female authors. By the late nineteenth century, the pattern for such collections was clear: white men and women would be literary insiders, but writers of color would be banished to the status of outsider. In 1896, Vanderbilt University professor William Malone Baskervill began publishing his collection in serial format, with each issue addressing a single writer through biography and critical analysis. The first issue addressed the work of Sidney Lanier, but later issues were devoted to prominent female authors such as Margaret J. Preston, Grace King, and Sherwood Bonner. From its earliest conceptual stages, then, the *LSL* could rely on a number of previous attempts to erect literary monuments that would memorialize the Lost Cause, defend the literary production of the region in response to New England critics, and remind white southerners themselves of the contributions rendered by their forebears. The editors of the *LSL* had all of these goals very much in mind as they began planning the massive collection.

From the beginning, the endeavor was closely aligned with the University of Virginia, which was the region's flagship academic institution as well as the home of Edwin Alderman, one of the chief movers behind the collection. A North Carolina native born just weeks after the cannons rang out at the battle of Fort Sumter, Alderman was the president of the University of Virginia and a noted speaker on higher education. By the time of the publication of the *LSL* in 1909, he had already served as the president of the University of North Carolina and of Tulane. Alderman's coeditors, Joel Chandler Harris and Charles W. Kent, were equally well known in the region. Harris had earned fame in the 1880s for his *Uncle Remus* stories that collected African American folktales, particularly the tales of Br'er Rabbit and Br'er Fox, using black dialect in a demeaning way that delighted white southern audiences. Kent, the author of several academic books, was an expert in poetry who had helped bring the works of Edgar Allan Poe to popular southern audiences. Together, Alderman, Harris, and Kent were a formidable group, the ideal collaboration that would bring the history of southern literature to national prominence.

Although the University of Virginia featured prominently in the pre-publication publicity, the *Atlanta Constitution* became the leading promoter of the volumes. Henry W. Grady, one of the region's most visible advocates of the new postwar South, which in Grady's campaign would be a national leader in education reform, had transformed the *Atlanta Constitution* into a regional powerhouse in the 1880s. As a city that had become a key example of the economic potential of the New South, and as Harris's home, Atlanta was a logical cheerleader for the *LSL*. The paper's literary editor, Samuel W. Dibble, made sure that readers knew of this "Epoch-Making Publication."[8]

Though the editors claimed not to be motivated by sectional jealousies, even before the volumes appeared, southern journalists and opinion makers were already staking claims to the recovery of the true greatness of a regional corpus of prose and poetry that had been (in the minds of white southerners) badly neglected by the elite literati of New England and the northeast. It mattered to southern journalists that publisher Martin and Hoyt was based in Atlanta and had earned the respect of regional authors by offering distinctly southern works to the public. The publishing house was well positioned, the *Charleston Courier* declared, to "establish for the South the place it deserves in the domain of American letters." The editors of the *Courier* agreed with fellow journalists that, in fact, the volumes would be "a monument to the memory and genius of the makers of Southern history and literature." At the same time that white southern communities were commissioning statues of Confederate soldiers, monuments that would be installed in town squares and city halls throughout the region, the *LSL* would be the intellectual equivalent, a paper testament that would honor the South's intellectual leaders to stand alongside the stone and bronze statues honoring the likes of Robert E. Lee and Stonewall Jackson.[9]

During the early twentieth century, the South embarked on a massive campaign to memorialize the men and ideology of the Confederacy, and the region's intelligentsia was enlisted in the effort, just as leading thinkers and writers such as William Gilmore Simms defended antebellum slavery. While a glance at southern history might lead one to think that white southerners in the nineteenth century cared little what northerners or Europeans thought of the region, evidence suggests quite the opposite. In fact, it is not too much to say that concern over external opinion was the prime motivator of southern intellectual history. White southerners had long seen themselves as outsiders, apart and distinct from the main currents of western civilization, a self-perception that drove the proslavery Simms and the racist Kent to defend the region against attacks from without. White southerners, ever concerned about outside opinion, had expended much of the region's creative and intellectual energy on defending slavery and segregation.

In fact, as the *LSL* began publication in the spring of 1909, other writers and editors grew concerned that the wave of publicity and praise for the new volumes would overwhelm works of regional justification already in progress. The Southern Historical Society issued a public declaration that it had not endorsed either the *LSL* or another collection titled *The South in the Building of the Nation*, a parallel effort to bring national attention to the South's economic contributions.[10]

The publishers and editors, of course, were hardly above playing on regional prejudices, and advertisements for the collection told readers it was "high-time" that the South finally receive the literary respect it had been long due. Lucian L. Knight penned a hyperbolic series of essays on the forthcoming publication, declaring that the South now stood "in the daybreak of an era, whose coming has been too long delayed; an era for which her scholars have longed, of which her minstrels have sung, and to which her prophets have pointed; an era whose compensating tribute will be, in part at least, the recognition of her just desserts." In fact, Knight hoped, the *LSL* would not only resurrect the long-forgotten authors of the Old South but would stimulate young writers to unprecedented literary production. Just as important, literate southerners would finally be able to hold their heads high when discussing the nation's intellectual output, no longer hiding in the shadows of Poe and Simms and shrinking from comparisons to the giants of New England. In Knight's vision, the nation as a whole would be forced to appreciate the region's signal contributions to American intellectual life.[11]

Publisher Martin and Hoyt embarked on an ambitious publicity campaign to ensure that southern schools, libraries, and individual members of the reading public could not fail to learn about the collection. Ads for salesmen appeared in papers throughout the region, and from the beginning, the firm made clear that southern white women would play important roles in promoting the collection.[12] Since the 1880s, women had been active in local and national clubs and organizations, an ideal target for the advertising staff of Martin and Hoyt. The *Atlanta Constitution* informed its "club women" readers that the collection deserved their patronage. Large cities such as Atlanta, Baltimore, St. Louis, and Nashville were key sites of heavy advertising, but the firm also sent women into smaller towns to drum up publicity and increase readership. For example, the firm paid Jeanette Moscrip, an unmarried woman from Atlanta, as a "special representative" to travel through southern towns such as High Point, North Carolina. There Moscrip remained for more than a week to meet with librarians, middle-class housewives, and churchwomen to garner customers.[13]

Libraries in all corners of the region were obliged to purchase the collection, from university holdings and private libraries to local public institutions. The smallest towns were not to be left out. The *Waxahachie Daily Light* in Texas boasted of its library's purchase just weeks after the first five volumes went on sale in July 1909.[14] Whether they were deluxe copies with ornate gilt lettering on the spines or the more common versions with less decorative bindings, the volumes generated widespread interest, with local authors and their communities excited to see whether they had appeared in the final production. Each volume offered readers a different sepia-toned picture of a famous author and a colorful title page. In the first volume of the thirteen alphabetically arranged books, the picture featured Joel Chandler Harris, who had passed away just before the *LSL* appeared in print, together with other photographs such as that of Jewish politician and thinker Judah P. Benjamin. At the outset of the collection the editors stated their objective: the *LSL* was designed for ease of use, reference, and study.

Each author treated in the collection was provided with a short essay combining biographical information with literary criticism, followed by stories, poems, and excerpts from novels. Poe is featured prominently with two critical essays, one by James A. Harrison, who had written an early book-length biography of Poe. Harrison had also edited multivolume collections of Poe's works, along with new editions of Greek classics.

The common thread in Harrison's career had been a commitment to promoting what he called "Anglo-Saxon Literature," which consisted of work by white Europeans, so his scholarly proclivities fit perfectly with the literary whiteness of the *LSL*. Virginia native William P. Trent, a professor at Sewanee and then Columbia, had penned the other essay on Poe, whom Trent called the greatest writer in the South's long history. The volume also included full reprints of famous poems such as "The Raven" and "To Helen" but also provided readers the whole text of "The Cask of Amontillado" and some of Poe's criticism. The editors elected not to include Poe's more macabre works such as "The Tell-Tale Heart," likely because such selections would clash with the collection's intention of providing a range of works of interest to families.

They were also clear that the volumes, while welcoming women into their pages, would be for whites only. As a staunch segregationist, and so as to leave no question about the intent, Kent argued, "The South is a single, homogenous people."[15] Nowhere would appear works by important antebellum black authors, such as the North Carolina poet George Moses Horton, an enslaved man whose poems "Ode to Liberty" and "Lines to My—" had appeared in the *Southern Literary Messenger* in 1843, or any number of prominent and important black authors of the postbellum era. Horton had also published his poems in 1829 in a volume titled *The Hope of Liberty*, and his regional reputation would certainly have been known to the editors of the *LSL*. By omitting even the most well-known black authors, Alderman, Kent, and Harris made clear that people of color would only appear as caricatured subjects, as plantation stereotypes in the works of white southern writers.[16]

White southern women, however, appeared in the first volume as biographical subjects and as writers of individual biographies. Excerpts from fiction writer Amelia E. Barr appeared in volume 1, with an introduction to Barr's work by Clara D. Sevier. Mississippi writer Sherwood Bonner, whose promising career had been cut short by breast cancer, also figured prominently in the first volume. Born in Holly Springs, Mississippi, in 1849, Katherine Sherwood Bonner became well known after the Civil War by her pen name, Sherwood Bonner, and met famous writers such as Longfellow while she resided in Boston. She wrote letters and commentary that were published in southern newspapers back home, as well as novels such as *Like unto Like* (1878). One of her more popular works was the collection *Suwannee River Tales*, and the *LSL* included an excerpt from that volume titled "Gran'Mammy": "In our southern home we were very fond of our old colored mammy, who had petted and scolded and nursed and coddled—yes, and spanked us—from the time we were born. She was not a 'black mammy,' for her complexion was the color of clear coffee; and we did not call her 'mammy,' but 'gran'mammy' because she had nursed our mother when a delicate little baby—loving her foster child, I believe, more than her own, and loving us for our dear mother's sake."[17]

Given the racial sentimentality Bonner exhibited, common in late nineteenth-century southern literature, it is not a surprise to learn that she was a great reader of Joel Chandler Harris. Similarly, subsequent female authors included in the series tended to be those who promoted the Lost Cause or otherwise remained unquestioning when it came to traditional assumptions about race and gender. The second volume included lengthy sections on Kate Chopin and Mary Bayard Clarke, while other volumes displayed the work of women essayists such as Louisa McCord. Throughout the collection, women usually contributed biographies and excerpts about female authors, but a number of articles covering female subjects were penned by leading male professors and authors. Sepia images of Varina Davis and Augusta Jane Evans even appeared alongside the likes of Robert E. Lee, John C. Calhoun, and Alexander Stephens. Among the hundreds of works excerpted and scores of writers praised, the *LSL* paid homage to white female poets and essayists.

It should be noted, however, that while the subject matter reflected in the selections by female authors was surprisingly diverse, few writers evinced critical engagement with the region and its conventions. McCord wrote freely on political economy in the South, justifying slavery and reiterating racist tropes that depicted people of African descent as naturally better suited to toiling in the rice and cotton fields than white laborers. Mary Bayard Clarke and other post–Civil War women hailed the Lost Cause in their poems and short stories, never questioning the racial conventions that had led to Jim Crow segregation and mass lynchings. So while the inclusion and even embrace of southern white literary women is abundantly evident in the collection, the sum total of that collective contribution is to reinforce rather than to undermine conservative interpretations of racial and gender traditions.

White women were also heavily involved in promoting the collection, and publisher Martin and Hoyt used every opportunity to draw upon their energy and excitement. The UDC incorporated lectures and book discussions into its programming while also holding contests for the best essays on southern history and literature. One contest in Alabama offered a prize for the best paper by a young woman on "The Confederate Indians of Alabama." In a sly bit of advertising, Martin and Hoyt even sent a full set of the collection to the Georgia Federation of Women's Clubs, knowing that the gift would be publicly acknowledged in the press. But, remaining true to the general thrust of southern intellectual culture, segregation and racial exclusion prevailed. Contest rules specified that blacks were ineligible to apply. For years after the original publication of the *LSL*, contest submission guidelines stated flatly that participants had to be "white persons twenty-one years old, and over."[18]

While the biographies and excerpts made up almost all of the thirteen main volumes of the collection, Alderman intended the *LSL* to be debated and discussed, and three additional volumes were added to the collection to accomplish this goal. The sixteenth volume, for example, included histories and descriptions of all of the flagship southern state universities, as well as no fewer than fifty suggested courses for reading and discussing regional literature. The courses included collections with titles such as *Negro Dialect Stories* and *Stories of Cracker Life* and were to serve as focal points for book clubs and literary debating societies. The fourteenth volume published historically significant letters, anecdotes, epitaphs, and quotations. The resulting mammoth collection thus laid before readers the most ambitious and comprehensive work of southern white writers that had ever been printed. How would the world react?

White southern readers and journalists took the regional honors a step further, calling attention to local and state authors honored through their inclusion in the collection. The *Tuscaloosa News* crowed that Samuel Minturn Peck, one of its local authors, had made it into the collection, while the press as far away as Missouri considered the inclusion of native authors a great honor. Southern newspapers also boasted when their local female writers had attracted the eye of the *LSL* editors. The *Baltimore Sun* proclaimed the news that local novelist and poet Katherine Pearson Woods "received the distinction" of inclusion in the thirteenth volume.[19]

The publication of the *LSL* also sparked a lengthy and wide-ranging debate over the South's place in national print culture. Southern white readers acknowledged that perhaps antebellum New England authors might be considered more prolific than their southern counterparts, but writers in the postbellum South had surpassed those in other American regions. The excellence of southern writers since the Civil War, they argued, was due in no small part to the suffering caused by the physical and economic destruction of the former Confederacy. In an essay on the *LSL*, the *Arkansas Democrat* claimed that "the war created great havoc in the South, but it paved the way for southern literature. In its wake it left a strange compound of pathos, humor, tragedy and drama, which in the course of time the bright minds of the South turned to literary account." The paper pointed specifically to Edith Wharton as "the literary par excellence" of postwar America. What made Wharton such a powerful writer, according to the paper, was her ability to express pain and suffering, which the defeated citizens of the Confederacy could particularly offer modern readers. Of course, the *Arkansas Democrat* could emphasize the wounds wrought by the Union's victory in the war without a hint of irony regarding the suffering of the 4 million people enslaved by the Confederate states.[20]

The *LSL* prompted an especially vigorous debate over the quality of antebellum southern literature. White southerners were fairly confident in the notion that during the late 1800s the region had produced a number of excellent poets and especially short-story writers and novelists. In addition to boasting of poetry by Henry Timrod and Sidney Lanier, southern intellectuals pointed with pride to the novels of Joel Chandler Harris, Mark Twain, and Thomas Nelson Page or to Kate Chopin's short story collections such as *Bayou Folk* (1894). The region had even cultivated highly respected literary critics and academics such as Alderman. But white southerners were not quite so sure that the authors of the Old South matched up with the likes of northern giants Herman Melville, Nathaniel Hawthorne, and Emily Dickinson. Poe and Simms were often mentioned as the leading Old South writers, but beyond them lay many lesser-known authors such as Paul Hamilton Hayne, Mary Elizabeth Lee, and Caroline Gilman.

Though it included dozens of excerpts from antebellum southerners, the *LSL* did little to convince national critics that there was a previously unknown trove of original and important works from the era of slavery. On the contrary, northern reviewers continued to make the free-labor case that slavery had retarded southern intellectual development in virtually all areas of cultural life, from education to fiction writing. Chicago's magazine of literary criticism, the *Dial*, remarked that while the *LSL* had achieved its goal of collecting southern works in one collection, it would ultimately fail in its larger ambition of rewriting the history of American literature.[21]

In fact, southern intellectuals viewed the publication of the *LSL* as an opportunity to raise the profile for and respect of literary pursuits. Regional authors and thinkers had long complained that their fellow southerners valued military or business careers much more than the life of the mind. But the widespread publicity the *LSL* generated provided an ideal opportunity for academics, poets, playwrights, and others to emphasize the liberal arts. As a Vicksburg newspaper reminded readers, "The South's progress and its value to the welfare of the Nation, depends not only upon its deeds and its history—but in great measure upon the mind and imagination" of intellectuals.[22]

Despite the favorable attention to southern print culture generated by the *LSL*, southern partisans still fretted that the region would be disrespected when compared to other sections of the nation. Just as in the antebellum era, when white southerners complained that school textbooks published in the northeast were unreliable sources on southern history and culture, so, too, did the press in the decades after the Civil War bemoan what it considered to be slights. In a review of a new American literature textbook just a few years after the *LSL* appeared, the *Richmond Times-Dispatch* protested bitterly that the textbook offered contributions from only two dozen southerners in a collection of nearly 300 authors and only two portraits of twenty-eight total were of southern background. The Alabama historian for the UDC denounced the collection as "falsely labeled like strawberry jam made of turnips, grass-seed, glucose, and dyes." Even more troubling was the fact that the *LSL* was supposed to have remedied this kind of dismissiveness in the national discourse. "In quantity, beauty, permanence, and style," the Richmond paper proclaimed, "the South has for two centuries made a better showing than the North." The editorial went on to compare specific writers, arguing that Virginia's John Esten Cooke was "more of a realist" than James Fenimore Cooper and that women such as Mary E. Johnston had used southern themes and settings in their successful novels.[23]

The response of literary critics in the North, however, was mixed. The *Philadelphia Inquirer*, much to the dismay of southern writers, not only dismissed the importance of the *LSL* but scoffed at claims of southern intellectual achievements. In fact, the *Inquirer* argued, the region had not produced any significant poets aside from Poe and Sidney Lanier, and it warned that "southern people do not buy books; they read little; they talk a great deal." Such slights raised the hackles of the southern press, and the *Baltimore Sun* responded with a defense of the region's print culture both before and after the war. It was true, the *Sun* allowed, that the Old South had few book publishers, but after the war the region could count Martin and Hoyt among its growing publishing industry. Such verbal assaults on southern intellectual life could hardly be surprising from a North that had come to regard the region "as well nigh illiterate."[24]

The *LSL* also sparked an internal debate in the South, as commenters harshly criticized Alderman and the other editors for ignoring state and local writers. Inevitably, the editors came under attack for omitting authors, particularly poets. Eugene Didier, a Baltimore native and a widely respected Poe scholar, lashed out at the *LSL* for snubbing Maryland's literature. The collection was a "mockery" for only including twelve authors from that state, and Didier listed both male and female writers, including Anne Seemuller and Kate Rowland, who might have been included. "A Student," writing to the newspaper, responded to Didier's criticism by emphasizing that while any reader could point to writers whose works were omitted, the virtue of the *LSL* was its breadth and scope and therefore accused Didier of missing the point of the collection. Didier responded angrily in another letter to the editor, beginning with criticism of "A Student" for "skulking" behind anonymity. The Poe scholar reiterated his complaint that numerous Maryland authors were left out, "while men who had not the slightest claim to literary distinction were included, such as Andrew Johnson, David Crockett, Sam Houston, etc."[25]

Although contemporary criticism of the collection tended to quibble about which authors of minor fame were left out of the series, no one complained about how the region itself was depicted in the selected works. In fact, there is little in the entire publication to which the most sensitive white mind might object. While statesman Henry Clay apparently warranted forty pages, there were no references to Cassius M. Clay, the fellow Kentuckian who called for the abolition of slavery. And although the works of several academics are presented, no mention was made of University of North Carolina professor Benjamin S. Hedrick, fired in the 1850s for daring to vote Republican. Yet sections were devoted to proslavery writers and thinkers, not just men such as Simms, George Frederick Holmes, and William Alexander Caruthers but prominent female defenders of bondage such as Caroline Lee Hentz and Caroline Gilman. Essays and excerpts appeared for military and political figures such as Robert E. Lee and Andrew Jackson but almost nothing that might be interpreted as critical of the region's history, ideology, or institutions.

In fact, the same is true for the white women included in the volume. Radical women such as Virginia native Anne Royall, who left behind a trove of travel and political essays as well as scores of editorials from the newspapers she edited before the war over a career that spanned several decades, were left out of the inclusion process. A critic of organized religion and societal traditions and conventions, Royall edited an important political newspaper in the nation's capital called the *Huntress*. Yet in the eyes of the *LSL*'s editors, Royall only merited a paragraph in the biographical volume, which appeared as volume 15, after the excerpts. Yet even here Royall is described in far less than glowing terms: "Her eccentricities were numerous, and she became the terror of the congressmen by reason not only of her vitriolic pen but of her grotesque appearance. Finally she was indicted by the Grand Jury as a scold and sentenced to be ducked in the Potomac River."[26]

Women like Royall, critical of the region, were not welcome in the pages of the series, even though Royall's literary prominence meant that she could not be left out of the biographical section. Herein lies the chief reason why scholars have not found the series as useful as the original editors intended it to be. In short, the major critical problem with the *LSL* was the same fundamental problem that had plagued southern literature since the colonial era. One of the characteristics of New England authors during the "American Renaissance" was their willingness to criticize, rather than defend, the hypocrisies and contradictions they observed in the society around them. When Henry David Thoreau lived on Walden Pond or when he protested the Mexican War by refusing to pay taxes, he offered fellow New Englanders a critical examination of the increasingly impersonal urban industrial economy or the importance of individual action. When Nathaniel Hawthorne published *The Scarlet Letter*, readers recognized the sexual repression and religious control of New England's Puritan ancestors. But almost to a person, southern men and women defended a region that they believed lay under external attack. White southerners who dared scorn slavery were banished from the inner circle of southern life.

Like every human society, the nineteenth-century South, as reflected in the *LSL*, drew boundaries to identify "insiders" and to keep out "outsiders." Yet because the region devoted so much of its time to defending the region from outside criticism, it missed an opportunity to offer readers past and present a more creative and thoughtful literature, not to mention a more just society. The *LSL* presents a clear picture of which southerners lay within the circle of insiders: white men and women. Outside of this sacred circle were people of color, external denigrators of slavery or other southern norms, and even internal white southerners who dared question the status quo.

How could a society simultaneously be open, at least in the literary sphere, to gender equality but so adamant about racial inequality? The nineteenth-century South belies one of the basic tenets of modern liberalism: that a society is either reactionary, remaining closed to all progressive change, or openly democratic and embracing of reform. The South was neither. At once the region could consider the merits of greater roles for white women, particularly in the feminized spheres of poetry and novel writing, while steadfastly rejecting any claims that bondage was immoral or that black writers could ever appear as peers with white authors. As important as it was for white women to be recognized in the body of works included in the series, gender equality could only survive in this one small but important sector of public life. But even this small sign of progress stood as but a dim light when compared to the dark shadow of racial violence and segregation.

Can modern readers consider themselves "insiders" in the region's sacred circle? Reading through the selections in the *LSL* one feels sharply removed from the editorial choices made in the early 1900s. The status of insider was clearly reserved for those who saw only heroics in the thoughts and actions of the Confederates, who preferred the comforting but illusory dreams of the Lost Cause to the reality of slavery's viciousness. The editors and contributors to the *LSL* reveal more about their momentary place in time and the nuanced ideology on race and gender than they do about the power of the mind of the South.

NOTES

1. "The Library of Southern Literature," *Times-Democrat* (New Orleans), April 11, 1909, 8.

2. Sarah E. Gardner, *Reviewing the South: The Literary Marketplace and the Southern Renaissance, 1920–1941* (Cambridge: Cambridge University Press, 2017); Bill Hardwig, *Upon Provincialism: Southern Literature and National Periodical Culture, 1870–1900* (Charlottesville: University of Virginia Press, 2013); Michael Winship, *American Literary Publishing in the Mid-nineteenth Century: The Business of Ticknor and Fields* (Cambridge: Cambridge University Press, 1995).

3. The turn toward revealing the important work of black and female writers in the South began in the 1970s and 1980s and continues to the present day, constituting a

vast historiographical corpus that has fundamentally changed our understanding of southern literary culture. See, for just two examples, Canter Brown Jr. and Larry E. Rivers, *Mary Edwards Bryan: Her Early Life and Works* (Gainesville: University of Florida Press, 2015); and Vivian M. May, *Anna Julia Cooper, Visionary Black Feminist: A Critical Introduction* (New York: Routledge, 2007).

4. Thavolia Glymph, *Out of the House of Bondage: The Transformation of the Plantation Household* (Cambridge: Cambridge University Press, 2008); Michael O'Brien, *Conjectures of Order: Intellectual Life and the American South, 1810-1860* (Chapel Hill: University of North Carolina Press, 2004); Giselle Roberts, *The Confederate Belle* (Columbia: University of Missouri Press, 2003); Elizabeth R. Varon, *We Mean to Be Counted: White Women and Politics in Antebellum Virginia* (Chapel Hill: University of North Carolina Press, 1998).

5. See, e.g., Jonathan Daniel Wells, *Women Writers and Journalists in the Nineteenth-Century South* (Cambridge: Cambridge University Press, 2011).

6. Page quoted in Mildred Lewis Rutherford, *The South in History and Literature* (Athens, Ga.: Franklin-Turner, 1906), xxxv.

7. Rutherford, 147-50.

8. Samuel W. Dibble, "An Epoch-Making Publication," *Atlanta Constitution*, October 26, 1908, 4; "Knight Is Manager of Literary Bureau," *Atlanta Constitution*, November 3, 1908, 9.

9. "A Great Work Undertaken under the Auspices of the University of Virginia," *Charleston Courier*, December 7, 1907, 10. On Martin and Hoyt, see "Southern Literature," *Charlotte (N.C.) News*, May 21, 1908, 9.

10. R. A. Brock, "Notice," *Atlanta Constitution*, May 2, 1909, 8.

11. Lucian L. Knight, "The Library of Southern Literature," *Atlanta Constitution*, November 15, 1908, 2.

12. See ads for salesmen in *Washington Post*, May 3, 1910, 12; and *St. Louis Post-Dispatch*, October 4, 1910, 14.

13. "A Valuable Work," *High Point (N.C.) Enterprise*, November 13, 1909, 6; "Some Valuable Books for Southern Libraries," *Atlanta Constitution*, October 3, 1909, 4.

14. "New Books Added to the Free Public Library," *Courier-Journal* (Louisville, Ky.), May 23, 1909, 4; "Library Notes," *Waxahachie (Tex.) Daily Light*, July 30, 1909, 4.

15. Edwin Anderson Alderman, Joel Chandler Harris, and Charles William Kent, eds., *The Library of Southern Literature* (Atlanta: Martin and Hoyt, 1909), 1:xvi.

16. George Moses Horton, "Ode to Liberty" and "Lines to My—," *Southern Literary Messenger*, April 1843, 237-39. See also "A North Carolina Poet," *De Bow's Review*, December 1860, 738.

17. Excerpt from *Suwannee River Tales* reprinted in Alderman, Harris, and Kent, *Library of Southern Literature*, 1:445-46. For more on Bonner, see Hubert Horton McAlexander, *The Prodigal Daughter: A Biography of Sherwood Bonner* (Baton Rouge: Louisiana State University Press, 1981); and William L. Frank, *Sherwood Bonner (Catherine McDowell)* (Boston: Twayne, 1976).

18. "The United Daughters of the Confederacy," *Austin (Tex.) American-Statesman*, January 2, 1910, 15; "Mrs. Fitzpatrick," *Atlanta Constitution*, May 18, 1913, 8; "Letter from UDC State Historian," *Montgomery (Ala.) Advertiser*, January 21, 1914,

6; "Prize Essay Contest on Southern Literature," *Pensacola (Fla.) News Journal*, April 8, 1914, 5; "One Subject in All Divisions Essay Committee," *State* (Columbia, S.C.), April 5, 1914, 8.

19. "Samuel Minturn Peck in the Library of Southern Literature," *Tuscaloosa (Ala.) News*, December 15, 1909, 5; "Southern Literature Arrives," *Evening Missourian* (Columbia), January 7, 1910; "Gifted Poet of Texas is Given Recognition," *Dallas Morning News*, February 28, 1910, 4; "Mrs. Ottley in Library of Southern Literature," *Atlanta Constitution*, November 7, 1909, 10; "Baltimore Writer Honored," *Baltimore Sun*, April 10, 1909, 7.

20. "The Literature of the South," *Arkansas Democrat* (Little Rock), May 30, 1909, 16.

21. "The Literature of the South," *Dial*, May 16, 1909, 330.

22. "The Library of Southern Literature," *Vicksburg (Miss.) Evening Post*, April 25, 1908, 7.

23. "That Partial Brander Matthews," *Richmond (Va.) Times-Dispatch*, May 6, 1913, 4.

24. *Philadelphia Inquirer* quoted in "Scoffing at Southern Literature," *Baltimore Sun*, June 19, 1910, 6; "A Student," letter to the editor, *Baltimore Sun*, June 24, 1910, 6.

25. Eugene L. Didier, letter to the editor, *Baltimore Sun*, June 20, 1910, 6; Didier, "Letter to the Editor," *Baltimore Sun* (June 27, 1910). 6. See also the complaint in *Evening Sun* (Baltimore), June 29, 1910, 6.

26. See the brief biographical entry in Alderman, Harris, and Kent, *Library of Southern Literature*, 15:379.

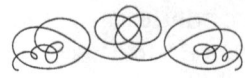

TONY JUDT AND MICHAEL O'BRIEN
Writing History

MICHAEL KREYLING

THE PROBLEM is that writing history (putting what happened in the human world into an often-uncontrollable yoke with its representation in written texts) makes history susceptible to the service of an idea or ideology (bad) or a feeling (worse). Both outcomes are simultaneously more and less than "events themselves": the chimera from which historians produce written histories. The problem has been familiar, and insoluble, to historians at least since the sixth century BCE when Archilochus made it a punch line: "The fox knows many things, but the hedgehog knows one big thing." Fox and hedgehog became Isaiah Berlin's mascots in his influential lecture on Tolstoy's view of history, *The Hedgehog and the Fox* (1953), and Berlin bore the care and feeding of them until the end of his life. "It was a joke, you know . . . purely . . . a *jeu d'esprit*," Berlin wrote, trying belatedly to deflect accountability.[1] His effort to walk back his allusion was in vain; the fox-hedgehog duality, admittedly oversimplified, has become a litmus test for evaluating historians as writers and writers as historians. The problem of disentangling history from history writing has survived to be summed up by Tony Judt in *Thinking the Twentieth*

Century: "A badly written history book is a bad history book."[2] Is that the end of the conversation between writing and writing history?

Despite Berlin's persistent attempts to escape his *jeu d'esprit*, the tail wags the dog because it awakens anxiety in almost every historian who thinks of his or her writing. Bad writing means bad history means hedgehog. Few historians seem to want to own up to the label of hedgehog; knowing "one big thing" carries connotations of ideological orthodoxy (knowing the conclusion in advance of the data) or, worse, dullness. It is cooler to be the fox, knower of many things, pursuing them all, and never being less than interesting: dangerously close to being more interesting than the subject matter. A compilation of many individual things, no matter how interesting, does not automatically add up to a well-written history book: "good" history. Without some organizing (hedgehoggian) principle, the result is inevitably "a badly written history book." The more the historian struggles with the dilemma, in other words, the more entangled he or she is in the process by which history becomes writing and inevitably writing becomes history.

Joseph Conrad's preface to *The Nigger of the Narcissus* (1897) is quoted almost as frequently as Berlin and Archilochus on the topic of making experience "real" through the medium of writing: "My task which I am trying to achieve is, by the power of the written word, to make you hear, to make you feel—it is, before all, to make you see. That—and no more, and it is everything. If I succeed, you shall find there according to your deserts: encouragement, consolation, fear, charm—all you demand; and, perhaps, also that glimpse of truth for which you have forgotten to ask."[3] Historians are rightly wary of Conrad's promise of affording meaning "there [in the written word] according to your deserts: encouragement, consolation, fear, charm—all you demand." Readers' "deserts," self- or group-interested "demands," inevitably corrupt the incontestability of "what happened" with questions of selection and arrangement. Simply stated, novels exist to make readers feel; history writing exists to make us think rather than feel.[4] Most historians, however, would rather be foxes, deploying "many things" to ward off the dangers of becoming captive to a one-size-fits-all orthodoxy, the curse of the doctrinaire.

Berlin thought he had found the ideal balance of fox and hedgehog in Leo Tolstoy. Tolstoy, with only his imagination, got closer to presenting what happened in *War and Peace* than most historians who had absorbed the entire archive of Napoleon's invasion of Russia. How did Tolstoy do it?

He was, according to Berlin, an instinctive amalgam of fox and hedgehog, a literary stylist attentive to words and things and a secret hedgehog with a big historical idea: the complexity of nineteenth-century history and Russia's unwilling encounter with it. Of course, Tolstoy also lived with the immediate fallout from what he wrote his novel about. Berlin proffers reading a novelist as a guide for reading (and writing) history; readable historians (the only good historians?) are inescapably hybrids of fox and hedgehog by employing, carefully, some (at least) of the tool set of the novelist.

Tony Judt and Michael O'Brien provide recent examples of the results of mixing fox and hedgehog. They make an apt pair, working toward the hybridity Berlin found in Tolstoy but from opposing directions and in two separate historians. Both O'Brien and Judt were born in Britain in 1948; Judt died in 2010, O'Brien in 2015. Both spent significant portions of their careers in U.S. academia. Both chose large, hedgehoggian ideas as the central objects of their historical research—huge intellectual areas populated with various viewpoints but, in different measure, receptive to control. Judt chose twentieth-century Europe as the organizing lodestone in his field; he capped his career with *Postwar: A History of Europe since 1945*, a finalist for the Pulitzer Prize.[5] O'Brien chose the intellectual history of the U.S. South to anchor his work, capping his career with the two-volume *Conjectures of Order: Intellectual Life and the American South, 1810–1860*, winner of the Bancroft Prize in American History.[6] But they handled the fox-hedgehog dilemma differently: Judt from the whole to the miscellany, O'Brien the other way.

"A BADLY WRITTEN HISTORY BOOK IS A BAD HISTORY BOOK"

Judt overtly and covertly resisted the pull of the literary. "Looking back, I am very glad I stuck with history and rejected the temptation urged upon me by schoolmasters and dons to become a student of literature and politics."[7] He became, instead, a student of *history* and politics, dismissing "literature" as a temptation to be overcome rather than an ally to be used. Judt does not mention Joseph Conrad in *Postwar*, his major work, although he does include literature in his coverage of Europe in the book. His later comments about writing history, compiled in *Thinking the Twentieth Century*, do, however, echo Conrad's anxiety about representing experience in written form. "To make clear that a certain event happened," Judt writes, there is also the requirement to make the readers "see the story in its plenitude."[8] It is not enough to write "what happened," Judt implies, although that aim looms very large in his intentions; in fact, one simply cannot write "what happened" without entailing the forms and traditions that enable readers to "see" what happened in a coherent form.[9] In other words, "literature" is a temptation that cannot be easily overcome, either in the writing or the reading. Judt moves into Berlin's quandary sideways.

Postwar begins with an attempt to blunt the edge of Berlin's "joke" by appropriating it:

> In his account of Tolstoy's view of history, Isaiah Berlin drew an influential distinction between two styles of intellectual reasoning, citing a famous line from the Greek poet Archilochus: "The fox knows many things but the hedgehog knows one big thing." In Berlin's terms this book [*Postwar*] is decidedly not a "hedgehog." I have no big arching theme to expound; no single, all-embracing story to tell. It does not follow from this, however, that I think the post–World War Two history of Europe has no thematic shape. On the contrary: it has more than one. Fox-like, Europe knows many things.[10]

Judt's disclaimer conflates a crucial trio of terms: the book (*Postwar*), the "I" designating the author, and the "big arching theme" ("Europe," paradoxically both author and subject) indulge in a round of exchanging identities, alternately assuming, then dodging, the fox-hedgehog dichotomy. None of the three, it seems, wants to wear the hedgehog's jersey. But for Berlin's "dichotomy" to work (in fact, for any written narrative to work), someone has to be the hedgehog (at the very least to designate Aristotelian beginning, middle, and end in a narrative) so that someone else can be the fox and disrupt the norm. Judt attempts to slip the yoke of the dichotomy by obfuscating human authorship, attributing the "shape" of his work to its subject matter, not to his representation of it. The Judt, or the "I" who owns to being the author of *Postwar* on its cover and title page, is indeed the hedgehog of the dichotomy, whose "style of intellectual reasoning," when he is operating as historian, is in fact to expound a "big arching theme," to tell a "single, all-embracing story." *Postwar* would be unmanageable without the narrative of "Europe" to shape it.

Judt's *Thinking the Twentieth Century* reveals the complicated struggle between fox and hedgehog in his work and the paradox of his denial in the introduction to *Postwar*. In the final stages of amyotrophic lateral sclerosis (ALS) in 2009, Judt could no longer summon the simple muscle control to write, but he could still think and talk about "the big arching theme" of his career: the travails of twentieth-century Europe—what he calls "The World We Have Lost" in the second chapter of an earlier posthumous text, *Ill Fares the Land* (2010).[11] *Thinking the Twentieth Century* (2012) is a collaboration between Judt and his friend and fellow historian Timothy Snyder, who recorded and transcribed weekly conversations between the two during the last year of Judt's life. As a collaborative text, *Thinking the Twentieth Century* complements Judt's "professional" history writing represented most notably by *Postwar*, as if the fox had infiltrated the hedgehog's project. In *Postwar*, Judt suppresses his personality as author, defaulting to an anonymous voice wary of the temptations of the literary, perhaps what Hayden White meant by "threads," disruptive and stubbornly occasional details that depart from the "centripetal" narrative that characterizes the hedgehog: "The threads are located and traced outward, into the circumambient natural and social space within which the event occurred, and both backward in time, in order to determine the 'origins' of the event, and forward in time, in order to determine its 'impact' and 'influence' on subsequent events."[12] In *Thinking the Twentieth Century* Judt takes full advantage of metahistorical "threads," weaving autobiographical memoir and historical commentary into a centrifugal, fox-like narrative in which he is both character and historian-narrator.[13] A stereophonic reading of the two Judts offers a gloss on the durable fox-hedgehog "joke" by revealing a historian enmeshed in the dichotomy Berlin described even as that historian (Judt) disclaims such involvement, striving to suppress in *Postwar* a voice that emerges in *Thinking the Twentieth Century* and his other memoir publications.

The heart of Judt's professional historical work is the retrieval, by means of historical research culminating in narrative writing, of "the lost world of central Europe," the world obliterated by a series of cataclysms: Nazism in Germany, World War II more widely, and (ironically) even more completely by the reconstruction of Europe by the victorious allied Western democracies that purportedly won in 1945.[14] *Ill Fares the Land*, another modest sequel to *Postwar*, echoes the mournful valediction to Judt's Europe—the idea that presides over *Postwar* and the lived experience of *Thinking*. It begins with the cry "Something is profoundly wrong with the way we live today."[15] The gone world of prewar Europe was marred by pogroms, ethnic and nationalistic jealousies, and social and economic inequity. Still, in Judt's memoir, it worked; it was the civilization heard and felt and tasted by his forebears. It was the world of Judt's parents and grandparents, Jews who had fled Eastern Europe in the first decade of the twentieth century, migrating across Europe to eventually become British citizens and the parents of the historian of their experience. Inescapably, it produced him as both rememberer and researcher, the writer and (to some extent) the written about. "The story in its plenitude" converts history into a form of autobiography that implicates Judt. But autobiographical implication and all forms of memory must be resisted, Judt claims in the final pages of *Postwar*. History might be a form of "disenchantment" and "discomforting," but it "does need to be learned—and periodically relearned."[16] The hedgehog in Judt claims the final say in *Postwar*, only to relinquish it when, dying of ALS, he constructs rooms of memory, which he judged "loosely articulated and yet more fully human than their deductively constructed, rigorously predestined forebears"—his history books.[17]

Thinking the Twentieth Century, alternatively, reverberates with echoes of an autobiographical novel, Charles Dickens's *David Copperfield* (1850). "I am born" locates both narrators, Tony Judt and David Copperfield, at the font of the narratives they create through the power of the written word. Copperfield is himself an increasingly successful novelist, although the line between what he "really" experiences and what he purportedly writes about is hopelessly (and interestingly) blurred. The blurring of autobiographical fiction and biographical fact suggests that literary "power" can, at times, work autonomously, beyond authorial intention. It spans generic boundaries, creating possibilities for the novelist and dilemmas for the historian.

Judt the hedgehog armors himself against such dilemmas in *Postwar*. Prewar Europe was, to echo Hayden White, "the circumambient natural and social space" to which Judt's history (and surreptitious autobiography) was organically connected, the world of "Judt himself," shaped by Holocaust memory among his kin and strategies of denial among the Europeans he professionally studied.[18] Judt lived what he studied: the Marshall Plan and the European Union, "austerity" and Thatcherite Britain, culture studies in U.S. academia, and late in his life (and ominously after his death) threats from within to the idea of Europe he cherished (authoritarian nationalism in Poland, muddled Brexit in the United Kingdom) and from without (Trumpism in the United States).[19] In *Thinking the Twentieth Century* and *The Memory Chalet* he admits all of this; in

Postwar, it is the part of the narrative thread known but cut off whenever it accelerates centripetally.

Thinking the Twentieth Century, like Dickens's *David Copperfield*, conflates author and protagonist, as Dickens projects himself onto Copperfield and Judt onto Judt. Judt's personal history as a nomadic historian of Europe (and its Western ally, the United States), in which he lived as a son of the long Jewish diaspora, complements the tale told by the professional historian in *Postwar*. Judt, the historian of *Postwar*, (his disclaimer notwithstanding) is predominantly the hedgehog who strives to know the one big thing, Europe and its vexed fate, that reflexively explains his own autobiography. Belatedly Judt, the subject of his own memoir, is the fox who knows many things by virtue of living them with an intensity approaching Tolstoy's "all-penetrating lucidity"—marriage and divorce, a balky Citroën DS19 in France and a Mustang convertible in California in the 1970s, and (not least) Groucho as well as Karl Marx—elements of his personal memory treated more fully in *The Memory Chalet*.

Such "charm" (echoing Conrad) lurking backstage in *Postwar* is produced—as it was for Berlin in Tolstoy's novel—by the friction of colliding genres. Is history writing a genre unto itself properly "marked off" against other kinds of writing? In *Writing in Society* (1983), Raymond Williams defined "writing" with deceptive simplicity as "putting words into conventional material form and being able to read them."[20] He then complicated his simple definition by drawing a fault line between "properties" (the knowledge that writing is *about*—the object of mimesis) and "qualities" (the affective powers of any particular writing's style to make you feel the real in its absence—the "power" or "charm" Conrad mentions).[21] Writing, Williams reminds us, must be taught and learned; how, to whom, by whom, when, and where are questions of social power and organization specific to times and places. In Williams's view, therefore, writing takes place in a mix of social formations (the autographical "I" and its narrative counterpart) like the events it strives to represent in words and forms. For Williams writing is compromised by circumstances; for White, by forms. To separate writing from history—to have a "view of history" as if from beyond it—is a move fraught with complications: "But between an enclosed kind of study of a body of writing marked off as 'literature' and a reduced kind of study of political, military, economic and generalized social facts marked off as 'history,' there is an important and neglected area of evidence and questions: in the practical history of writing and of forms of writing, and in what these can show us of how, in the increasingly important practice, people assumed, developed, extended, realized and changed their relationships."[22] For Williams writing is a historical event enmeshed in the social formations historians write about; it follows that written history is a hybrid creature as well. A version of the same paradox attracted Berlin to Tolstoy.

Timothy Snyder, Judt's collaborator (still another complication), registers the problem of genre in the first line of *Thinking the Twentieth Century*: "This book is history, biography, and ethical treatise."[23] Unwritten is the assumption that history is a genre of narrative writing rightly exclusive to itself, possessing rules that require "biography" to be set off as separate and distinct from history and (not least, for Judt is a strongly ethical writer) ethical treatise. The Europe Judt writes about would have existed whether or not Judt had written about it or had lived as one of the human "threads" of its general narrative. The "Tony Judt" Judt writes about, however, causes some perturbation in the genres' separate orbits. The object of history is and ought to be, both Snyder and Judt seem to assert, the focus of study; the writer who conjures the object is instrumental, not structural. But facts cannot speak for themselves; therein a dilemma stirs. What attracted Berlin to Tolstoy—what animates his fox-hedgehog dichotomy—is the suspicion that such "marking off" never really succeeds, that the personal voice always emerges, that dilemmas are energizing—in elements of style if not overtly in content.[24]

Although in much of his work Judt maintains separation between self and historian, "one" and "I," in *Thinking the Twentieth Century* he confronts the problem of authorship. "The problem with historical events which are intricately interwoven," he says, "is that, the better to understand their constituent elements, we have to pull them apart. But in order to see the story in its plenitude, you have to interweave those elements back together again."[25] "You" in this context is self-referential: the historian as writer (not entirely one and the same with the Tony Judt who appears in his various autobiographical narratives) encountering the "elements" of writing in his effort to tell "the story in its plenitude."[26] "Plenitude" is, however, a relative concept too. At times Judt echoes Sgt. Joe Friday: "The job of the historian is to make clear that a certain event happened. We do this as effectively as we can, for the purpose of conveying what it was like for something to have happened to those people when it did, where it did and with what consequences."[27] But to convey "what it was like for something to have happened," the writer of history enters what A. J. P. Taylor, in his contentious review of *The Hedgehog and the*

Fox, labeled a "strange borderland" where the historian must use a "conventional material form" shared with novelists. Is it possible, much less desirable, to "make clear" that something happened without "conveying what it was like" for that event to have happened? Where and how does the historian stop the flow from what happened to "those people when it did, where it did and with what consequences?" Berlin's meditations on Tolstoy became, in Taylor's hedgehoggian reading, too fox-like for the reviewer's trust.

Taylor took Berlin's joke as the signpost to "that strange borderland, the history of ideas, especially of ideas displayed in literature."[28] He opens with a tempered salute to what he sees as Berlin's excess: "One sometimes feels that he [Berlin] has more ideas than all the historical authors whom he sets out to illuminate. Voltaire no doubt had him in mind when he wittily remarked, 'it is neither literature nor ideas nor history.' Something rather in the nature of an intellectual firework display. . . . Mr. Berlin is lavish with his gifts."[29] Surplus and excess clearly mark Taylor's disapproval of the "qualities" of Berlin's prose; "more," "firework," "lavish," "gifts," and possibly "wittily" come from the contested vocabulary of excess. When there is "more" than enough to register the "properties" or knowledge of the content, the hedgehog senses the danger of the nonstop sentence that tracks all of the ramifications of "what happened." Taylor implies, with a hint of a smirk, that the object of Berlin's history is the mind of Isaiah Berlin himself, thrall to his own imagination and therefore distanced from "certain events as they happened."

Taylor is not mistaken. Berlin's style *is* his thought; form and content cohabit in his prose. A passage from *The Hedgehog and the Fox* captures excess at work:

> But, taken figuratively, the words [of Archilochus's saying] can be made to yield a sense in which they mark one of the deepest differences which divide writers and thinkers, and, it may be, human beings in general. For there exists a great chasm between those, on the one side, who relate everything to a single central vision, one system, less or more coherent or articulate, in terms of which they understand, think and feel—a single, universal, organizing principle in terms of which alone all that they are and say has significance—and, on the other side, those who pursue many ends, often unrelated and even contradictory, connected, if at all, only in some de facto way, for some psychological or physiological cause, related to no moral or aesthetic

principle. These last lead lives, perform acts and entertain ideas that are centrifugal rather than centripetal; their thought is scattered or diffused, moving on many levels, seizing upon the essence of a vast variety of experiences and objects for what they are in themselves, without, consciously or unconsciously, seeking to fit them into, or exclude them from, any one unchanging, all-embracing, sometimes self-contradictory and incomplete, at times fanatical, unitary inner vision. The first kind of intellectual and artistic personality belongs to the hedgehogs, the second to the foxes.[30]

Cut from a longer paragraph, these lines reveal the fox (Berlin himself) performing rather than describing his own "intellectual and artistic personality." Berlin's prose is distinctive for its periodicity: "on the one side" waiting on its other side, while Berlin's thinking stretches to accommodate ideas and their modifications in elastic syntax. "A single central vision" gives way to another metaphor, "system," that is then modified ("less or more coherent or articulate") before it is yet again renamed as "a single, universal, organizing principle." Even the centripetal habit of thinking Berlin attributes to hedgehogs becomes, in his style, centrifugal. "Unitary inner vision" (the harbor of the centripetal thinker) is postponed while its modifiers, perhaps like the fireworks Taylor imagined, sparkle in the delayed closure of the Berlinian sentence: "Any one unchanging, all-embracing, sometimes self-contradictory and incomplete, at times fanatical." It is not just the larger structures of genre that call for discipline but the smaller units of style—sentences.

Moreover, in Judt's case, "those people" to whom something happened are in fact his people—the Jewish people of central Europe of whom he is a scion and voice—and what happened to them (and in Judt's master narrative continues to happen) is the Holocaust and its long aftermath. How history felt for them reverberates in how it feels for Judt. He was named for a cousin of his father who was murdered at Auschwitz, so the "consequences" of historical events are always both personal and professional whether he acknowledges that connection or not.[31] The history Judt writes is the history that has happened to him and, in expanding circles of impact, continues to happen. "Plenitude," then, is a more furtive objective than the "certain event" or the comprehensiveness of historians' subject matter and research. The historian as writer is always chasing two ends: the recovery of the event and the writing, the "conveying" of the affect of the real, of "*what it was like* for something to have happened."

Tolstoy, in Berlin's essay, framed his "view of history" in a sweeping narrative that accommodated both voices, making the arbitrariness of the everyday the norm and the settled meaning of history the exception. Napoleon's invasion of Russia and Russia's defense can be known in many ways, not only by reading *War and Peace* (serialized 1865–67, published as a novel in 1869). And yet our way of knowing historical fact in *War and Peace* is different from the way we would know it in a work of history. Judt similarly animates *Postwar* with the sweeping narrative of a twentieth-century war but subordinates the fox-like options of narrative to control by history's demands for "Europe." The difference in genre—Tolstoy wrote a historical novel about a war, Judt a history of a war's aftermath—may account for the hedgehog direction of Judt's "style of intellectual reasoning." That is, without an array of fictional or semifictional characters such as those with whom Tolstoy works (and to whom Berlin pays extensive attention in his essay), Judt's history is rigorously reined to an "all-embracing story."

Judt the hedgehog speaks in *Postwar* in the third person, subordinating autobiography to the function of historian. Judt the person almost appears in the "coda" to part 1 of *Postwar*, "The End of Old Europe," when the historical territory he investigates catches up with the life he lived: "The present author, who grew up after the war in the inner-London district of Putney, recalls frequent visits to a murky sweetshop run by a wizened old woman who advised him reproachfully that she had 'been selling gobstoppers to little boys like you since the Queen's Golden Jubilee'—i.e. since 1887: she meant Victoria of course—*the* Queen."[32] Judt presents this vignette as if he had interviewed himself to get it. The "murky sweetshop" and the "wizened old woman"—not to exclude the little boy—are, in addition to being autobiographical data, furtive literary characters, products of reading and memory, threads reaching centrifugally to familiar Dickens narratives where little boys and old women abound in his representation of Victorian England. Evidence, if you will, of history yearning to be literature. The singular knowledge of the hedgehog might insist on relegating the author to the third person, but the fox is always agitating for a voice to disrupt the "all-embracing story" with the irrefutable personal fact.

Another example of the Dickensian subconscious in *Postwar* is better known to history than the proprietress of the London sweetshop. In his presentation of Charles de Gaulle as the metonymic figure for France (as

Churchill was for Great Britain and Joseph Stalin for the Soviet Union), Judt surreptitiously liberates an inner fox who nursed a stubborn distrust of France's national version of its own history and character.[33] Among the Allies arrayed against the Axis powers, France was never a full partner, even though it claimed such status. "As recently as 1938," Judt reports, France had been considered a bulwark on the continent against German and Soviet expansion:

> This image of France as a—*the*—European Great Power was shaken at Munich, but outside the chancelleries of Eastern Europe it was not yet broken. The seismic shock that ran through Europe in May and June 1940, when the great French army collapsed and fell apart before the Panzer onslaught across the Meuse and through Picardy, was thus all the greater for being unexpected.
>
> In six traumatic weeks, the cardinal reference points of European inter-state relations changed forever. France ceased to be not just a Great Power but even a power, and despite De Gaulle's best efforts in later decades it has never been one since. For the shattering defeat of June 1940 was followed by four years of humiliating, demeaning, subservient occupation, with Marshall Pétain's Vichy regime playing Uriah Heep to Germany's Bill Sikes.[34]

Allusions to Dickens's fictional characters surreptitiously open Judt's "big arching narrative" to literary detours. A few allusions, however, seem to be as far as Judt is willing to go in *Postwar* to disrupt the hedgehog's master narrative.

As a historian of Europe, Judt strives to know one big thing: the Europe of history. If the delegitimized "master narratives" of nineteenth-century European history writing had "withered away" after the two world wars of the twentieth century, a truncated "Europe" still survived as the armature of narrative and cultural meaning and was, significantly, the background of the narrative of Judt's all-too-brief life span as he looked back on it from the depths of ALS.[35] What Tolstoy did in one text, Judt did in two or three: suppressing the fox in *Postwar*, all but expelling it in the final pages of that book, but setting it free in *The Memory Chalet* and *Thinking the Twentieth Century*.

"THE SUBTLETIES OF INDIVIDUALITY ARE ENDLESS AND CRUCIAL"

Michael O'Brien (1948–2015) was less resistant than Tony Judt to the temptation of literary influences.[36] His career's worth of writing on the idea of the American South is replete with literary echoes: Virginia Woolf makes several cameo appearances; the usual suspects of southern literature such as Robert Penn Warren and Allen Tate are prominent; and others who mixed literature with regional politics—most notably C. Vann Woodward and W. J. Cash—figure centrally. O'Brien numbers literary critic Frank Kermode among his models.[37] O'Brien, in fact, embraced what Judt tried to shun. While in Judt's work the suppressed fox peeks out from the overarching dominance of "Europe" or is penned up in separate texts, in O'Brien's work the hedgehog exercises looser control over his expansive gallery of thinking and writing southerners, and the fox gets his say.

O'Brien is a fox by temperament, as comfortable with the coupling of literature and politics as Judt was not. He navigates easily in the "strange borderland, the history of ideas" where A. J. P. Taylor lost touch with Isaiah Berlin, and he often matches Berlin in literary "fireworks." Take, for example, the opening to his essay on Mary Boykin Chesnut, "The Flight Down the Middle Way: Mary Chesnut and the Forms of Observance."[38] The essay opens with a long paragraph, close to 500 words conspicuously lacking a conventional thesis statement. The first word of the paragraph is "She," and O'Brien allows readers to believe that the pronoun's referent is the southern woman, Mary Chesnut (1823–86), named in the title. The final word of the paragraph, though, out of the reader's sight until he or she turns the page, is "Bloomsbury." If we had been explicitly told to think of Mary Chesnut as precursor to Virginia Woolf (1882–1941), many readers might have questioned what a nineteenth-century South Carolina plantation mistress has to do with an early twentieth-century Bloomsbury literary modernist. In O'Brien's hands we have been "playfully" escorted into "the strange borderland" where literature and history commingle,[39] and we are the more effectively reminded that history inevitably becomes history writing with the first keystroke.[40]

A project of the scope of intellectual history and the U.S. South, however, cannot survive on *jeu d'esprit* alone; it requires a managerial system, some participation by a hedgehog to supply a "deductively constructed," if not "predestined," ultimate shape. O'Brien, like Judt, had a big arching story. As Judt depended on "Europe in the 20th century" to set the boundaries of his thinking, O'Brien used Romantic nationalism in the nineteenth century as the context for his gallery of southern thinkers and writers. Over the span of O'Brien's work, this arc combines synchronic and diachronic elements; it is a static definition of a "mind" that nevertheless moves from its heyday in the nineteenth century to decay and demise in the twentieth.

O'Brien adapted the "geist" theory of Romantic nationalism, attributed by Isaiah Berlin in "The Bent Twig: On the Rise of Nationalism" to Johann Gottfried Herder: "Human customs, activities, forms of life, art, ideas were (and must be) of value to men not in terms of timeless criteria, applicable to all men and societies, irrespective of time and place, as the French *lumieres* taught, but because they were their own, expressions of their local, regional, national life, and spoke to them as they could speak to no other human group."[41] Tribalism lurks in plain sight here; we have witnessed its physical and cultural violence in both Judt's Europe and O'Brien's South in the years since their deaths. Nevertheless, the stair-step "local, regional, national life" of Berlin's formula is the basic structural element of O'Brien's intellectual history of the South. At the level of the "local" it begins with personal/biographical character.[42] "Subtleties of individuality" in O'Brien's human subjects are then domesticated to a regional, political/cultural agenda enfolding slaveholding and southern nationalism and extending even to climate-producing diseases. The violent collision with "national life" functions as the conclusion to *Conjectures of Order*. Whereas Judt preferred Berlin's third step, "national life," and demoted the other two, O'Brien reverses the hierarchy.

To illustrate how much O'Brien relies on individual character, consider a contrast in Judt's wary use of the device. In *Thinking the Twentieth Century* Judt presents a partial portrait of one of his mentors, Annie Kriegel (1926–95), "the great historian of French communism," who entered the French Resistance in her teens and later became the authority on the origins of the Communist Party in France, a columnist for *Le Figaro*, and Judt's mentor at the University of Paris–Nanterre.[43] Kriegel was, Judt writes, "misleadingly diminutive—she stood four-foot-eleven" and is said to have displayed a submachine gun on the wall of her dorm room—a memento of her time in the Resistance.[44] There, however, Judt stops; the rest of his character of Kriegel is intellectual, touching on her influences and the historians whom she in turn influenced, including himself.

O'Brien takes the character device back to its eighteenth-century origins, fitting southern thought more thoroughly to individual bodies and temperaments. The essays in *The Idea of the American South*, exercises in tracing "the historiography of Southern self-consciousness" in actual minds, are the earliest place this technique appears in O'Brien's work.[45] O'Brien's "character" of W. J. Cash (1900–1941) is a case in point. Unfortunately for Cash, whose book *The Mind of the South* (1941) remains a popular synthesis of southern culture and thought, his attempt at synthesizing his own life "wreak[ed] havoc," a disorder that stubbornly clings to the character of Cash in O'Brien's subsequent work.[46]

In the second part of *Rethinking the South* (1988), O'Brien takes up the Cash character again, alluding more specifically to the man's private torments. O'Brien comes to see Cash as trapped in his own "Romantic image" of the South.[47] Significantly, Cash's Romanticism is embodied in his near-pathological physical and psychological woes. O'Brien quotes passages in which Cash falls into the idea of the South as into a "reverie," reminiscing about "opiates," "perfume," "languor," and "mourning."[48] The undead Poe, another but more calculated southern Romantic, is never far off. Ultimately, O'Brien disapproves of Cash: "There is much more of this kind of thing," he writes in dismissing a particularly inward passage of Cash's writing.[49] Although there is empathy in O'Brien's characters of southern thinkers, there are limits.

The central feature of O'Brien's use of character is the link between thinking and the thinker's physical body. If, as Judt claims, the historian of events is obliged to convey how it felt in the moment of the event, then O'Brien strives to convey how ideas felt in particular bodies: race, sexuality, height, weight, birth order. In his second essay on Cash, for example, O'Brien portrays a thinking Cash as "awkward with women and fear[ing] impotence. He had bad depth perception and was physically clumsy, famous enough for knocking things over that a hostess felt obliged to tape down her tablecloth, lest he wreak havoc. He dressed badly, had a pot belly, went bald."[50] Prufrock among southerners.[51]

History and ideas register differently upon each individual, O'Brien's technique suggests, and the body has a lot to do with it. This is what the fox knows. In O'Brien's work, history is like a character-driven novel. His most fully developed character is Hugh Swinton Legaré (1797–1843), a white South Carolinian in whose mind (and mortal body) intellectual life and the American South blended.[52] O'Brien is archly skeptical of post-Appomattox legends about Legaré brewed up by surviving family members. He counters with an in-the-round "character" of Legaré, lest we take the concept of intellectual life to be disembodied. Noting the odds that Hugh

Legaré's corporeal body could have survived to think for as many years as it did, O'Brien expresses an empathy that goes along with analysis of his subject's historical significance. This complementarity pervades O'Brien's work, widening toward Chekhovian empathy. It is no coincidence that he quotes *The Cherry Orchard* in the introduction to volume 1 of *Conjectures*.[53]

Hugh Legaré was barely four years old when he contracted smallpox, a gruesome disease in early nineteenth-century Charleston, South Carolina. Situating intellectual life in the midst of mortality is crucial to understanding the kind of historical narrative O'Brien composes: "Charleston, like other eighteenth-century cities, had habitually suffered from the devastations of smallpox: the incubation of two weeks, the feverish aching of three days, the swift pustular eruptions that blistered, opened, crusted, and lost their scabs. Half of its victims died, and the rest survived with deforming scars."[54] Young Legaré was among the half who survived but at a cost that made his subsequent life painful and, in the end, brief; he died in his forties. In his youth "he nearly died," O'Brien writes. "The virus turned confluent and attacked his joints, which broke out in ugly impostumes [abscesses], requiring constant redressing. . . . The child . . . shrank. He became so skeletal, thin, and wracked that his mother carried him about upon a pillow, as his legs were weakened and his arms diminished."[55] One might argue that such details constitute irrelevant excess; one of the three serial adjectives (skeletal, thin, wracked) would have been enough. To some intellectual historians, any mention of Legaré's mortal flesh would have been enough.

A stunted boy at puberty, Legaré's expected growth spurt seemed only to affect his head and torso. The physical effects of smallpox became or engendered psychological ones: he brooded, was given to fits of melancholy. Ruled out of much of the social and breeding sweepstakes by the disease and its aftereffects on his body, he channeled what was left into intellectual life. He was put to school in the Willington Academy, the seedbed, O'Brien attests, of the flower of southern intellectual life; among its graduates were John C. Calhoun, Augustus Baldwin Longstreet, Preston Brooks, Pierce Butler, and others whose names—and specters—still confront us today.[56]

The Willington curriculum was heavily influenced by Scottish common sense philosophy, one of the main strands of intellectual DNA in O'Brien's composite portrait of the American South—indispensable, in fact, for it was common sense reliance on classification as a way to make order of the world that clashed with Romantic habits of thought individualizing things and people (and thereby dissolving that order). In the "havoc" that resulted from this collision, the "mind of the South" journeyed from one "crooked" body (Legaré's) to another (Cash's).

The scope of *Conjectures of Order: Intellectual Life and the American South, 1810–1860*, presents a problem: How far can O'Brien's fox-like technique, given to digression and personal character, sustain a 1,202-page, two-volume work? The scale of a macrohistorical narrative might seem to disallow "the subtleties of individuality" as not much more than asides to the general narrative. Judt's practice is illustrative of the default to the overarching theme. The typical chapter of his *Postwar* moves with grave momentum. Chapter 12, "The Spectre of Revolution," is a fair example. The subject matter to be covered is "the Sixties" and "its mark upon History."[57] That "mark," Judt is quick to assert, was more significant in the minds of the putative revolutionaries themselves than the actual history merits: "The self-congratulatory, iconoclastic impulse—in clothing or ideas—dated very fast; conversely, it would be some years before the truly revolutionary shift in politics and public affairs that began in the late 1960s could take full effect."[58] Judt then moves through waves of census statistics representing the student populations en masse of various European countries and follows with a dyspeptic backward glance at the "Swinging London" look that, briefly in hindsight, swept the field of contemporary fashion when Judt himself was a teenager.[59]

Judt's survey eliminates "subtleties of individuality," as embarrassing as they might seem four decades later, for the stability of the big, arching story. The achievement of O'Brien's *Conjectures of Order* is immense and comprehensive too, but he allows for surprises. The "immensity" is physically obvious: the two volumes comprise over 1,300 pages, counting notes, index, and illustrations. Within the years of its domain (1810–60) there is scarcely a (white) southern intellectual whose writing, at least in part, is not digested and placed in O'Brien's genealogy of ideas. His method is exhaustive but relaxed in its narrative discipline. "Idiosyncrasy matters here, as it must in any rigorous intellectual history," O'Brien writes early in the first of his two volumes, and the interplay of "idiosyncrasy" and "rigorous[ness]" gives *Conjectures* a kind of energy that Judt's *Postwar* sacrifices to its "predestined" purpose.[60]

In volume 1, chapter 5, "Types of Mankind," is an apt example of O'Brien's looser narrative, his attention to idiosyncratic character and its generative influence in historical narrative, and his propensity to follow "threads"—as Hayden White observed—"into the circumambient natural and social space within which the event occurred." In this chapter O'Brien recuperates the process by which race was created as a concept in the intellectual life of Europe ("the event") and was then filtered through the "natural and social space" of slave society in the American South to be used by proslavery voices in justification of their barbarous practices. O'Brien's focal character is Josiah Nott (1804–73) of Mobile (born in South Carolina and educated in Philadelphia and in Paris: a global southerner), researcher of the insect-borne origins of yellow fever—for which he might have been honored in history had he not also been the author of several papers arguing for the inferiority of the Negro as a race.

Nott absorbed Lamarckian ideas on the inheritance of acquired characteristics as they had been filtered by Darwin, and he transformed them into a theory of the separate origins of the races in the human species (later disavowed by Darwin in *The Descent of Man* [1871]). Nott's thinking on race was derived from the work of Johann Friedrich Blumenbach (1752–1840), who wrote the first of several editions of his treatise on classifications of mankind, *De Generis Humani Varietate Nativa*, in the resonant year of 1776. As *De Generis* evolved through several subsequent editions, however, what began in the 1770s as merely descriptive categories of human types ended in the 1830s as hierarchical and prescriptive rankings under the newly coined term "race," with the Caucasian (not accidentally, for it was Caucasians who made the lists) at the top.[61] It was this "science" of race that found a socket in southern thinking in the 1830s and 1840s. "By the 1830s," O'Brien writes after tracking the hardening of Blumenbach's race theorizing in the serial editions of *De Generis*, "the ethnic categories of Anglo-American and Romantic thought had collided with the natural science of Blumenbach and his heirs, to produce habitual disquisitions on the 'Types of Mankind.'" In these disquisitions—in southern classrooms, books, periodicals, and orations—the "natural order of man was divided [by race], hierarchical, organic."[62] Nott himself was a creature of this collision and added to its racist damage with a book he coauthored (with George Gliddon) further disseminating Blumenbach's thinking: *Types of Mankind* (1854).[63]

There was a traceable process that accounted for the mind of the American South in any given historical moment. That process was materially and intellectually shaped by "the subtleties of individuality" before it became visible to the historian. Those subtleties included, but were not limited to, the particular body hosting the brain (male or female, hale or infirm, always literate and educated), the circumstances of a certain historical moment and place, and the history of knowledge as it arrived to a certain person in a certain moment.

CODA

Eugene D. Genovese's major project mirrored O'Brien's: a study of "the intellectual culture of the Old South" that remained unfinished at Genovese's death in 2012.[64] Reviewing Genovese's *The Slaveholders' Dilemma: Freedom and Progress in Southern Conservative Thought, 1820–1860*, O'Brien, not surprisingly, but acutely, positioned his own work in the same endeavor against Genovese's.[65] Berlin's *jeu d'esprit* makes a sly reappearance to mark the differences O'Brien sees distinguishing his work from Genovese's. O'Brien reminds us that Genovese (like O'Brien himself) "has characteristically been an essayist," that most of his published work has appeared in that literary form and is "necessarily prone to miscellaneous thoughts, and [that] Genovese has not always resisted the blandishments of the form. However, though a fox in his choice of form, Genovese has been a hedgehog in his standpoint."[66] Genovese's overarching story is the introduction of "Gramscian concepts of hegemony into American thought" and (in the specific late 1980s Reaganite moment of the work under review) to locate "the origins of that anti-capitalist Southern conservatism" that Republican politicians have cultivated ever since.[67] And thus, O'Brien notes, to purchase "cogency," a hedgehoggian focus, by "small acts of exclusion," the jingling currency of the fox.[68] The price for some hedgehoggian history, O'Brien implies, is meted out in "small acts of exclusion," a currency O'Brien is loath to use.

NOTES

1. Isaiah Berlin, *The Hedgehog and the Fox*, ed. Henry Hardy, 2nd ed. (Princeton, N.J.: Princeton University Press, 2013), 101.

2. Tony Judt, *Thinking the Twentieth Century*, with Timothy Snyder (New York: Penguin, 2012), 263.

3. Joseph Conrad, *The Nigger of the Narcissus*, ed. Robert Kimbrough, Norton Critical Editions (New York: W. W. Norton, 1979), 147.

4. The proper historian, in Judt's view, is obliged to engage with readers as "citizens," a public oriented to civic action and understanding, rather than fulfilling, "demands" for feeling. See Judt, *Thinking*, 154.

5. Tony Judt, *Postwar: A History of Europe since 1945* (New York: Penguin, 2005).

6. Michael O'Brien, *Conjectures of Order: Intellectual Life and the American South, 1810-1860* (Chapel Hill: University of North Carolina Press, 2004).

7. Judt, *Thinking*, 397. Judt had made this point earlier in *The Memory Chalet* (New York: Penguin, 2010), 11.

8. Judt, *Thinking*, 268.

9. On the shared infrastructure of writing and reading history, see Hayden White, *Metahistory: The Historical Imagination in Nineteenth-Century Europe* (Baltimore: Johns Hopkins University Press, 1973).

10. Judt, *Postwar*, 7.

11. Tony Judt, *Ill Fares the Land* (New York: Penguin, 2010). Judt's passion for "Europe" echoes George Smiley's uncharacteristic outburst in John le Carré, *A Legacy of Spies* (New York: Viking, 2017): "I'm a European, Peter [Guillam—Smiley's surrogate son in "the Circus"]. If I had a mission—if I was ever aware of one beyond our business with the enemy, it was to Europe. If I was heartless, I was heartless for Europe. If I had an unattainable ideal, it was of leading Europe out of her darkness towards a new age of reason. I have it still" (262).

12. White, *Metahistory*, 18.

13. For another example of this sort of history writing, see Michael O'Brien, "Autobiography," in *Placing the South* (Jackson: University Press of Mississippi, 2007), 79-85. O'Brien's brief essay is both discussion and demonstration of the way "threads" move in the process of writing history.

14. Judt, *Thinking*, 13.

15. Judt, *Ill Fares the Land*, [1].

16. Judt, *Postwar*, 830.

17. Judt, *Memory Chalet*, 11.

18. White, *Metahistory*, 18.

19. For a useful refraction of Judt's subject matter and point of view, see Thomas Piketty, *Capital in the Twenty-First Century*, trans. Arthur Goldhammer (Cambridge, Mass.: Belknap Press of Harvard University Press, 2014). Piketty, from his foundation in economic data, labels Judt's territory "the enchanted world of the postwar decades" (409), in which growth in wealth stemming from labor increased at a greater rate than growth in wealth from inheritance—an anomaly in the history of capital. Piketty deals with the "temptation" of literature by enlisting Jane Austen and Honoré de Balzac as allies in his economic analyses.

20. Raymond Williams, *Writing in Society* (London: Verso, 1983), 3.

21. Williams, 1.

22. Williams, 2.

23. Judt, *Thinking*, ix.

24. The issue of genre seems to have nagged at Judt. In *Memory Chalet* he wonders, "I don't know what sort of genre this is" (10).

25. Judt, *Thinking*, 43.

26. Illustrating the point of the bifurcated Judts, the index to *Thinking the Twentieth Century* contains thirteen lines of mentions of "Judt, Tony."

27. Judt, *Thinking*, 268.

28. A. J. P. Taylor, "Thoughts on Tolstoy," review of *The Hedgehog and the Fox*, by

Isaiah Berlin, *New Statesman and Nation*, December 12, 1953, 768; published as "A. J. P. Taylor's Review" in Berlin, *Hedgehog and the Fox*, 94–96.

29. "A. J. P. Taylor's Review," 94. In Taylor's text, the words attributed to Voltaire are noted as "untraced" by the editor of the volume.

30. Berlin, *Hedgehog and the Fox*, 2.

31. Judt, *Thinking*, 3.

32. Judt, *Postwar*, 226.

33. See also Tony Judt, *Past Imperfect: French Intellectuals, 1944–1956* (Berkeley: University of California Press, 1992); and Tony Judt, "Paris Was Yesterday," in *Memory Chalet*, 111–18.

34. Judt, *Postwar*, 113.

35. Judt, 7.

36. The quote that begins this section is from Michael O'Brien, *The Idea of the American South, 1920–1941* (Baltimore: Johns Hopkins University Press, 1979), 220.

37. O'Brien, ix.

38. O'Brien, *Placing the South*, 159–79.

39. O'Brien, 160.

40. O'Brien's fascination with Virginia Woolf has been noticed by others. See Nicholas Guyatt, "Cool Brains," review of *Conjectures of Order: Intellectual Life and the American South, 1810–1860*, by Michael O'Brien, *London Review of Books*, June 2005, 27–28.

41. Isaiah Berlin, *The Crooked Timber of Humanity*, ed. Henry Hardy (Princeton, N.J.: Princeton University Press, 2013), 260.

42. In this context, "character" refers to the literary genre attributed to Joseph Addison (1672–1719) and Richard Steele (1672–1729), authors of *The Spectator* (1711–12). "Characters" were essay-length portraits of representative social figures.

43. Judt, *Thinking*, 143.

44. Judt, 144.

45. O'Brien, *Idea*, xiii.

46. O'Brien, 215.

47. Michael O'Brien, *Rethinking the South: Essays in Intellectual History* (Baltimore: Johns Hopkins University Press, 1988), 183.

48. O'Brien, 184.

49. O'Brien, 184.

50. O'Brien, 187.

51. For comparison, see Richard King's assessment of Cash in *A Southern Renaissance: The Cultural Awakening of the American South, 1930–1955* (New York: Oxford University Press, 1980). King frames Cash's writing life with his "Oedipal problems" (156), distancing Cash from his body with the Freudian framework King uses to organize his narrative of southern thinking.

52. Michael O'Brien, *A Character of Hugh Legaré* (Knoxville: University of Tennessee Press, 1985).

53. O'Brien, *Conjectures of Order*, 5.

54. O'Brien, *Character of Hugh Legaré*, 5–6.

55. O'Brien, 6.

56. O'Brien, 13.
57. Judt, *Postwar*, 390.
58. Judt, 390.
59. Judt, 396–97.
60. O'Brien, *Conjectures of Order*, 7.
61. O'Brien, 230.
62. O'Brien, 237.

63. Josiah Nott appears in Louis Menand, *The Metaphysical Club: A Story of Ideas in America* (New York: Farrar, Straus and Giroux, 2001), 109–12. Menand places Nott as a disciple of Louis Agassiz. See his chapter "Agassiz," 97–116.

64. Michael O'Brien, "Eugene Genovese," in *Placing the South*, 223; originally published as Michael O'Brien, "Conservative Thought in the Old South: A Review Article," review of *The Slaveholders' Dilemma: Freedom and Progress in Southern Conservative Thought, 1820–1860*, by Eugene D. Genovese, *Comparative Studies in Society and History* 34, no. 3 (July 1992): 566–76.

65. Eugene Genovese, *The Slaveholders' Dilemma: Freedom and Progress in Southern Conservative Thought, 1820–1860* (Columbia: University of South Carolina Press, 1992).

66. O'Brien, *Placing the South*, 224.
67. O'Brien, 222–23.
68. O'Brien, 227.

CONTRIBUTORS

MICHAEL T. BERNATH is Charlton W. Tebeau Associate Professor in American History at the University of Miami. He is the author of *Confederate Minds: The Struggle for Intellectual Independence in the Civil War South* (2010).

STEPHEN BERRY is Gregory Professor of the Civil War Era at the University of Georgia and the author or editor of six books on nineteenth-century America. He directs the web project CSI:Dixie (csidixie.org) and coedits the UnCivil Wars series at University of Georgia Press with Amy Murrell Taylor.

JOHN GRAMMER is professor of English at the University of the South, where he also directs Sewanee's interdisciplinary program in southern studies. He is the author of *Pastoral and Politics in the Old South* and of essays appearing in *American Literary History*, the *Sewanee Review*, *Oxford American*, and other periodicals.

MICHAEL KREYLING is Gertrude Conaway Vanderbilt Professor of English, emeritus, at Vanderbilt University. He is the author of several books and articles on southern literature and literary culture, most recently *The South That Wasn't There: Postsouthern Memory and History* (2010) and *A Late Encounter with the Civil War* (2014).

SCOTT ROMINE is professor of English at the University of North Carolina at Greensboro. He is the author of *The Narrative Forms of Southern Community* (1999) and *The Real South: Southern Narrative in the Age of Cultural Reproduction* (2008) and coeditor, with Jennifer Rae Greeson, of *Keywords for Southern Studies* (2016).

BETH BARTON SCHWEIGER is a historian in Seattle, Washington. Her most recent book is *A Literate South: Reading before Emancipation* (2019).

MITCHELL SNAY is professor emeritus at Denison University in Granville, Ohio. He is the author of three books on nineteenth-century southern, political, and intellectual history, including *Gospel of Disunion: Religion and Separatism in the Antebellum South* (1993).

MELANIE BENSON TAYLOR is professor of Native American studies at Dartmouth College. She is the author of *Disturbing Calculations: The Economics of Identity in Postcolonial Southern Literature, 1912–2002* (2008), *Reconstructing the Native South: American Indian Literature and the Lost Cause* (2012), and *The Indian in American Southern Literature* (2020) and serves as executive editor of *Native South*.

JONATHAN DANIEL WELLS is professor of history in the Departments of Afroamerican and African Studies and History and in the Residential College at the University of Michigan. He is the author or editor of several books, including, most recently, *Blind No More: African American Resistance, Free-Soil Politics, and the Coming of the Civil War* (2019) and *The Kidnapping Club: Wall Street, Slavery, and Resistance on the Eve of the Civil War* (2020). He lives in Detroit, Michigan.

TIMOTHY J. WILLIAMS is associate professor of history at the University of Oregon. He is the author of *Intellectual Manhood: University, Self, and*

Society in the Antebellum South (2015) and coeditor of *Prison Pens: Gender, Memory, and Imprisonment in the Writings of Mollie Scollay and Wash Nelson, 1863–1866* (2018).

Editors

SARAH E. GARDNER is Distinguished University Professor of History at Mercer University. She is the author of *Blood and Irony: Southern White Women's Narratives of the Civil War, 1861–1937* (2004) and of *Reviewing the South: The Literary Marketplace and the Southern Renaissance, 1920–1941* (2017).

STEVEN M. STOWE is professor emeritus of history at Indiana University, Bloomington. He is the author, most recently, of *Keep the Days: Reading the Civil War Diaries of Southern Women* (2018).

INDEX

Abbeville Press, 105
abolitionism: lower-class whites and, 172–73; post–Harpers Ferry threat of, 36–39, 41, 42, 44, 46, 47
Adair, George, 96
African American Intellectual History Society, 2
African Americans: Anthropocene and, 122, 123–24, 128–29; as authors, 184, 185, 186, 187, 188, 192; book history and, 57–58, 59, 61, 64, 71n5; labor of, devaluated, 104–6; Native blood and, 128–29; opposition to immigration, 103–4; spiritual songs and, 69–70. *See also* freedmen
African Methodist Episcopal Church, 69
African Native heritage, 128–29
Afro-pessimism, 122

Alabama & Chattanooga Railroad, 107
Alabama Female College, 39
Alderman, Edwin, 182, 183, 188–89, 192, 194, 197. See also *Library of Southern Literature, The*
Alexander v. Holmes County Board of Education, 154–56
Alibar, Lucy, 124
Allen, Richard, 69
All the King's Men (Warren), 152
American, 145
American Anti-Slavery Society, 46–47
American Labyrinth, 4
American Review, The, 24
American Revolution and printing, 57
Angel in the Cloud, The (Fuller), 82
"Angel in the Cloud, The" (Fuller), 81

Anthropocene: about, 7, 119–21; in southern literature (*see* literature and the Anthropocene, southern)
antinorthernism, 36–39, 48–49. *See also* Boggy Swamp incident
"arche-fossil," 134
Archilochus, 202, 205, 210
Archipelagic American Studies (Roberts and Stephens), 130–31
archipelagic influence, 130–32
Arkansas Democrat, 195
Arkansas Freeman, 108
Arkansas River Valley Immigration Company, 96, 97, 107
Armies of the Night, The (Mailer), 141
Atlanta Constitution, 189, 191
Auden, W. H., 28
Augusta Dispatch, 37
autobiographical fiction, 207, 208, 212–13. See also *Sea-Gift*
autochthonizing, 126
Awiakta, Marilou, 120
Ayers, Edward L., 167

bacchanalian whirl, 165
Baker, Catherine A., 64–65
Baltimore Collection, 69
Baltimore Sun, 194, 196–97
Barbour, Jeppie, 156
Bard, Samuel, 103
Barnaby Rudge (Dickens), 15–17, 18, 24
Barney, Mary Chase, 185
Barnsley, Veronica, 124
Barr, Amelia E., 192
Baskervill, William Malone, 188
Bass, Rick, 125
"Bear, The" (Faulkner), 121–22
Beasts of the Southern Wild (Zeitlin), 124
Beaufort Republican, 99
Bender, Thomas, 10n5
Benítez-Rojo, Antonio, 131
Benjamin, Judah P., 191
"Bent Twig, The" (Berlin), 215

Berkeley, William, 56–57
Berlin, Isaiah: about, 202–4, 205, 209, 210–12, 215, 220; *The Hedgehog and the Fox*, 202, 209–11
Berry, Stephen W., 85
Berry, Wendell, 125, 126, 127
Best and the Brightest, The (Halberstam), 141–42
Bethel Church (Philadelphia), 69
Bibles, 60, 68, 69, 73n24
Billion Black Anthropocenes or None, A (Yusoff), 121
Biloxi-Chitimacha tribe, 124
Black Diamonds Gathered in the Darkey Homes of the South (Pollard), 171–72, 176, 180n57
"Black Indians," 128–29
Bloom, Harold, 32n9
Blumenbach, Johann Friedrich, 219
body, the: biopolitical vulnerability of, 216–17; in McAdams's poetry, 129–30, 132; O'Brien and, 216–17, 218; "throwaway," 122–23
Boggs, Belle, 136–37
Boggy Swamp incident, 36–51; aftermath of, 50–51; background and overview of, 36, 39–40; defenders and accusers, 40–45, 53nn28–29, 53–54nn36–37; Dodd and, 42, 44–45; Hamilton-Logan dispute and, 41–42, 43–44; press and, 45–47, 50; southern intellectual life and, 49–50
Bone, Martyn, 131
Bonner, Sherwood, 187, 188, 192–93
book history in the South, 56–70; book buying and, 57, 61–62, 63; human voice and, 65–66, 67–70, 75n49; overview of, 56–60, 70; print culture and, 66–67, 74nn36–37; region and culture and, 60–65
Boston Daily Atlas, 27
Bradford, John, 68
Bradley, James, 41
Bradley, S. J., 41, 44–45

Bragg, Rick, 163
Breslin, Jimmy, 143
Brewster, William, 49
Briggs, Charles Frederick, 15, 27
Broadway Journal, 27
Broomall, James J., 77
Browning, Elizabeth Barrett, 25
Bryan, Mary Edwards, 184, 185
Bryant, William Cullen, 101
Burton, Pierce, 103
Burton, Vernon, 55n55
Butler, Judith, 122
Butler, Leslie, 94–95
Byrd, Willie, 145
Byron, Lord, 28

Cabell, E. Carrington, 96
Caleb Williams (Godwin), 18–19
Calhoun, John C., 67, 166, 193, 217
Capitalocene, 120, 128
Carey, Henry C., 101
Carlyle, Thomas, 19
Carter, Forrest "Asa," 127
Case, Meigs, 39
Cash, Wilbur J., 10n8, 161, 214, 216, 218, 222n51
"Cask of Amontillado, The" (Poe), 192
Cedar Swamp Soldiers' Aid Society, 51
Cedar Swamp Troop, 45
Charleston, South Carolina and book history, 64
Charleston Courier, 50, 189
Charleston Daily Republican, 101, 108
Charleston Mercury, 41, 43, 46, 50
Chesnut, Mary Boykin, 214
Child, Lydia Maria, 20–21
Chinese immigrants, 97, 107–8, 109, 112n9, 115nn34–35
chivalry, 46–47, 79, 168, 175–76
Chopin, Kate, 5, 193, 195
civil rights movement and journalism, 8, 142, 145–48, 153
Clansman, The (Dixon), 89
Clarke, Mary Bayard, 193

Clay, Cassius M., 197
Clay, Henry, 197
Cole, Thomas, 85
Coleman, Tom, 146
Collection of Spiritual Songs and Hymns, Selected from Various Authors, A (Allen), 69
colonialism, settler, 122–23, 127–28
colonies, free labor, 100–101
Colored American, 103
Confederados, 88
Confederate memorialization, 79, 186, 188, 189–90
Confessions of a White Racist (King), 145, 154
Confessions of Nat Turner, The (Styron), 141
Conjectures of Order (O'Brien), 204, 215, 217, 218–19
Conrad, Joseph, 203, 204, 208
Cooke, John Esten, 196
Cooper, Anna Julia, 184
Couthard, Glen Sean, 122
Cowles, John, Jr., 141, 142, 158
Crackers, 126
Crane, Hart, 29
"crowd upon the word *South*," 161–62, 164, 177

Dabbs, James McBride, 176
Dabney, Thomas Smith, 48–49, 55n57
Daily New Era, 98, 99, 102, 103
Daniels, Jonathan, 146
Darnton, Robert, 3, 58
Darwin, Charles, 219
David Copperfield (Dickens), 207, 208, 212–13
Davidson, James Wood, 187–88
Davis, Richard Beale, 1
Davis, Varina, 193
Day, Iyko, 122
"Death in Lowndes County, A" (Morrisroe), 146
De Bow's Review, 107, 178n18

decontinentalization, 130–31
Decter, Midge, 142
de Gaulle, Charles, 212–13
De Generis Humani Varietate Nativa (Blumenbach), 219
Democrats and immigration, 95, 96, 104–6, 107–8, 109
Dew, Thomas Roderick, 165
Dial, The, 195
Dibble, Samuel W., 189
Dickens, Charles: American tour of, 17–18; *Barnaby Rudge*, 15, 16–17, 18, 24; *David Copperfield*, 207, 208, 212–13; Grip and, 15–17; Poe and, 18–20, 21–24, 25, 27, 34nn16–18
Didier, Eugene, 197
Didion, Joan, 143
Dimock, Wai Chee, 131
Dirt and Desire (Yaeger), 122
disaster narratives, 123–25
Dispatches (Herr), 144
distinctiveness of the South, 4–5, 56, 57, 166, 168–69, 182, 185
Dixie National Baton Twirling Institute, 148–49
Dixon, Thomas, 89
Doaks, Michael, 151
Dodd, Eunice, 51
Dodd, W. J., 36, 40, 42, 44–45, 47, 51
Dorson, Richard M., 65–66
Down to Now (Watters), 146–47, 157
"Dreaming, the Book of" (McAdams), 129
dreamland state, 79, 89

ecocriticism, 119, 128
Ecology of a Cracker Childhood (Ray), 126
Education of Little Tree, The (Carter), 127
Eisenstein, Elizabeth, 66, 74n36
E. J. Hale and Son, 76
"Elegy, An" (Fuller), 84
Elliott, William, 29–30
Ellison, Ralph, 165

Emerson, Ralph Waldo: about, 19–20, 23, 26, 28, 57; "The Humble Bee," 19, 23, 34n22; Poe and, 19–20, 32n9
environmental injustice, 125
environmentalism, 119–20, 123, 125
Esquire, 143, 144
European immigrants, 102, 105, 108
Evans, Augusta Jane, 185, 193
Evening Mirror, 24–25
Evening Post, 47
Everglades, the, 135
exile, 82, 83, 88, 89

fantasies: Anthropocene and, 125, 132, 136; Fuller and, 7, 78, 79–80, 83, 88, 89
Faulkner, Mississippi (Glissant), 131
Faulkner, William: about, 5, 119–20, 137n2; "The Bear," 121–22; Indigenous peoples and, 126; Wrecking Crew and, 143, 149, 152, 153, 155
Fear and Loathing in Las Vegas (Thompson), 144
Feral (McAdams), 129–30, 132
Fichte, Johann Gottlieb, 166
Fitzhugh, George, 165, 167
"Flight Down the Middle Way, The" (O'Brien), 214
Florida Improvement Company, 100
Foner, Eric, 102, 107, 109, 112n9
Ford, Jesse Hill, 151–52, 153
Foreign Quarterly Review, 22–23, 34nn16–18
Fort Smith New Era, 103
fox-hedgehog. *See* hedgehog-fox dichotomy
Fourth South Carolina Calvary, 51
Frady, Marshall: about, 8, 142, 143, 144–45; "Judgment of Jesse Hill Ford," 151–52; *Southerners*, 146; Tom Wolfe and, 148, 149. *See also* Wrecking Crew, the
France, Tony Judt on, 212–13
"Frank Sinatra Has a Cold" (Talese), 144

freedmen: labor of, devaluated, 104–6; immigration dissent of, 103–4, 108, 109; literacy and, 61; Republican Party and, 102–3, 109

freehold farmers, 99–102, 106–7, 109–10, 114n31, 115n38

free-labor colonies, 100–101

free-labor ideology, 98, 100–102, 103, 108

Free Land and Colonization Company, 96

Free-Soilers, 101

Free State Colony, 101

Fuller, Anna Long Thomas, 81

Fuller, Edwin Wiley: about, 81–82, 88–89; *Sea-Gift* (see *Sea-Gift*)

Fuller, Jones, 81

future-oriented perspectives, 78, 79

Gara, Larry, 173

Gardner, Dave, 149–51, 152

Geertz, Clifford, 3

gender: *LSL* and, 8, 183–86, 192–94, 198–200n3; southern literary history and, 187–88. *See also* masculinity; women writers, white

Genovese, Eugene D., 220

Georgia Federation of Women's Clubs, 194

German Homestead Association of Cincinnati, 100

German immigrants, 95–96, 100, 102, 105

"Ghost Ranch" (McAdams), 132–33

Gift, J. C., 97

Giles, Paul, 131

Gilman, Caroline, 185, 195, 197

Glasgow, Ellen, 119–20, 137n2

Gliddon, George, 219

Glissant, Édouard, 131

globalization of the South, 108–9, 131

Godard, Charles W., 99

Godwin, William, 18–19

Gordon, D. E., 45

Gordon, John B., 106

Grady, Henry W., 176, 189

Graham, George Rex, 27

Graham's Magazine, 17, 26, 34n22

"Gran'Mammy" (Bonner), 192–93

Great Chain of Being, 3

Greeley, Horace, 101

Greenberg, Amy, 88

Grip, 15–17, 24, 25

Griswold, Rufus, 19

Gross, Robert, 60

Guterl, Matthew Pratt, 108

Hagar, Sarah, 47–48

Haile, Israel, 37

Halberstam, David, 141–42

Hall, David D., 56

Hamilton, R. A. P., 36, 40, 41–42, 43–45, 53n30

Hammond, James Henry, 165, 167

Harper, William, 179–80n57

Harper's Magazine, 141–43, 145, 154, 158, 183

Harris, Joel Chandler, 182, 183, 187, 188–89, 191–92, 193, 195. See also *Library of Southern Literature, The*

Harris and Ashby, 96

Harrison, James A., 191–92

Hawthorne, Nathaniel, 195, 198

Hedgehog and the Fox, The (Berlin), 202, 209–11

hedgehog-fox dichotomy: background and overview of, 202–4; Berlin and, 202–4, 205, 209, 210–11; Genovese and, 220; Judt and, 204, 205–6, 212–13, 214; O'Brien and, 204, 214, 220

Hedrick, Benjamin S., 197

Heise, Ursula, 125

Helper, Hinton Rowan, 45, 57, 172–73, 180n62

Herder, Johann Gottfried, 215

heroism, 78, 199

Herr, Michael, 144

Hersh, Seymour, 141

Higham, John, 3

Historical Magazine, 82
history of books in the South. *See* book history in the South
History of the Book in America, A, 66
history writing. *See* writing history
Hoard, Charles B., 101
Hollinger, David, 3
Homestead Company, 101
honor, 86–87
Hope of Liberty, The (Horton), 192
Horton, George Moses, 192
Houston, R. E., 97
Houston Union, 101–2, 103
Howe, Julia Ward, 25
human voice and books, 65–66, 67–70, 75n49
"Humble Bee, The" (Emerson), 19, 23, 34n22
Hunt, H. L., 150–51
Huntress, 198
Huntsville Advocate, 103
Hurricane Katrina, 123–24
Hutton, J. S., 105, 113n29
hymnbooks, 59, 62, 68–70
Hymns and Spiritual Songs for the Use of Christians, 69

Idea of the American South, The (O'Brien), 216
identity, southern: conclusions on Pollard and, 176–77; defense of, 198; ideas and, 163–65, 177n9; O'Brien and, 161–64; Poe and, 21; print and, 66–67; Romantic nationalism and, 166–67; southern defensiveness and, 165–66; southern superiority and, 167–69; tradition and, 169, 178–79n34; white superiority and, 170–73, 180n57; Wrecking Crew and, 143, 153. *See also* southern mind
Ill Fares the Land (Judt), 206, 221n11
I'll Take My Stand (Twelve Southerners), 126
"illusion of continuity," 172, 173

imaginary and Anthropocenic histories, 125, 126, 129, 130
imagination: postwar, 77–78, 79–80, 169–70; Wrecking Crew and, 153, 158
immigration crusade: background and overview of, 95–97, 112n9; Chinese laborers and, 97, 107–8, 109, 112n9, 115nn34–35; conclusions on, 108–10; dissent against, 103–4, 106–7; reasons for failure of, 97–98; Republicans and, 96–97, 98–103, 106, 108, 109; Southern Democrats and, 104–6, 107–8, 109
Impending Crisis, The (Helper), 45, 172–73, 180n62
Independent Monitor, 107
Indigenous peoples: Anthropocene and, 122–23, 124, 126–30, 131–34, 137; "Black Indians," 128–29; oral culture and, 67, 68
Industrial and Immigration Association of Middle Florida, 102
insiders: background and overview of, 4, 5, 8–9; Dickens as among, 20; southern identity and, 162, 163, 173; southern literary collections and, 8, 186, 188, 198–99
intellectual history: Anthropocene and, 120; identity and, 162–63, 164, 177n9; O'Brien and, 80, 162–63, 204, 214–15, 217–18; overview of South's, 1–6, 9n2, 10nn7–8; Reconstruction and, 94–95; *Sea-Gift* as, 80, 89; southern literary history and, 182, 183, 186, 190, 196–97; southern outsiders and, 190
Isle de Jean Charles, 124

Jackson, Leon, 58
J. B. Lippincott, 63
Jefferson, Thomas, 1, 172, 180n62
Johns, Adrian, 66
Johnson, Willard, 128–29
Johnston, Mary E., 185, 196

Jones, J. Robert, 150–51
journalism: civil rights movement and, 8, 142, 145–48, 153; New Journalism (*see* New Journalism); partisan, 50, 95. *See also* press, the; *and specific newspapers*
"Judgment of Jesse Hill Ford, The" (Frady), 151–52
Judt, Tony: about, 204, 221n19; autobiography and, 207–8, 209, 211, 212; hedgehog-fox dichotomy and, 204, 205–6, 212–13, 214; history writing overview and, 204–7; *Ill Fares the Land*, 206, 221n11; master narratives and, 212–13; *Memory Chalet*, 207–8, 213; plenitude and excess and, 209, 211; *Postwar: A History of Europe since 1945*, 204–5, 206–8, 212–13, 218; themes and, 205–6, 218; *Thinking the Twentieth Century*, 202–3, 204–8, 209, 213, 215, 220n4

Kansas-Nebraska Act, 88
Karp, Matthew, 88
Kelley, Harold, 155
Kent, Charles W., 182, 183, 184, 188–89, 190, 192. See also *Library of Southern Literature, The*
Keowee Courier, 37, 105
Kermode, Frank, 214
King, Elisha J., 70
King, Larry L.: about, 143, 144–45, 146, 152, 153; *Confessions of a White Racist*, 145, 154; *Harper's* and, 145, 153–54, 158; "Whatever Happened to Brother Dave?," 149–51. *See also* Wrecking Crew, the
King, Martin Luther, Jr., 150
King, Richard, 222n51
Kingstree incident. *See* Boggy Swamp incident
Kingstree Star, 36, 39, 41, 42, 45, 53–54n37
Klibanoff, Hank, 147–48
Knight, Lucian L., 190
Kriegel, Annie, 215
Kuhn, Thomas, 3
Ku Klux Klan, 89

labor, immigrant. *See* immigration crusade
"Labor Question of the South, The," 95
Lancaster Ledger, 46
Land, Immigration, and Colonization Society, 96
land and immigration companies, 96
land reform, 99–102
Lanier, Sidney, 80, 91n20, 188, 195, 196
Latour, Bruno, 120, 134, 164–65
le Carré, John, 221n11
Lee, Robert E., 189, 193, 197
Lee, Spike, 124
Legacy of Spies, A (le Carré), 221n11
Legaré, Hugh Swinton, 216–17
Le Vert, Octavia, 188
Liberation of Lord Byron Jones, The (Ford), 151
Library of Southern Literature, The (*LSL*): background and overview of, 8, 182–86; content of, 191–93, 194–95, 197–98; discussion and courses of, 194; editing and publicity of, 188–91, 193–94; gender and, 183–86, 192–94, 198–99, 199–200n3; race and, 183–84, 192–93, 199–200n3; reaction to, 194–99
Like unto Like (Bonner), 192
"Lines to My—" (Horton), 192
Lippincott's, 175
literacy, 57–58, 59, 60, 61, 62, 71n5
Literary Gazette, 28
literary history, southern, 5–6, 10n8, 183–86. See also *Library of Southern Literature, The*
literary studies, 67–68, 75n42, 120
literature, Lost Cause. *See* Lost Cause literature

literature and the Anthropocene, southern, 119–37; African Americans and, 122, 123–24, 128–29; archipelagic influence and, 130–32; background and overview of, 119–22; Boggs and, 136–37; disaster narratives and, 123–25; environmental injustice and, 125; hidden features of, 125–26; Indigenous peoples and, 122–23, 126–30, 131–34, 137; McAdams and, 129–30, 132–34, 137; Ray and, 125, 126, 127; Russell and, 134–36; settler colonialism and, 122–23, 127–28

Living Female Writers of the South (Tardy), 188

Livingston Journal, 104

Living Writers of the South (Davidson), 187–88

Lloyd, Christopher, 123

Logan, Richard Columbus, 41–46, 50

Longfellow, Fanny, 26

Longfellow, Henry Wadsworth, 19, 23, 27

Longstreet, Augustus Baldwin, 33n11, 59, 217

Look Homeward, Angel (Wolfe), 152

Lost Cause, The (Pollard), 165, 167–69, 174, 176, 178–79n34

Lost Cause literature, 79, 82, 169, 186–87, 188, 193. See also *Lost Cause, The*; *Lost Cause Regained, The*; *Sea-Gift*

Lost Cause Regained, The (Pollard), 170–71, 172, 176, 180n62

Lovejoy, Arthur O., 3

Lowell, James Russell, 28, 32–33n11

Lower Bridge Soldiers' Aid Society, 51

Lowry, David Shane, 122

Loyal Georgian, 103

LSL (*The Library of Southern Literature*). See *Library of Southern Literature, The*

Lynch, James, 103–4

Maddex, Jack P., 172, 173, 174

magazine subscriptions, 62–63

Mailer, Norman, 141

Malone, Mary E., 82

Manifest Destiny, 88

Manly, Louise, 188

Marker, Michael, 127

Marrs, Cody, 79

Martin and Hoyt Company, 186, 189, 191, 193–94, 197

masculinity, 77–78, 79–80, 83, 85, 88, 89, 154

Master Humphrey's Clock, 15

Mattaponi Queen (Boggs), 136–37

Maurice, Samuel W., 50

Maury, Jesse, 48

May, Robert E., 88

McAdams, Janet, 129–30, 132–34, 137

McCarthy, Cormac, 125

McCord, Louisa, 188, 193

McCurry, Stephanie, 40

McKenzie, D. F., 65

McLuhan, Marshall, 66

Meillassoux, Quentin, 134

memorialization, Confederate, 79, 186, 188, 189–90

memory: Judt and, 207–8; southern, 169–70, 174, 179n35

Memory Chalet (Judt), 207–8, 213

Menand, Louis, 142

Mencken, H. L., 161

Meredith, James, 149

Methodist Episcopal Church, South, 64

Mind of the South, The (Cash), 10n8, 216

Minges, Patrick, 128

Mobile, Alabama, 64–65

Mobile Tribune, 106

modernity, 121, 127–28, 132, 133, 167

Montgomery Advertiser, 105

Moore, MariJo, 136

Morning News, 105–6

Morris, Willie: about, 8, 142–43, 145–46, 153–54, 158–59; Faulkner and, 152; *Harper's* and, 141–42, 154, 158; *North Toward Home*, 143, 154; *Yazoo*, 154–58. *See also* Wrecking Crew, the
Morrisroe, Richard, 146
Moscrip, Jeanette, 191
Moxon, Edward, 22
Murray, Albert, 142, 154
mythologizing, 82, 85, 89, 121, 124–25

narrative threads, 206, 208, 209, 212, 219, 221n13
Nashville, Tennessee, 64
nationalism, 87, 166–67, 168, 171, 172, 215
Native Americans. *See* Indigenous peoples
"Native Hill, A" (Berry), 127
"Negro in the South, The" (Pollard), 175, 176
New Directions in American Intellectual History, 2–3
New Era, 104
New Hanover Agricultural Society, 96
New Journalism: background and overview of, 141–44; civil rights movement and, 144–48; Tom Wolfe and Southern and, 148–49, 152–53; Wrecking Crew and (*see* Wrecking Crew, the)
New Mind of the South (Thompson), 163
"News from the Imaginary Front" (McAdams), 129
New South, 98–99, 108–10, 112n9, 189
New Southern Studies, 6, 121, 131
newspaper subscriptions, 62–63
Newsweek, 146
Newton, Willoughby, 106
New World, 25
New York Herald, 47
New York Tribune, 28

Nigger of the Narcissus, The (Conrad), 203
nissology, 130–31
Nixon, Rob, 121, 123, 125
Norfolk Virginian, 104–5
Northern immigrants, 100–102
northern teachers. *See* teachers, northern
North Toward Home (Morris), 143, 154
nostalgia, 82, 87, 125, 155
Notes on the State of Virginia (Jefferson), 172, 180n62
Nott, Josiah, 219, 223n63
nullification crisis, 41, 53n28

O'Brien, Michael: about, 9n2, 10n8, 204, 214; *Conjectures of Order*, 204, 215, 217, 218–19; "Flight Down the Middle Way," 214; Genovese and, 220; hedgehog-fox dichotomy and, 204, 214, 220; *Idea of the American South*, 216; individual character and, 215–20; on intellectual history, 80; literary influences on, 214; *Rethinking the South*, 177n8, 216; Romantic nationalism and, 215; on the South, 60, 94; southern identity and, 161–64, 165, 166, 167, 177n9
"Ode to Liberty" (Horton), 192
Old South, 83, 169, 186, 195
Ong, Walter J., 66
"On the Steps of the Pentagon" (Mailer), 141
oral tradition, 59, 65–66, 68–70, 75n49
Orangeburg Southron, 37
Orr, John, 104
outsiders: background and overview of, 4; immigration and, 95; northern teachers as, 36–37; southern literary collections and, 8–9, 188, 190, 198–99; Wrecking Crew and, 148, 155, 156
Owens, Delia, 124

Oxford History of Popular Print Culture, The (Kelly), 67

Page, Thomas Nelson, 169–70, 186, 195
Patterson, Orlando, 129
Pearson, Katherine, 194
Peck, Samuel Minturn, 194
People's Press, 104
perception and reality, 163–64, 177n8
periodical subscriptions, 62–63
Philadelphia Inquirer, 196
Phillips, Ulrich B., 173
Pickens, Francis W., 104
Pike, James Shepherd, 174, 175
Piketty, Thomas, 221n19
plantation system: eradication of, 99–100, 121; immigration and, 105, 107–8; in literature, 5, 131; memory and, 169–70
planters: Boggy Swamp incident and, 40, 42–43, 44, 47–49, 55n55; immigration and, 95–99, 104, 106–8, 109
plenitude, 209, 210–11
Podhoretz, Norman, 142
Poe, Edgar Allan: about, 28–29, 31–32; abyss of progress and, 29; Boston poetry reading of, 27–28; "The Cask of Amontillado," 192; death and, 24, 28, 31; Dickens and, 18–20, 21–24, 25, 27, 34nn16–18; Emerson and, 19–20, 32n9; Longfellow and, 27; *LSL* and, 191–92, 196; "The Raven," 24–27, 192; southernness of, 20–21, 32–33n11, 33n13; "To Helen," 192
Poets and Poetry of America (Griswold), 19
"Polar Journeys" (McAdams), 130
political thought in the South, 5, 10n7
Pollard, Edward A.: about, 8, 165; *Black Diamonds Gathered in the Darkey Homes of the South*, 171–72, 176, 180n57; conclusions on, 176–77; *The Lost Cause*, 165, 167–69, 174, 176, 178–79n34; *The Lost Cause Regained*, 170–71, 172, 176, 180n62; "The Negro in the South," 175, 176; subintellectual history and, 163; tradition and, 169, 178–79n34; two civilizations and, 167–68, 172; *The Virginia Tourist*, 174, 176; war of ideas and, 168–69; white supremacy and, 170–73, 175
Pollard, H. Rives, 179n35
Postwar: A History of Europe since 1945 (Judt), 204–5, 206–8, 212–13, 218
Povinelli, Elizabeth, 121, 123, 134
Pratt, Scott, 128
Presidential Reconstruction, 96, 103, 107
press, the: Boggy Swamp incident and, 45–47, 50; establishment of Republican, 103; travel and, 88. *See also* journalism; *and specific newspapers*
Preston, Margaret J., 188
Primitive Baptists, 68
print culture, 66–67, 70, 74nn36–37
printed texts and oral tradition, 65–66, 67–70, 75n49
printing, 56–57, 60, 62, 63, 64–65, 72n12, 73n21
Printing Press as an Agent of Change, The (Eisenstein), 66, 74n36
"private confederacies," 77–78, 79, 80, 89
Proslavery Argument, The (Harper), 179–80n57
Prostrate State, The (Pike), 174
Public Ledger, 17
Publishers Weekly, 82
publishing trade, 60, 62–65, 183–84, 197. *See also* Martin and Hoyt Company

race: labor and, 96, 98, 99, 102–6, 107–8, 113n29; *LSL* and, 183–84, 192–93, 199–200n3; Nott and, 219; O'Brien and, 219; *Sea-Gift* and, 84;

race (*continued*)
  southern literary history and, 185, 186, 187, 188
Race Beat, The (Roberts and Klibanoff), 147–48
racial hierarchies, 172, 176, 180n62, 219
racial integration, 154–56
Radical Reconstruction, 96–97, 98
"Raven, The" (Poe), 24–27, 192
ravens, 15–17, 24–27
Ray, Janisse, 125, 126, 127
reading, teaching of, 57, 62
Reconstruction: globalization of, 108–9; immigration crusade and (*see* immigration crusade); intellectual history and, 94–95; literature and, 77, 78–80, 89, 95, 121; Presidential, 96, 103, 107; Radical, 96–97, 98
Reed, Rex, 148
Renan, Ernest, 171, 179n48
Republican, 98
Republican Party: establishment of press and, 103; immigration crusade of, 96–97, 98–103, 106, 108, 109; Pollard and, 176; white supremacy and, 173
Rethinking the South (O'Brien), 177n8, 216
rhetorical mode of the South, 168–69, 177–78n11
Rhett, Robert, 46
Richardson, Frank, 62
Richmond Times-Dispatch, 196
Road, The (McCarthy), 125
Roberts, Brian Russell, 130–31
Roberts, Gene, 147–48
Romanticism, 31, 68, 161, 163, 175–76, 216
Romantic nationalism, 166–67, 168, 171, 172, 215
Royall, Anne, 185, 198
Rozier, Albert L., 148
Rubin, Joan Shelley, 58–59
Rural Carolinian, 107

Russell, Karen, 134–36
Rutherford, Mildred Lewis, 185, 187

Sacred Harp, The (King and White), 70
sacred song, 59, 66, 68–70
Salters, John A., 51
Salvage the Bones (Ward), 124
Salvo, T. A., 37
Saturday Evening Post, 16
Scarlet Letter, The (Hawthorne), 198
Schivelbusch, Wolfgang, 79, 89
Schurz, Carl, 96
Sea-Gift (Fuller): background and overview of, 7, 76–80; cultural and intellectual history and, 88–89; dreaming and, 79, 83, 85; masculinity and, 77–78, 79–80, 83, 85, 88, 89; reviews of, 82; story and themes of, 82–88
secession, 47, 50, 78
sectional hostilities, 40
selling books, 57, 61–62, 63
settler colonialism, 122–23, 127–28
Sevier, Clara D., 192
Shaw, Henry D., 40–41, 42, 44–45
S. H. Goetzel and Company, 65
Shields, Rudy, 155–56
Simms, William Gilmore, 49, 190, 195
Skinner, Quentin, 3
Slaveholders' Dilemma, The (Genovese), 220
slaveowners. *See* planters
slavery: about, 88; book history and, 57–58, 59, 61, 64, 71n5; defense of, 40, 41, 44, 165–66, 167–68, 171–73, 179–80n57, 190; immigration as a substitute for, 97, 99, 106, 109; literary compilations and, 187, 197; in *Sea-Gift*, 77, 84–85; white supremacy and, 172–73, 180n62
Slave Songs of the United States, 69–70
slow violence, 121, 123, 125
smallpox, 217

Smith, Elizabeth Oakes, 25
Smith, Jon, 119–120, 121
Smith, Mark, 109
Smith, Seba, 59
Snyder, Timothy, 206, 209
Society for U.S. Intellectual History, 2
"Solid Souths," 164
song, sacred, 59, 66, 68–70
Southern, Eileen, 69–70
Southern, Terry, 143, 148–49
Southern Argus, 95
southern "concrete," 161–62
Southerners (Frady), 146
Southern Field and Factory, 96
Southern Harmony (Walker), 70
Southern Historical Society, 190
"southern home," 83, 84, 85, 87, 88
southern idea, 162, 163–64, 177n9
Southern Intellectual History Colloquium, 9n2
Southern Literary Messenger, 25, 26, 192
southern mind, 78–79, 161–62, 164, 171, 216
southern nationalism, 87, 166–67, 168, 171, 172, 215
Southern Reach (VanderMeer), 125
Southern Republican, 103
southern superiority, 167–68, 194–95
South Georgia Times, 106
South in History and Literature, The (Rutherford), 185, 187
South in the Building of the Nation, The, 190
South to a Very Old Place (Murray), 154
speech, 65–66, 67–70
Spirit of the Times, 23
Sports Illustrated, 144
Spoth, Daniel, 123
Standing Bear, 128
state governments and immigration, 97, 104
Stephens, Alexander, 193
Stephens, Michelle Ann, 130–31

Stern, Madeleine, 63
Stevens, Wallace, 177
"strange borderland," 210, 214
Styron, William, 141, 142, 153
subscriptions, periodical, 62–63
Sunday school libraries, 73n19, 92
Suwannee River Tales (Bonner), 192
Swamplandia! (Russell), 135–36
Swedish immigrants, 97

Talese, Gay, 143, 144
Tales of the Grotesque and Arabesque (Poe), 18
Tallahassee Sentinel, 100
Tardy, Mary T., 188
Tate, Allen, 126, 169, 214
Taylor, A. J. P., 209–11, 214, 222n29
teachers, northern, 36, 37–40, 48–49, 51, 55n55. *See also* Boggy Swamp incident
teaching reading, 57, 62
Telegraph (Macon), 99, 104
Tellico Dam project, 120
Texas Observer, 142
textbooks, 196
"Thatcher's Letter," 38
Thayer, Eli, 101
Thinking the Twentieth Century (Judt), 202–3, 204–8, 209, 213, 215, 220n4
Thomas, Anna Long, 81
Thompson, Hunter, 143, 144, 148, 153
Thompson, John Reuben, 26
Thompson, Tracy, 163, 169
Thoreau, Henry David, 31, 198
threads, narrative, 206, 208, 209, 212, 219, 221n13
throwaway body, 122–23
Tiger Lilies (Lanier), 80, 91n20
Tocqueville, Alexis de, 22
"To Helen" (Poe), 192
Tolstoy, Leo, 202, 205, 209; *War and Peace*, 203–4, 212
Tourgée, Albion, 174

Trachtenberg, Alan, 128
tradition, oral, 59, 65–66, 68–70, 75n49
tradition, southern, 142–43, 166–68, 169, 178–79n34
Trent, William P., 192
Trescot, William Henry, 166, 178n18
Tupper, Martin Farquhar, 28, 35n28
Tuscaloosa News, 194
Twelve Southerners, 121, 126, 137n7
"Twirling at Ole Miss" (Southern), 148–49
"Types of Mankind," 218–19

Uncle Remus (Harris), 187, 189
Underwood, John C., 101
United Daughters of the Confederacy (UDC), 186, 193–94
United States, growth of, 29–31
University of North Carolina, 81
University of Virginia, 76, 81, 188, 189

Vanderbilt Agrarians, 121, 137n7
VanderMeer, Jeff, 125
Vernon, Zackary, 119
vigilance committees, 37, 38–39, 45
violence and journalism, 147
Virginia Tourist, The (Pollard), 174, 176
Voltaire, 210
Voyage of Life, The (Cole), 85

Wagner, John W., 105
Walker, William, 70, 88
War and Peace (Tolstoy), 203–4, 212
Ward, Jesmyn, 124
Warmoth, Henry Clay, 97
Warner, Michael, 66
war of ideas, 168–69
Warren, Robert Penn, 142, 152, 153, 214
Water Valley Manufacturing Company, 97
Watson, Jay, 125
Watters, Pat, 146–47, 157

Watts, Isaac, 69
Waxahachie Daily Light, 191
Weekly Mississippi Pilot, 99, 100, 101, 106, 108
Wee Nee Volunteers, 50
Wells, Jonathan, 61
Wharton, Edith, 195
"What Ever Happened to Brother Dave?" (King), 149–51
When the Levees Broke (Lee), 124
Where the Crawdads Sing (Owens), 124
White, Benjamin Franklin, 70
White, Hayden, 206, 207, 208, 219
White Citizens Council, 145
whiteness, 8, 33n13, 84, 105, 154, 171, 172, 192
white supremacy: labor and, 104–6, 113n29; southern identity and, 170–73, 174–75, 176, 180n57
Whitman, Walt, 20
Wilderson, Frank B., III, 122, 129
Wiley and Putnam, 26
Williams, Raymond, 3, 208–9
Williamsburg Presbyterian Church, 40–41, 53n26
Willington Academy, 217
Willis, Nathaniel Parker, 24–25
Wingspread conference, 2–3, 10n5
Wise, Henry, 38
Wolfe, Patrick, 122
Wolfe, Thomas, 5, 157
Wolfe, Tom, 143–44, 148, 152–53
women writers, white, 184–86, 187–88, 191, 192–94. *See also specific white women writers*
Woodward, C. Vann, 122, 142, 214
Woolf, Virginia, 214
Worlds of American Intellectual History, The, 3–4
Wrecking Crew, the: background and overview of, 141–43; Cowles and, 141–42; Faulkner and, 149; Frady and (*see* Frady, Marshall); *Harper's* and, 141–42, 158–59; King and (*see*

Wrecking Crew, the (*continued*)
King, Larry L.); method of, 154; Morris and (*see* Morris, Willie); privilege and, 153–54; Tom Wolfe and, 148, 152–53

writers, white women. *See* women writers, white

writing history: autobiography and, 207–8, 209, 211, 212; background and overview of, 202–4; individual character and, 215–20; Judt overview and, 204–7; master narratives and, 212–13; O'Brien overview and, 214–15; plenitude and excess and, 209–11; Williams and, 208–9

Writing in Society (Williams), 208–9

Wyllis, Harold, 44–45

Yaeger, Patricia, 122, 125

Yazoo: Integration in a Deep-Southern Town (Morris), 154–58

Yeats, William Butler, 26

yeoman farmers, 99–102, 106–7, 109–10, 114n31, 115n38

Yusoff, Kathryn, 121

Zeitlin, Benh, 124

www.ingramcontent.com/pod-product-compliance
Lightning Source LLC
Chambersburg PA
CBHW020247310525
27492CB00007B/583